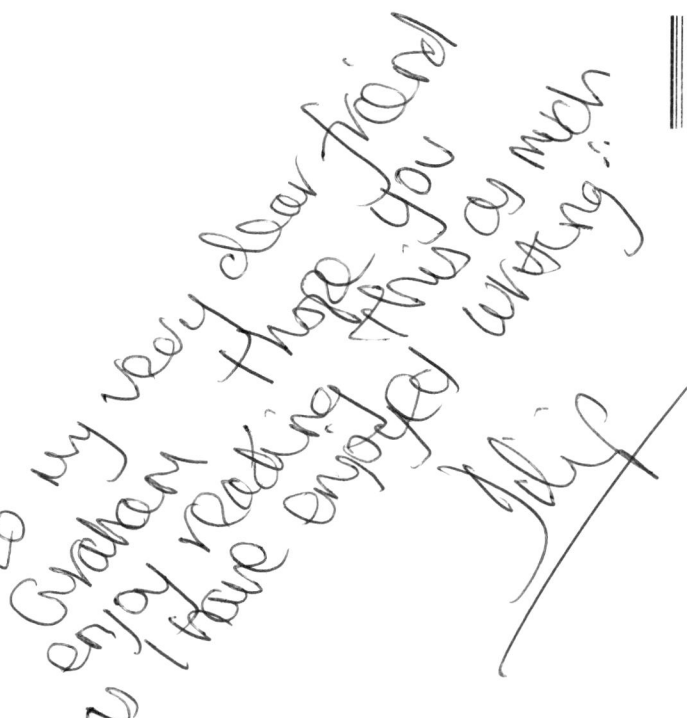

To my very dear friend Graham, I hope you enjoy reading this as much as I have enjoyed writing it.

ENEMY SIGHTED

All the ascendancy of the Hurricanes and Spitfires would have been fruitless, but for the system which had been devised, and built before the war. It had been shaped and refined in constant action, and all was now fused together into a most elaborate instrument of war, the like of which existed nowhere in the world.

Winston Churchill

ENEMY SIGHTED

THE STORY OF THE BATTLE OF BRITAIN BUNKER AND THE WORLD'S FIRST INTEGRATED AIR DEFENCE SYSTEM

DILIP AMIN

AIR WORLD

ENEMY SIGHTED
The Story of the Battle of Britain Bunker and the World's First Integrated Air Defence System

First published in Great Britain in 2023 by
Airworld
An imprint of
Pen & Sword Books Ltd
Yorkshire – Philadelphia

Copyright © Dilip Amin, 2023

ISBN 978 1 39904 930 6

The right of Dilip Amin to be identified as Author of this work has been asserted by him in accordance with the Copyright, Designs and Patents Act 1988.

A CIP catalogue entry for this book is available from the British Library.

All rights reserved. No part of this book may be reproduced or transmitted in any form or by any means, electronic or mechanical including photocopying, recording or by any information storage and retrieval system, without permission from the Publisher in writing.

Typeset by SJmagic DESIGN SERVICES, India.

Printed and bound in the UK by CPI Group (UK) Ltd.

Pen & Sword Books Ltd includes the Imprints of Atlas, Archaeology, Aviation, Discovery, Family History, Fiction, History, Maritime, Military, Military Classics, Politics, Select, Airworld, Frontline Publishing, Leo Cooper, Remember When, Seaforth Publishing, The Praetorian Press, Wharncliffe Local History, Wharncliffe Transport, Wharncliffe True Crime and White Owl.

For a complete list of Pen & Sword titles please contact

PEN & SWORD BOOKS LTD
George House, Units 12 & 13, Beevor Street, Off Pontefract Road,
Barnsley, South Yorkshire, S71 1HN, England
E-mail: enquiries@pen-and-sword.co.uk
Website: www.pen-and-sword.co.uk

or

PEN AND SWORD BOOKS
1950 Lawrence Rd, Havertown, PA 19083, USA
E-mail: uspen-and-sword@casematepublishers.com
Website: www.penandswordbooks.com

Contents

Acknowledgements vi
Introduction vii
Chapter 1   An Evolving Threat – 'Britain is No Longer an Island' 1
Chapter 2   A Three Dimensional Challenge – 'To Catch a Fly' 5
Chapter 3   Integrated Air Defence – 'Weaving the Web' 10
Chapter 4   Essential Elements – 'Signal & Capture Threads' 14
Chapter 5   Fighter Aircraft – 'Capture Thread' 17
Chapter 6   Fighter Command – 'Capture Thread' 29
Chapter 7   Radio Detection and Ranging (Radar) – 'Signal Thread' 39
Chapter 8   Observer Corps – 'Signal Thread' 57
Chapter 9   Anti-Aircraft Guns & Searchlights –
            'Signal & Capture Threads' 68
Chapter 10 Balloon Command – 'Capture Thread' 75
Chapter 11 The Underground Operations Room –
            'Down the Spider Hole': Part One 79
Chapter 12 The Underground Operations Room –
            'Down the Spider Hole': Part Two 89
Chapter 13 The Locus Above – 'Over the Spider Hole' 114
Chapter 14 Major Campaigns & Engagements –
            'Dynamo' to 'Seelöwe' 126
Chapter 15 Battle of Britain Day – 'The Prelude' 161
Chapter 16 Battle of Britain Day – 'The Finale' 182
Chapter 17 The Continuing & Immeasurable Contribution 193
Endnotes 200
Index 220

Acknowledgements

Writing this remarkable story has been a labour of love and immensely rewarding. I would like to thank volunteers and staff at the Battle of Britain Bunker, in particular Dr Rachael Abbiss, Principal Curator for Military History, and Fiona Sweet, Operations Manager for Museums & Historic Sites.

I would like to thank my family without whose support this book would not have been realised, especially my four children, Matthew and Nicholas for your encouragement, and Christopher and Stephanie for your professional assistance. Finally, my wife Jane for the patience and tolerance you have shown on so many early mornings, late nights, and even while we were on holiday.

Introduction

This is the story of how Britain developed the world's first integrated air defence system, and how that avant-garde framework was skilfully wielded to thwart invasion over eighty years ago. Fundamental to its telling, is the 11 Group Operations Room, commonly referred to as the 'Battle of Britain Bunker', and the people who worked there, deep below Royal Air Force Uxbridge. Without their involvement, Fighter Command's pilots could not have routed the Luftwaffe during the Battle of Britain, and so would have been unable to prevent Operation *Seelöwe* or *Sealion*, the German invasion of Britain. If the Nazis had been permitted to land on British soil, then no doubt its people, inspired by their wartime leader Winston Churchill, would have fought stoically on the beaches and on the landing grounds. However, Hitler's army, the German Heer, was not only vastly superior in numbers, but also possessed more heavy armament than the British, who had been forced to abandon much of their equipment in France. If Britain had been subjugated, then the course not only of British, but also world history, would likely have been reconstructed. It is therefore difficult to overstate how important the Bunker's role was in frustrating the Nazis' obsession of creating a Third Reich, and their appetite for world domination.

The Führer had declared that before invasion could take place, 'The English Air Force must be beaten physically and morally to a point that they cannot put up any show of attacking force worth mentioning.'[1] To bring this about, the Luftwaffe needed to gain air superiority over the English Channel and intended landing grounds. The battle would therefore be predominantly fought over London and south-east England. It was the area covered by the Bunker, and it would come to be known as 'Hell Fire Corner'. At its closest point, between Dover and Calais, the stretch of water separating Britain and Nazi Occupied France is just under twenty-one miles (thirty-three km). I have been privileged to fly in a Spitfire over the White Cliffs of Dover and can attest to the fact that the French coastline can clearly be seen

ENEMY SIGHTED

from Dover. The distance, in aeronautical terms, really is extremely short, capable of being traversed by German aircraft in around five minutes.

It was for this reason that the greater part of the Hurricanes and Spitfires involved in the fighting during this conflict were controlled from the Bunker. They would shoot down over 1,300 of the 1,733 enemy aircraft claimed destroyed during the battle. Their contribution not only helped Britain to survive during the early part of the Second World War, but also ensured that it could, in due course, be used as the springboard from which to launch Operation *Overlord*, the assault on Hitler's 'Fortress Europe'. Indeed, it was having visited the Bunker, when the Battle of Britain was at its height, that stirred Prime Minister Winston Churchill to declare he had 'Never been so moved', and first utter the immortal words: 'Never has so much been owed, by so many, to so few.'

With the advent of powered flight at the turn of the twentieth century, Britain was no longer an island in the sense that the sea was no longer an absolute barrier to invasion. The Royal Navy could not, on its own, be expected to guard against future incursions. Aircraft approaching Britain would be flying within a vast three-dimensional domain, making the task of detecting and intercepting them more difficult than was the case with ships. This is because only knowledge of two dimensions, both existing on a horizontal plane, is required to detect and intercept ships. The first is the direction from which they are approaching, the azimuth angle on the horizon, which is described in degrees. The second is their distance from the defending forces, the length of which is described in miles and feet, or kilometres and metres. Aircraft travel along these two dimensions, plus an additional third dimension on a vertical plane – height. If their height is unknown, then they cannot be successfully intercepted. A further challenge, in the case of aircraft, is a significantly reduced period in which to detect and intercept them. This is because they are travelling much faster than ships, and unlike ships they do not stop on reaching the coast, but instead continue their journey inland, at speed.

The challenge, therefore, was to create a system capable of detecting approaching enemy aircraft early enough to alert ground defences, and get fighter aircraft not only into the air, but also to the right place and at the right height. The solution was neither straightforward, nor immediate. Like in the Battle of Britain, which in reality was won by the 'many', and not the 'few', there were 'many' without whom the system would not have been realised. However, if credit is to be given to one individual, then that person is Hugh Caswall Tremenheere Dowding, who, as Air Member for Supply

INTRODUCTION

and Research and then for Research and Development, helped to oversee its development, and then as Air Officer Commanding, Fighter Command, directed its use during wartime. It is in recognition of this contribution, that the integrated air defence system is more simply and widely referred to as the 'Dowding System'.

The system of air defence was integrated, meaning that for it to operate successfully, all elements were essential, and all needed to operate in unison. The aim was to develop a shared understanding of what was happening, in other words to develop a 'recognised air picture'. So for example, the Senior Controller, sat sixty ft (eighteen metres) below ground at Uxbridge, to the west of London, was able to track German raiders as they crossed the English Channel, and could metaphorically 'see' when they approached Dover, some eighty-three miles (133 km) away. He had before him information on the raid's direction of travel, height, strength and even whether it was composed of bombers, fighters, or both. He would be cognisant of the prevailing weather over Dover and even how high the barrage balloons were. It was as if he was looking out of the window, allowing him to make informed decisions on how best to deploy his finite resources. This was all possible due to an arrangement of teleprinter, telephone and radio telephony networks, established across the entire system. To those of us today, in the era of interconnected computers, this would appear unremarkable, let alone extraordinary, but we need to remind ourselves that this achievement was even more exceptional in a world without computers, or the internet.

There were six essential elements within the integrated air defence system. The first element was formed by the fighter aircraft that were directed to intercept enemy raids. The majority of these were Hurricanes and Spitfires; second was Fighter Command itself, providing a fighter control network through an organisational infrastructure of Sector and Satellite airfields or aerodromes, and Operations Rooms at Headquarters, Group and Sector level; third were the Chain Home and Chain Home Low Radio Detection and Ranging (Radar) stations. The 'all seeing eye' that informed Fighter Command, as to when and where the raiders would attack; fourth was the Observer Corps, whose members monitored and reported on the composition and movement of enemy raiders once they had crossed the coastline. They performed a vital role by mitigating Radar's weakness at that time, which was the inability to detect aircraft once they had flown overhead and were continuing over Britain itself; fifth was Anti-Aircraft Command, whose anti-aircraft guns protected Britain from the ground, and whose searchlights exposed enemy aircraft prowling in the night sky; and

ENEMY SIGHTED

lastly, Balloon Command, which offered protection at strategic locations and to vulnerable targets, by hindering the enemy's ability to carry out low-level attacks.

By coming together, these individual elements all combined to present an immediate and unified response when faced with threats from the air. Radar detected enemy aircraft, often as they were gaining height over Northern France, and so provided early warning of an imminent raid. The information from Radar stations would be passed to the Filter Room at Fighter Command Headquarters, where it was 'filtered', or tidied up, before being shared across the system. As enemy aircraft crossed the British coast, their location, direction of travel, height and strength were reported on and shared by the Observer Corps. Details of raids entering 11 Group's area were passed on to the Bunker at Uxbridge, from where anti-aircraft guns, searchlights, balloons and fighter aircraft were alerted and deployed.

As well as denying the Luftwaffe the air superiority it needed to invade Britain, what is perhaps less well known is the significant role performed by the Bunker, during some of the other major campaigns and engagements of the Second World War. The decisions made here helped slow down the Nazi invasion of France and the Low Countries; protected the embattled troops being evacuated from Dunkirk; supported the exploratory raid on Dieppe; shielded the troops landing in Normandy; and defend against Hitler's *Vergeltungswaffen*, or Vengeance Weapons, the V1 and V2. These moments would influence not only British, but world history, and they are deservingly acknowledged in this account.

This book takes the reader from a time when Britain was subjected to attacks purely from the sea, to when the threat emanated from both sea and air. This fundamental shift in how the threat presented itself necessitated the creation and implementation of a new and radical system of defence. An exploration follows of not only what this new system was, but also how it was created, and how it was effectively deployed. Central to the operating of this system, was the 11 Group Operations Room at Uxbridge, or, as it is more commonly referred to today, 'The Battle of Britain Bunker'.

Chapter 1

An Evolving Threat

'Britain is No Longer an Island'

The Operations Room at Fighter Command's 11 Group Headquarters was pivotal to Britain's defence, at a time in its history when a malevolent foreign power, Nazi Germany, attempted to conquer and subjugate it. But why was it considered necessary, even before that conflict, that this island kingdom needed to be defended against the threat of attack? What evidence was there that Britain could, or would, be invaded by forces from beyond these shores? To understand the threat, we need to examine Britain's past and ultimately how the sea, a natural barrier, was to become superfluous and made redundant by advances in aviation technology.

Hostile armies and large raiding parties have attempted to invade the British Isles throughout history. In some instances, they were able to land successfully on these shores, and on other occasions, they were comprehensively repulsed. In the year 55 BC, Emperor Julius Caesar landed with an army in Thanet, Kent, on the south-east coast of Britain, ushering in almost 400 years of Roman rule. Then, between 793 and 1066, marauding Vikings from Scandinavian countries repeatedly carried out raids along the north and east coast of Britain.

In 1066, King Harald Hardrada of Norway landed with an army on the east coast of Britain and fought King Harold of England, at the Battle of Stamford Bridge. Having defeated the invading army, the English King then travelled south to engage with William, Duke of Normandy, who had landed with his army in Pevensey Bay, Sussex, on the south-east coast. King Harold was killed at the Battle of Hastings and the Normans went on to rule England for over half a century.

In 1545, King Francis I of France ordered the French fleet to invade Britain, but its attempt to land on the south coast at Portsmouth was thwarted by King Henry VIII's navy, led by his flagship *Mary Rose*. Unable to land in mainland Britain, the French then invaded the Isle of Wight and landed successfully at St Helens, Bonchurch and Sandown, where they remained until they themselves were vanquished by the English defenders.

ENEMY SIGHTED

An armada sent in 1588 by King Philip II of Spain, against Queen Elizabeth I of England, was defeated at sea by the English navy, led by Sir Francis Drake. This victory prevented the invasion army, which was waiting in Calais, from embarking and crossing the English Channel. On this occasion, a network of beacons positioned at high points along the coast were lit to warn the English defenders of an impending invasion, and for them to mobilise their response. This 'chain' of highly visible fires represented a fledgling system, being used to give early warning of an attack from the sea. During the Battle of Britain 352 years later, the British Isles would again rely on a 'chain' system of Radar masts and observation posts to provide early warning of an attack, not from the sea but from the air. It is noteworthy that the crest of the Royal Observer Corps, which played such a pivotal role in the defence of this country during the Second World War, honours its predecessors by depicting an Elizabethan Coast Watcher, in breastplate and helmet, holding a flaming torch in his raised right hand, and using his left hand to shield his eyes. He is standing on a cliff next to a flaming beacon, against a background of sea and a coastline with beacons. The central relief is surrounded by a pale blue enamel border, on which the motto *Forewarned Is Forearmed* is etched in silver.[1]

In 1688, a Dutch army led by William of Orange successfully landed in Devon, on the south coast of Britain, and marched on London. The invading fleet was many times larger than the Spanish Armada, which had attempted an invasion 100 years before. The Dutch were able to land because of the support given to them by several English peers, in what would come to be known as 'the Glorious Revolution'. Was this an invasion, or was it an invitation?

In 1797, the newly formed French Revolutionary Government, 'the Directory', sent an invasion force of 1,400 men, under the command of an Irish American, Colonel William Tate. The original plan was to land at Bristol, but adverse weather meant the invading army landed near Fishguard in south-west Wales. Many of the invaders were convicts who had been recruited for the task, and soon the rabble became drunk and unwilling, or incapable, of fighting. Such was the situation that a local cobbler's wife, Jemima Nicholas, armed only with a pitchfork, detained twelve of the invaders by herself, and the remaining invaders surrendered to a local militia force within two days of their landing.

In 1805, Admiral Horatio Nelson's British fleet defeated the French and Spanish fleets at Trafalgar, off the coast of Spain. This British victory denied the French Emperor, Napoleon Bonaparte, control of the English

AN EVOLVING THREAT

Channel, and so thwarted his plans for invading the British Isles. Britain would, as a result, maintain dominance of the seas for the next 100 years, and thereby possess the means to protect herself against attacks launched from foreign shores.

Regardless of whether these assaults on the British Isles had been successfully realised or not, they all shared two features from which lessons could be learnt and applied to address future maritime and airborne threats.

The first is that to engage aggressors and successfully repel them, either at sea or after they have landed, an attack must be identified at the earliest opportunity, and communicated speedily and effectively across the defending force. Meeting this requirement would become more challenging when facing threats from the air, where aircraft, unlike ships on the surface of the sea, could travel and, importantly, hide, in a three dimensional domain at any given height on a vertical plane stretching many thousands of feet.

The second, is that Britain was an island. The invaders in every case had needed to successfully navigate a body of water to reach Britain, and the only means of doing so had been by using seaborne craft, or ships. Ships had also been used defensively against attacks, and from the sixteenth century, the Royal Navy possessed a formidable array of seaborne craft … Britannia did indeed rule the waves. However, when Britain became accessible by aircraft, it became no longer an island in an aeronautical sense, and therefore the Royal Navy alone was not enough. Britain needed to defend herself against the evolving threat from aircraft. She needed an air force, with an array of aircraft operating within an integrated air defence system, in order to detect intruders and successfully challenge any incursion.

In 1908, the *Daily Telegraph* newspaper reported on the Royal Aero Club's annual dinner, held at the famous Ritz Hotel, in London, with the headline, 'Airship squadrons. Peril of the future'. The Duke of Argyll had referred to the 'necessity of considering the possibility of having every part of a country visited and inspected by transient visitors who might or might not have hostile intentions', and 'the precautions that needed to be taken against intrusions by aeroplanes'. It was in response to this, that Charles Rolls, who had entered into partnership with Henry Royce, said that 'England was no longer an island and that to maintain her supremacy she must now not only have the command of the sea, but that of the air as well.'[2]

Then, in 1909, an event occurred that would transform the nature of any threat which Britain was likely to face in the future. Lord Northcliffe, founder and proprietor of the *Daily Mail* newspaper, had issued a challenge the year before, offering a prize of £1,000 to the first person to fly across the

ENEMY SIGHTED

English Channel.[3] On 25 July 1909, Louis Blériot attempted the crossing in a fragile plane he had constructed from ash and cloth, and which was held together by piano wire. The machine's modest 25hp engine could produce only a fraction of the power generated by a typical push-along garden lawnmower today. The flight, over some twenty-five miles (forty km) of water, between the port of Calais and the port of Dover, was completed in thirty-seven minutes. This achievement was a monumental landmark in aviation history, one worthy of Neil Armstrong's words sixty years later, when he flew to the Moon: 'one small step for man, one giant leap for mankind'. It demonstrated man's ability to use machines to travel through the air, thereby circumventing the natural barriers of land and sea. These thirty-seven minutes had shown that Britain could be reached more rapidly and less conspicuously. There was now an added sense of renewed urgency to the threat prophesied by Argyll and Rolls, some seven months earlier.

The Literary Digest made an ominous prediction that, 'If one machine bird can migrate from the continent to the island kingdom, why not 10,000?' As if to support this premonition, it also reported on the congratulatory telegram sent to Blériot by Lord Roberts, Commander in Chief of the British Army, in which he stated: 'It is impossible to imagine the far reaching effects of the feat. It may lead the way to great changes in the conduct of future wars.'[4]

Only five years after Blériot's historic crossing, the country found itself embroiled in 'The Great War'. Mainland Britain was attacked from the air for the first time on the morning of Christmas Eve 1914, when a German *Friedrichshafen* FF29 seaplane dropped four 4 lb (2 kg) bombs over Dover. The raid caused only minimal damage and minor injuries to civilians, but it had a disproportionate effect on the national psyche, creating a sense of helplessness and fear among the British public.

Lord Roberts' forewarning of 'great changes' being necessary was proven to be correct, and the island kingdom deliberated on how best to defend itself against future aerial attacks from German airships and bombers ... the threat had evolved, and so too would the response.

Chapter 2

A Three Dimensional Challenge

'To Catch a Fly'

The evolving threat from the air greatly complicated Britain's ability to defend itself from attack. Observation posts in isolation were no longer a sufficient means of surveillance, and the race was on to find and implement a more commensurate, integrated system of air defence. In order to understand the challenges of defending against air attack, we need to think about it in terms of space and time.

This view was affirmed in instructions issued to Fighter Command Controllers during the Second World War:

> To meet enemy aircraft in the air, other than by purest chance, fighter aircraft must have the guidance of a Controller to direct them in space and time into the enemy's vicinity. The Controller must know the position of the enemy in space and time; know the position of his fighters in space and time; and have the means of communicating with his fighters in the air.

This is the essential control in the air, for which the whole Fighter Operational Control System is designed.[1]

It is appreciated that enemy aircraft can occupy any one of an infinite number of positions in the sky, which is a vast three-dimensional domain. They are almost always likely to have an intended target, which can be approached from different directions, on a horizontal plane, and different heights, on a vertical plane. If defending fighter aircraft, or ground-based anti-aircraft artillery are successfully directed to a precise position within a horizontal plane, currently occupied by enemy aircraft, they may still fail to make contact if they are not at the same height as the enemy, its position on a vertical plane. Both horizontal and vertical planes are attributes of the element defined as space. In addition, the defending aircraft or ground-based anti-aircraft artillery, will always aim to intercept the enemy aircraft before they reach their target, so they need to know precisely where the enemy is at any given moment, and therefore when the interception can be made, this is the element of time.

To help understand the challenge of effectively locating, and successfully intercepting enemy aircraft, entering territorial airspace, we can use the analogy of a spider catching a fly in a room, where the former is synonymous with the defender, and the latter, the intruder.

The spider needs to spin a web in order to catch the fly. It does this intuitively, regarding both the fly's likely position within a room, on a horizontal plane, and how high its prey is likely to be flying, its position on a vertical plane. Both these two planes represent the element of space. By spinning a web in a suitable location, it will hope to get lucky and snare its prey. The spider does not need to know where the fly is at all times, it only needs to know when the fly becomes ensnared in the web, at which point the vibration will alert the spider and allow it to attack, this is the element of time. Unlike the spider, however, defending fighter aircraft or ground-based anti-aircraft artillery need always to be alerted and aware of the 'fly' while it is in the 'room'. The 'web', that needs to be spun to effectively locate and successfully intercept enemy aircraft, therefore needs to cover the entire 'room', which in reality would encompass both the vast territorial airspace being defended, and adjoining airspace likely to be used by the enemy when approaching it.

The position of the enemy in 'space and time' was not readily gaugeable at the outbreak of the First World War. Radar had not yet been developed, and so Britain was unable to gain early warning of an attack. Its ability to effectively direct defending fighters and communicate vital information immediately, across all parts of the defence system, was rudimentary.

Existing facilities such as railway stations, military camps, police stations and lighthouses were engaged as 'reporting posts', to provide limited early warning of any possible raid on London. Not all these locations were equipped with a telephone, and messages would have to be relayed by a runner to another site, from which the information could be forwarded. All reports eventually led through to a central administration point at the Admiralty, and then had to be translated into instructions for the most appropriate airfields.[2]

The only option available to sight the enemy as they entered British airspace, was to mount permanent 'standing patrols', in which defending aircraft would fly along the English Channel and North Sea coast, hoping to see the attacking aircraft. This was costly in terms of resources and

A THREE DIMENSIONAL CHALLENGE

tactically flawed, because if defending aircraft had used most of their fuel by the time they spotted the enemy, then they were not able to engage them.

To compound the problem, there was insufficient coordination between the Royal Flying Corps (RFC), which was under the direction of the Army, and the Royal Naval Air Service (RNAS), both of which were involved in defending Britain against aerial attack. The RNAS claim that defending Britain against invaders had always traditionally been a naval responsibility was refuted by the RFC. This infighting led to a great deal of antagonism between the two arms of the military, resulting in a diminution of their collective capability to provide aerial defence. The issue was resolved for the time being, when responsibility for combating the threat from the air was ceded to the British Army in February 1916.

The challenge of defending against the aerial raiders became more pressing as the attacks intensified. By the end of 1916, German Zeppelin airships had killed 500 civilians, and 17,000 servicemen had been diverted from other duties to deal with the raiders. In the summer of 1917, long-range German Gotha bombers struck London, killing and wounding nearly 600 people in the initial raid. The fear felt on the streets spread upwards.[3]

During three raids in July 1917, over 120 British fighters took to the air over London to challenge German Gotha GIV bombers of 'The England Squadron', but only one defending aircraft was able to find and shoot at the raiders.[4] Britain was shown to be woefully inadequate in defending its capital, and the Prime Minister, Lloyd George, commissioned General Jan Smuts to lead an inquiry to examine two distinct but interdependent issues: 'The defence arrangements for home defence against air raids', and 'The air organisation generally and the direction of aerial operations.'[5]

In the first part of the report, Smuts identified that 'no system of unified command in the air existed', with little or no coordination, and 'because of the fragmentation of command and the importance of the London anti-aircraft guns that a senior officer be appointed'.[6] The recommendations were approved and Brigadier General 'Splash' Ashmore was recalled from France 'to work out schemes of air defence for this area'.[7] This scheme would form the catalyst of the world's first integrated air defence system.

In the second part of his report, Smuts addressed the issue of air organisation generally and the direction of aerial operations. He recommended that an Air Ministry be created, to oversee Air Staff who would be responsible for the working out of war plans, the direction of operations, the collection of intelligence, and the training of Air personnel. In addition, he proposed that the Air Ministry and its staff proceed to work out the arrangements necessary for the amalgamation of the RNAS and RFC.[8] This resulted in the formation of the Royal Air Force, which was inaugurated in April the following year, a move which would ensure that Britain's ability to defend itself against aerial attack would no longer be undermined by political rivalry between her army and navy.

Ashmore, now a Major General, took command of the newly formed London Air Defence Area (LADA), which covered Suffolk, London and Sussex. The LADA system was fully operational by September 1918, and brought together a network of observers, listening posts, anti-aircraft artillery, balloons, and fighter squadrons. Reports from the units were fed through to twenty-six sub control centres, and then onwards to Major General Ashmore's Operations Room at Horse Guards, in London. Here, plotters stood around a map table, moving symbols representing British fighters and enemy aircraft, which were referred to as 'air bandits'. The evolving picture on the map would then determine which fighter aircraft should be scrambled, and in which areas public air raid warnings should be issued.[9]

The LADA system had brought together all the essential elements that were technologically possible at the time, in order to create an integrated air defence system. Cessation of hostilities in 1918 resulted in an immediate reduction in military expenditure, but Britain needed to learn the lessons from its past and forge a structure capable of withstanding any future attack from the air.

A THREE DIMENSIONAL CHALLENGE

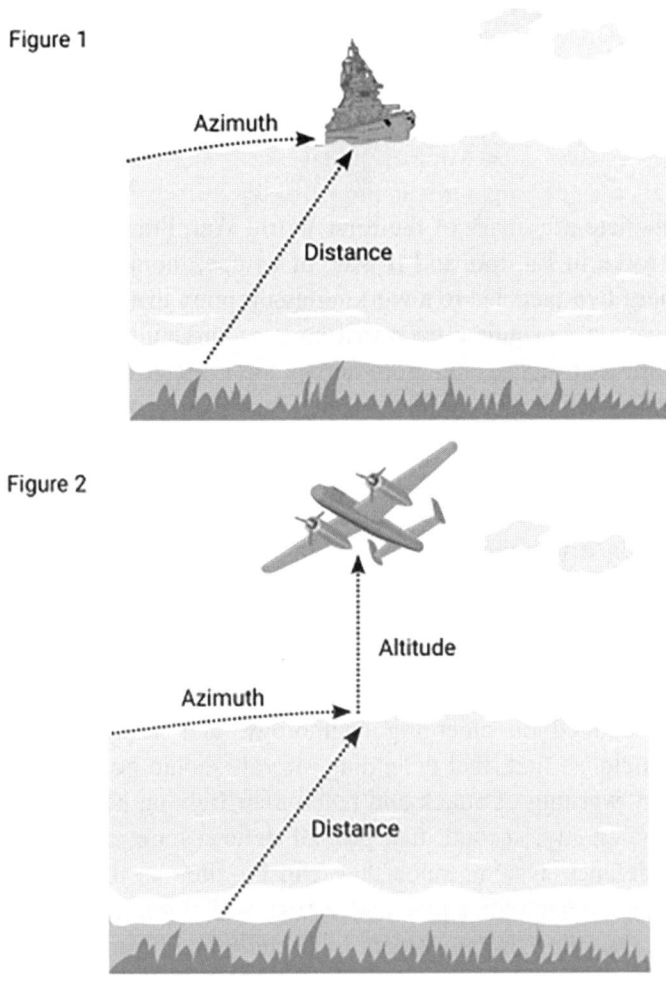

A comparison of the challenges when defending against a seaborne invasion (figure 1), where ships operate within a two dimensional domain, and an airborne invasion (figure 2), in which aeroplanes operate within an additional third dimension. © Dilip Amin

Chapter 3

Integrated Air Defence

'Weaving the Web'

In the immediate aftermath of the First World War, France possessed the largest air force in Europe, and it was, of course, the country nearest to Britain. These two facts led to a working assumption that any future threat from the air would originate from that country, targeting Britain's capital and the south-east of England from across the English Channel. In time, however, Adolf Hitler and his Third Reich, not France, would come to be seen as the likely aggressors. London continued to be viewed as the prime target for air attack, a belief reaffirmed by Winston Churchill in typical animated language, 'With our enormous Metropolis here, the greatest target in the world ... a valuable fat cow tied up to attract the beasts of prey.'[1] Although the source of the threat was morphing, it was still present, and Britain persevered with the development of its air defence, in order to keep watch over its 'valuable fat cow'.

The air defence system being forged would be cast from the existing structure, fashioned on emerging technology, and influenced by three constant principles: first, that defending aircraft should be able to receive the necessary warning of attack and reach their fighting height before the arrival of the enemy; second, that ground defences are an essential part of any air defence system, since they can be sited as direct protection for important vulnerable points and areas; and third, information and intelligence regarding the movement of friendly and hostile aircraft must be collected and distributed to all parts of the defence system, as quickly as possible.[2]

Two reports, one by the Steel-Bartholomew Committee in 1923, and the other a year later by the Romer Committee, were to significantly influence and shape the air defence of Great Britain. The first report identified Artillery and Aircraft Fighting Zones to protect not only London and the south-east, but also other parts of Britain. The second report outlined measures such as observation posts to improve the raid intelligence system, so that defending aircraft could have the maximum period of warning in order to successfully engage the enemy.[3]

The first person to be vested with responsibility for all decisions regarding air defence, both on the ground and in the air, was Sir John Salmond, Air Officer Commanding-in-Chief, Air Defence Great Britain (AOC-in-C, ADGB). Salmond's Headquarters opened at Hillingdon House, Uxbridge, in 1926, from where he presided over the Home Defence fighter squadrons, searchlights, anti-aircraft artillery, and observer units. Information was filtered at Uxbridge, to paint a complete picture of all enemy air activity over Britain, and this would be displayed on a plotting table, which would be used by all those needing a clear view of the air situation.[4] Hillingdon House can still be seen on the approach to the Battle of Britain Bunker. Under Salmond's control was the Air Officer Commanding Fighting Area, who was charged with the immediate control of defensive operations. This function was coordinated from a control room situated in a wooden hut at Uxbridge. The room standardised the sequence of incoming information, using a system of reference counters, which were displayed on a gridded map table.[5] It would be the precursor to the Bunker, Fighter Command's 11 Group underground Operations Room.

In 1930, Hugh Caswall Tremenheere Dowding was appointed Air Member for Supply and Research, and then for Research and Development. Although he did not have a technical background, he would go on to demonstrate a shrewd ability for recognising the merits of emerging technology. He understood the inherent strategic and operational challenges involved in aerial warfare, having led a squadron in France during the First World War and gained personal experience of aerial combat. As a result, Dowding was able to exercise sound judgement and empathise with his 'chicks',[6] the fighter pilots he would go on to direct during the Battle of Britain as AOC-in-C, Fighter Command, after it had superseded ADGB.

In 1934, Britain was again alarmed by the threat posed from a rampant, unrestrained Germany. Dowding understood the need to improve the effectiveness of fighter aircraft, which would be available to Britain in any future conflict with Germany. He championed technological change, by visualising and framing Air Ministry specifications F.37/34 and F.36/34 accordingly. The specifications were for fighter aircraft and so, in addition to speed, they were required to be armed with eight machine-guns and fitted with an enclosed cockpit. Aircraft manufacturers were encouraged to think innovatively, beyond the obsolete biplane designs of the past, and instead to focus on contemporary monoplane structures, more comparable to the Schneider Trophy-winning Supermarine monoplane racing seaplanes designed by Reginald J. Mitchell. Mitchell would respond with a design for what is perhaps the most renowned fighter aircraft of all time. Dowding's involvement resulted in the development of two aircraft on the frontier of aeronautics in the early 1930s, Reginald Mitchell's Supermarine Spitfire and Sydney Camm's Hawker Hurricane. Together, they would present a formidable challenge to Hitler's ambition of achieving air superiority over Britain.[7]

In the same year, a Sub-Committee to the ADGB was formed with a brief to review the reorientation of the air defence system. The Sub-Committee was of the view that an 'air attack would probably synchronise with, or indeed form the commencement of hostilities, and so the air defences of the country must be fully ready when war was about to break out'.[8] It was also recognised that new technology needed to be developed and harnessed, to 'offset the advantage so clearly held by the attacker'.[9] A group of scientists were brought together to form the Committee for the Scientific Survey of Air Defence (CSSAD), with a brief by the Air Ministry, to identify how technology could be used to provide adequate warning of enemy aircraft approaching British airspace. The chairperson of this committee was a highly regarded physicist, Henry T. Tizard.

In 1935, Tizard's Committee considered a historic document titled, 'Detection and Location of Aircraft by Radio Methods', put forward by Robert Watson-Watt, the Superintendent of the National Physical Laboratory's Radio Research Station at Slough. Dowding and H.E. Wimperis, a member of Tizard's Committee, met Watson-Watt, and a demonstration was arranged in a field near to the BBC shortwave overseas radio transmitter at Daventry, in the East Midlands. The trial was to see if a green spot on a screen would be deflected by the radio signal reflected from a Heyford bomber aircraft. The trial was successful and a device was born which was, in large measure, to decide the fate of Britain and the world. In Watson-Watt's words, 'Britain became once more an island'.[10]

Later that year, the ADGB Sub-Committee identified several elements that needed to be present in order to create an effective integrated air defence system. Many of the elements already in place within the existing system were underdeveloped, with enormous scope for enhancement, combining fighter aircraft; anti-aircraft guns and searchlights; balloon aprons; and the Observer Corps. Importantly, the ADGB Sub-Committee's report also contained two further elements that would take the system to the next level, in fact to the level of best in the world. The first, was to embed a comprehensive system of telephone communications across the entire air defence network. The second element referred to 'an intelligence system comprising other means of detecting aircraft movements, some of which were only in the first stages of development'.[11] This was a reference to the device, born following the earlier trial in Daventry, which was described as Radio Detection and Ranging, and later referred to as Radar.

In 1936, the Air Defence of Great Britain evolved into Fighter Command, with a new Headquarters at Bentley Priory, RAF Stanmore, and a new Commanding Officer, Hugh Dowding. The decision to appoint Dowding was insightful. Who better to deploy Britain's newly constructed air defence system than the man who had been instrumental in its development? Others, such as Ashmore, Tizard, Wimperis and Watson-Watt, should be recognised for their role in 'spinning the spider's web', but Dowding was central to its inception. The newly formed Fighter Command had a leader who understood, perhaps better than anyone else, how the system of air defence would work in the military context of a theatre of operations. For these reasons it is unsurprising, and fitting, that the system would also become known as 'The Dowding System'.

Chapter 4

Essential Elements

'Signal & Capture Threads'

What were the essential elements of Britain's air defence system, which, when woven together, formed an indomitable 'web' to guard against Nazi aggression? How did each contribute to the system's overall effectiveness, and to what degree were they interdependent?

Identified four years earlier by the ADGB Sub-Committee, the essential elements of Britain's integrated air defence system were further developed and refined, in preparation for the war with Nazi Germany, which many thought inevitable. There were six essential elements within the system, and these were the fighter aircraft that would be sent up to engage with German raiders; Fighter Command, with its Sector and Satellite airfields, and Operations Rooms at Headquarters, Group and Sector level; Radio Detection and Ranging stations; the Observer Corps; Anti-Aircraft Command, comprising both guns and searchlights; and Balloon Command. Information needed to be shared rapidly and reliably between all essential elements, and so an arrangement of teleprinter, telephone and radio telephony networks was established across the entire system. These were, to use the spider's web analogy, the 'silk' holding the 'web' together.

The essential elements were all interdependent, needing to work in unison, for the system to operate effectively. There was limited redundancy within the air defence system, and where there was a contingency in place, it would likely have reduced the effectiveness of, or compromised the process. A case in point is the prerequisite for communication to be maintained between different locations across the air defence system, regardless of the situation. So, for example, if the telephone and teleprinter lines between the Operations Room at Uxbridge and its respective Sectors were unable to be repaired following the all too frequent Luftwaffe raids on 11 Group's airfields, then both sites would continue to communicate through radio transmissions, using the equipment already installed at each location.[1] However, the number of instructions and acknowledgements would have to be restricted because of the volume of information needing to be shared, and the additional risk of that information being intercepted by German Signals Intelligence.

To help understand each essential element's individual and combined role in helping to thwart aerial attacks, we can return to the analogy of a spider spinning a web in order to catch a fly and consider how the spider constructs its web. A typical web will have a number of sticky threads, called 'capture threads', which radiate out from the centre. Their purpose, as the name implies, is to catch a fly that is unfortunate enough to come into contact with the web. In addition, some spiders incorporate a remote sensing technique by using a 'signal thread' to transmit vibrational sensory information. This allows it to hide and lie in wait in a spider hole. When a fly becomes entangled, the vibration alerts the waiting spider, which runs along the signal thread to capture its prey.[2] In applying this analogy to the context of Britain's air defence system, the 'signal thread' function is comparable to the role performed by Radio Detection and Ranging, the Observer Corps, searchlights, and teleprinter and telephone communications, all of which announce the presence of the enemy. The 'capture thread' function is provided by the fighter aircraft, under the control of Fighter Command's multi-layered Operations Rooms; anti-aircraft guns; and Balloon Command, which all serve to make contact with, and overwhelm the enemy.

We can further scrutinise the role of each of the six essential elements within Britain's air defence system by examining the situation from when Britain declared war on Nazi Germany, on 3 September 1939, and thereafter.

ENEMY SIGHTED

A. Radar
B. Observer Corps
C. Search lights
D. Telephone network
E. Teleprinter network
F. Fighter aircraft
G. Anti-aircraft guns
H. Balloons
I. Sector Operations Rooms & airfields
J. Group Operations Room

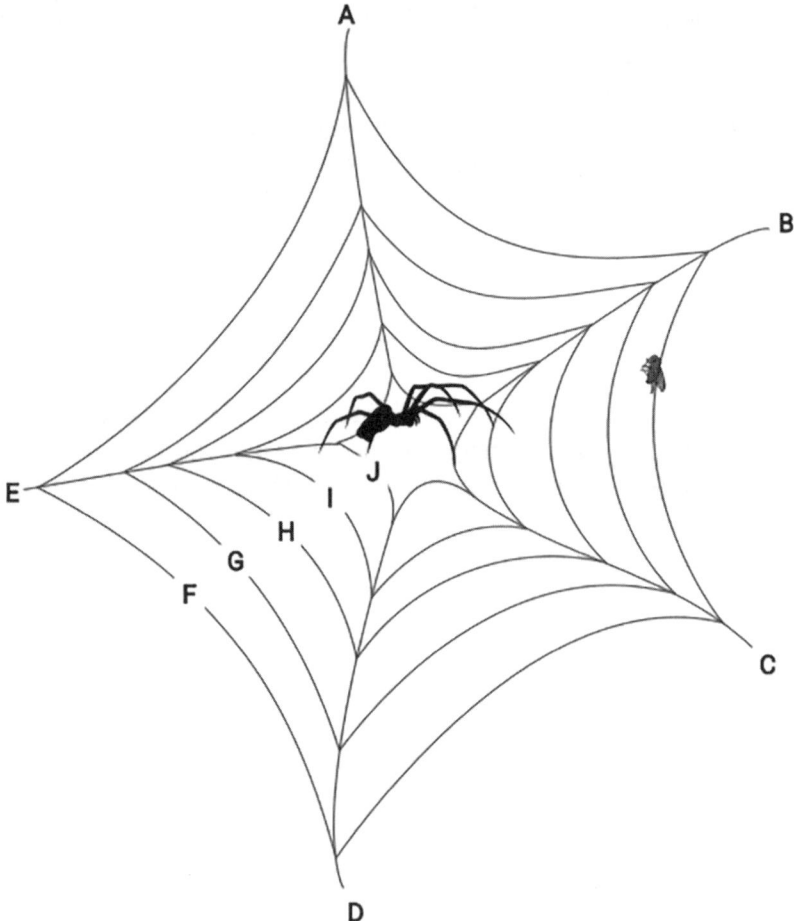

A comparison of Britain's integrated air defence system with how a spider constructs a web of interconnected signal and capture threads to capture its prey. © Dilip Amin

Chapter 5

Fighter Aircraft

'Capture Thread'

The first, and most observable, essential element within Britain's integrated air defence system, was the fighter aircraft. Britain had planned for an establishment of fifty-seven fighter squadrons by April 1940, but at the outbreak of war, possessed only thirty-nine. The 'fighter force was in the comparatively early stages of a considerable programme of expansion'.[1] To compound this shortfall, four squadrons were despatched within a week to support the British Expeditionary Force in France, as part of what Dowding called the 'Field Force'. Britain's air defence was left dangerously depleted, and vulnerable to aerial attack. The 'Home Base' now stood at only thirty-five squadrons, all in various stages of efficiency and readiness. Of these squadrons, twenty-five were formed by the regular Royal Air Force, and fourteen by the Royal Auxiliary Air Force,[2] which were assembled from volunteer airmen and groundcrew. The conduct of the latter, in the forthcoming battle, would show conclusively that they were coequal to their regular comrades in arms.

A fighter squadron was expected to field twelve aircraft, which were arranged into two 'flights', A and B, each with six aircraft. The 'flights' were further divided into 'sections' of three aircraft, and each 'section' was identified by the colours blue, red, yellow, or green. So, Britain's 'Home Base' of thirty-five squadrons totalled a mere 420 fighter aircraft available for defending the British Isles.

Fortunately for Britain, two events were to provide a temporary relief, while the programme of expansion continued apace. The first event to buy time, was the compromise reached in Munich a year earlier between British Prime Minister, Neville Chamberlain, and German Führer, Adolf Hitler, which slowed down the road to war. The second was the hiatus known as the 'phoney war', the name given to the period before the British Expeditionary Force saw military action in France and Belgium. Both episodes brought much needed time for Fighter Command to increase the number of squadrons it had at its disposal for the aerial fighting that lay ahead.

ENEMY SIGHTED

Dowding placed great importance on the expansion of his fighter force, and firmly expressed this view in letters to the Air Council during the first two months of war:

> The best defence of the country is the fear of the fighter. If we were strong in fighters, we should probably never be attacked in force. If we are moderately strong, we shall probably be attacked, and the attacks will gradually be brought to a standstill. During this period considerable damage will have been caused. If we are weak in fighter strength, the attacks will not be brought to a standstill and the productive capacity of the country will be virtually destroyed ... the continued existence of the nation and all its services, depends upon the Royal Navy and the Fighter Command.[3]

This discord was not uncommon for the forthright Dowding, and his candid assertions would later come to jeopardise his position with the Air Council.

Four days after the Germans launched their offensive in France and Belgium, Britain accelerated its programme of expansion, with a newly formed Ministry, and Minister for Aircraft Production. The decision to appoint Lord Beaverbrook, a media tycoon and close friend of Churchill, to this vital position was shown to be well judged, as the number of fighter aircraft being produced began to increase. Five days before the Battle of Britain officially commenced, Fighter Command held a reserve of 222 Hurricanes, 119 Spitfires, and thirty-two Defiants, ready for immediate issue.[4]

Beaverbrook had previous experience of getting things done, having built the *Daily Express* into the most successful mass-circulation newspaper in the world, with sales of 2.25 million copies a day across Britain. Notably, as he was putting British fighter aircraft into the sky, his own son, Max Aitken, a Fighter Command pilot, was knocking German aircraft out of the very same sky. He was credited, over the course of the Battle of France and the Battle of Britain, with the confirmed destruction of five, probable destruction of a further three, and causing damage to one more enemy aircraft.

At the time when war was declared in September 1939, Fighter Command had several different types of aircraft in service. These were the Bristol Blenheim Mk IF; Boulton Paul Defiant Mk I; Gloster Gladiator; Hawker Hurricane Mk I; and Supermarine Spitfire Mk I. The Luftwaffe had two

FIGHTER AIRCRAFT

fighters at its disposal, the single engine Messerschmitt Me 109, and twin-engine Messerschmitt Me 110. Both German machines were manufactured by the Bavarian Aeroplane Company, *Bayerische Flugzeugwerke*. The descriptor 'Bf', acknowledging the manufacturer, or 'Me', acknowledging the designer, Willy Messerschmitt, are interchangeable. Both aircraft would prove to be formidable adversaries, when flown by experienced Luftwaffe pilots, but the Messerschmitt Me 109 was by far the more lethal, and the British rapidly discovered which of their aircraft were up to the task, and which were not.

The Bristol Blenheim Mk IF, a twin-engine, low-wing, all metal monoplane, was a long-range fighter variant of the Blenheim Mk I light bomber. It had five forward-facing Browning .303 inch machine-guns, and one rear-facing turret mounted Browning machine gun. Although it had a long range, it was slow, too slow, with a top speed of only 260 mph (418 kph). It was also not very manoeuvrable. These deficiencies in performance and agility put the Blenheim at a serious disadvantage when pitted against Luftwaffe day fighters. However, Fighter Command was responsible for protecting Britain's airspace during both day and night, and so the Blenheim was reassigned to a night fighter role, soon to be equipped with new technology, Airborne Interception (AI) radar. The redeployment was foresighted, as the Blenheim was shown to be more suited to its nocturnal role, where it successfully intercepted Luftwaffe night bombing raids.

The Boulton Paul Defiant Mk I, another low-wing monoplane, was designed in the belief that Luftwaffe bombers carrying out raids over Britain, would be unescorted by fighters, as they lacked the range to fly from Germany. Consequently, the Defiant was configured not for dogfighting with enemy fighters, but instead, for intercepting unescorted, less lethal bombers. Unfortunately, the German blitzkrieg and rapid subjugation of Western Europe, resulted in Luftwaffe fighters being able to operate from captured French airfields. The Defiant's vulnerability was soon exposed, following clashes with Messerschmitt Me 109 and 110s, first over France, and then over Britain itself.

The Defiant had three main weaknesses, when clashing with enemy fighters. The first was its low top speed of 304 mph (489 kph), which prevented it from being able to catch, or escape from the much faster German fighters. The second weakness was that it did not have any forward-facing armament, and only a hydraulic powered rear-facing turret, armed with four .303 inch machine-guns. This led to the third weakness, which was that the pilot and gunner had to think in unison, whereby the pilot had to manoeuvre the Defiant into a position where the gunner was able to engage the enemy aircraft. Defiants did, however, enjoy initial success during their first encounters with Messerschmitt Me 109s over Dunkirk, when German pilots, mistaking them for Hurricanes, carried out attacks from behind, only to be engaged by the Defiant's rear facing machine-guns. This success was to be short lived once the German pilots realised the Defiant's vulnerability to a frontal attack. They, like the Blenheim, also suffered unacceptable losses during daytime engagements, and were also reassigned to a night fighter role. As an AI radar-equipped night fighter, the Defiant did extremely well, shooting down more raiders per interception than any other night fighter in the winter of 1940–41.[5]

The Gloster Gladiator was the last biplane to see frontline service with Fighter Command, although it was the first RAF aircraft to have an enclosed cockpit. It was more effectively armed than the Defiant, with four forward-facing Browning .303 inch machine-guns, two in the wing and two in the fuselage. However, being able to achieve only 253 mph (407 kph) and having non-retractable wheels, they were inferior in speed and manoeuvrability, to not only the German fighters, but also to the bombers. The Gladiator did see action against the Luftwaffe in Norway, and although the British pilots fought bravely, they were tactically disadvantaged. Despite their being obsolete, Gladiators were used during the Battle of Britain to defend the Naval Dockyard at Plymouth, because the local grass airstrip was too short for Fighter Command's other fighters. Fortunately, Plymouth's location in the south-west of England, meant that it was beyond the range of the Luftwaffe's Messerschmitt Me 109 fighters.

The Gloster Gladiator was designed in response to F.7/30, the Air Ministry's unambitious specification for a new fighter aircraft, and it was selected over designs submitted by both Hawker and Supermarine. Undeterred, both Hawker and Supermarine continued through private enterprise, to design a more effective fighter. Hawker would go on to develop the Hawker Hurricane, under specification F.36/34, and Supermarine entered private collaboration with Rolls-Royce, to develop the world beating Supermarine Spitfire, with its Rolls-Royce Merlin powerplant, under specification F.37/34. It is sobering to reflect on what might have happened if this work had not been so tenaciously undertaken, and if the Air Ministry had not been persuaded to issue further specifications. Fighter Command would have had to meet the Luftwaffe over France and Britain, not in formidable modern monoplanes, but instead, in vastly inferior and obsolete biplanes, incapable of engaging with the enemy on equal terms.

FIGHTER AIRCRAFT

The Hawker Hurricane Mk I would come to be known as the 'workhorse' of Fighter Command. It was a low-wing monoplane, constructed using a tubular metal structure and fabric covering throughout, although the wings in later marks would subsequently be covered in metal. The Hurricane's construction meant that it could be built quickly and in large numbers, an assertion borne out by the fact that it would form two thirds of Fighter Command's strength during the Battle of Britain. Importantly, the Hurricane was able to tolerate significant damage during aerial combat, which could often be patched up at the Sector airfield by ground crew. The consequence of it not having to be sent away to a maintenance depot for lengthy repair was that it remained available for operations.

The Hurricane Mk I had a top speed of 312 mph (502 kph), and the Hurricane Mk IIA, which became available towards the end of the Battle of Britain, increased that to 342 mph (550 kph). The Hurricane Mk I was slower than both the Messerschmitt Me 109E, at 354 mph (570 kph) and Messerschmitt Me 110, at 340 mph (547 kph). However, it was more manoeuvrable than its adversaries, and so a skilled Hurricane pilot could out turn both rivals in a dogfight, gaining a tactical advantage that allowed him to get behind his adversary and take the shot. The Hurricane Mk I was faster than the enemy's bombers and to capitalise on this tactical advantage they would, where possible (and often it was not possible) attack the slower, lower bomber formations.

The Hurricane Mk I was fitted with eight .303 inch Browning machine-guns, concentrated in a tight configuration of four guns in each wing. This arrangement made the aircraft a very stable gun platform, providing an effective concentration of firepower capable of downing enemy aircraft, especially bombers. On both the Hurricane's manoeuvrability and firepower, Douglas Bader, an indefatigable figure within Fighter Command, commented, 'I grew to love it. It was strong, highly manoeuvrable, could turn inside the Spitfire, and of course the Me 109. Best of all, it was a marvellous gun platform. The aeroplane remained rock steady when you fired.'[6]

The Supermarine Spitfire Mk IA was Fighter Command's fastest interceptor monoplane, and indeed, with a top speed of 355 mph (571 kph), it was more than capable of matching the speed of the Messerschmitt Me 109E. It was constructed from metal, had a streamlined design, and became easily recognisable by its eye catching elliptical wing. However, it took longer for a Spitfire to roll off the production line than it did a Hurricane, and unlike a Hurricane, a Spitfire that suffered battle damage could not readily be patched up at its Sector airfield, and instead had to be sent away.

ENEMY SIGHTED

The Spitfire Mk IA was the mainstay mark during the Battle of France, and Battle of Britain. It, like the Hurricane Mk I, was equipped with eight .303 inch Browning machine-guns. The guns, however, were arranged differently, with one near the fuselage, two near the middle, and one further out. This configuration, albeit deadly, did not achieve the same concentration of firepower as that delivered by the Hurricane. For this reason, and because of its higher speed, the Spitfire would, if possible, be tasked to engage the Messerschmitt Me 109 fighters escorting Luftwaffe bombers over Britain.

The Supermarine Spitfire Mk I would combine with the Hawker Hurricane Mk I to present the greatest threat to Luftwaffe aircrew. At the outbreak of war, Fighter Command's Home Base consisted of ten Spitfire squadrons and twelve Hurricane squadrons. Within six months, as the relative calm of the phoney war crescendoed into 'blitzkrieg', there would be a further nine Spitfire squadrons and seven Hurricane squadrons available, to operate both defensively and offensively from the British Isles.[7]

To compare the Spitfire and Hurricane in equestrian terms, the former would be a sleek racehorse, with its creditable stablemate more akin to a sturdy draft horse. Although the Hurricane fought in greater numbers in the opening phase of the war, it is the Spitfire that would undoubtedly come to personify Fighter Command, and its David and Goliath struggle with the Luftwaffe. This was due to several reasons: in part, its mesmerising aesthetic qualities; partly, its fearsome reputation among Luftwaffe adversaries (leading many to exhibit 'Spitfire Snobbery', and wrongly insist they had been shot down by a Spitfire), and also partly due to its ability to supercharge public involvement and support for the aerial battle overhead. There were many 'Spitfire Funds', but no similar funds for its erstwhile stablemate; it exemplified 'the best of British', and served as an ideological rallying point for a beleaguered nation.

Although there were more Hurricanes in service at the beginning of the Second World War, the Spitfire would go on to be produced in greater numbers and become the predominant British fighter. Being so versatile, it would be the only British fighter aircraft to remain in production throughout the Second World War, with over 20,000 being constructed. In total, there were twenty-four marks of Spitfire developed, during which time the power more than doubled, from the Mk I's 1,050 horsepower Merlin II to the Mk 24's, 2,340 horsepower Griffon 84. Maximum speed increased by around a third, from 362 mph (583 kph) in the Mk I, to 454 mph (735 kph) in the Mk 24. The maximum rate of climb more than doubled, from 2,195 ft (669 metres) per minute in the Mk I, to 4,900 ft (1,494 metres) per minute in the Mk 24. The maximum take-off weight more than doubled, from the Mk I's 5,720 lb (2,595 kg) to the Mk 24's 10,920 lb (4,953 kg).[8]

Widespread adulation for the Spitfire and Hurricane, and nexus with the Group Operations Room at Uxbridge, necessitate further commentary. Several enhancements were made to both aircraft, improving their performance during the Battle of Britain. The first was the propeller, or airscrew, which can either efficiently, or inefficiently, use the power generated by an engine. A propeller whose angle of attack, that is the angle at which it meets oncoming air, cannot be altered in flight is like driving a car without being able to change gears, regardless of differing conditions. Early Spitfires and Hurricanes were fitted with De Havilland two-bladed wooden propellers, which had only two settings: fine for take-off, and coarse for all conditions during flight. This resulted in a serious limitation in the aircraft's performance. Werner Molders, a leading Luftwaffe pilot, wrote after trialling a captured Spitfire, 'and because the propeller has only two pitch settings (take off and cruise), in a rapidly changing air combat situation the motor is either over speeding, or else is not being used to the full'.[9] The British needed their fighters to be equipped with constant speed propellers, like those fitted to their adversary, the Messerschmitt Me 109. A constant speed propeller allows an aircraft to take better advantage of the power supplied by an engine, in the same way that changing gears in a car does.

Beaverbrook approached Geoffrey De Havilland just over two weeks prior to the commencement of the Battle of Britain, and instructed him to fit all Spitfires, Hurricanes and Defiants, in that order, with constant speed metal propellers. Astonishingly, all Spitfires and Hurricanes were modified by 16 August, resulting in a reduced take off run, from 1,260 ft (384 metres), to 675 ft (206 metres), an increased rate of climb, and a greater top speed.[10] Importantly, the new propellers were shorter, and so reduced the occasions during take-off when a Spitfire's propeller would accidentally plough into the ground as its tail lifted.[11]

Another enhancement, resulting from a joint venture between the British Air Ministry and American petroleum suppliers, developed 100 octane fuel. The previously available eighty-seven octane fuel, restricted the Spitfire and Hurricane's Merlin engine to only 1,000 horsepower, well below the 1,140 horsepower Daimler Benz engine powering their nemesis, the Messerschmitt Me 109. Known as BAM 100/130, the new fuel delivered 30 per cent more horsepower, providing British fighters with more power when taking off, climbing, and dogfighting with the Luftwaffe.[12]

ENEMY SIGHTED

The criticality of this new fuel was commented on three years later:

> It is an established fact that a difference of only thirteen points in octane number made possible the defeat of the Luftwaffe by the RAF in the fall of 1940. This difference, slight as it seems, is sufficient to give a plane the vital edge in altitude, rate of climb, and manoeuvrability that spells the difference between defeat and victory.[13]

The enhancements to both propeller and fuel greatly assisted Fighter Command pilots when engaging with the Luftwaffe during 1940, but there was one problem they continued to experience, which would not be resolved till the following year. Fighter Command pilots reported, that as soon as they got on the tail of a Messerschmitt Me 109, it would go into a sharp dive to get away. When they attempted to follow, the manoeuvre would starve the Merlin engine's float-controlled carburettor, causing it to momentarily cut out, and so allow their adversary to escape. The same problem arose when British fighters entered a steep dive, while attacking bomber formations below them. Werner Molders, when trialling a captured Spitfire, wrote, 'as a fighting aircraft, however, it is miserable. A sudden push forward on the stick will cause the motor to cut.'[14] The reason why the German fighter pilots did not experience the same problem was because, unlike their pursuers, the Mercedes Benz engine benefited from direct fuel injection, rather than relying on a carburettor. The operational tactic to compensate for this problem was for the pilot to roll the aircraft, as he commenced his dive. The technical solution was to fit a restrictor in the fuel supply line, and a diaphragm known as 'Shilling's Orifice', or 'Shilling's Penny', named after its designer Beatrice Shilling, a scientist at the Royal Aircraft Establishment, Farnborough. Later enhancements would involve moving the fuel outlet from the bottom of the carburettor, to halfway up, and the use of fuel injection using a Stromberg pressure carburettor, and finally an SU injection carburettor.[15]

Surprisingly, pilots flying early Spitfires and Hurricanes had no frontal protection from enemy fire. Dowding complained to the Air Ministry stating, 'If Chicago gangsters can have bulletproof glass in their cars, I see no reason why my pilots cannot have the same.'[16] As a result, both types of aircraft were fitted with 1-inch (2½ cm) thick bulletproof windscreens, although unfortunately, the programme of work to do so was not completed until towards the end of the Battle of Britain. Later, pilots would also receive protection against attacks

FIGHTER AIRCRAFT

from the rear with the inclusion of armour plating behind their seat. 'These two measures were to save the life of more than one fighter pilot in combat.'[17]

Both Spitfire and Hurricane were originally armed with wing-mounted .303 inch (7.69 mm), rifle calibre machine-guns. In truth, a shot on target was unlikely to do serious damage, unless the pilot was seriously hurt, or killed, or if critical parts such as the engine, fuel tank or control cables were hit. Their adversary, the Messerschmitt Me 109, was more heavily armed in one of two configurations, either with four .312-inch (7.92 mm) rifle calibre machine-guns, of which two were wing-mounted, and two were over the engine, or alternatively with two .312-inch (7.92 mm) rifle calibre machine-guns above the engine, and two wing-mounted .787-inch (20 mm) MG FF cannon. The cannon round was in essence an explosive shell, much larger than the rifle round, and capable of causing more serious damage. During the Battle of Britain, some Spitfires and Hurricanes were fitted with French design Hispano .787 inch (20 mm) cannon, built under licence by the British Manufacturing and Research Company (BMRC). Because the cannon were wing-mounted, they had to be installed on their side in the Spitfire, due to its narrow wing profile. This resulted in frequent stoppages, caused by problems with ammunition feed, and spent-case ejection.[18] However, once the initial problems were overcome, cannon-equipped Spitfires would go on to reap havoc among Luftwaffe formations.

Many people may wonder why the smooth elliptical wings on some Spitfires were clipped, and the answer is that it was necessary in order to survive. In the autumn of 1941, a new Luftwaffe fighter, the Focke-Wulf Fw 190, began to challenge Fighter Command for aerial dominance. Its German name was *'Würger'*, meaning 'butcher bird', and alarmingly the 'butcher bird' began despatching Spitfires, which were particularly vulnerable at lower altitudes due to their lower roll rate and airspeed. A captured Fw 190 was trialled against a Spitfire Mk V by the Air Fighting Development Unit (AFDU), which reported 'in the starkest terms the measure of the inferiority of Fighter Command's principal fighter type during the third year of the war'. Clipping the wings on some Spitfire Mk Vs, helped improve their manoeuvrability, especially during low altitude combat. 'Her wings were clipped, and her supercharger blades cropped for better low-level work, and the outraged bird was dubbed the clipped and cropped spitty.'[19]

Later Spitfires, such as the Mk LFIXe, 'LF' denoting low altitude fighter, and 'e' denoting clipped e type wing, were purposely built with clipped wings, low altitude two stage superchargers, and intercooler Merlin 63 engines, to take on the Fw 190 in low altitude combat below 25,000 ft (7,620 metres).

ENEMY SIGHTED

The force acting on a pilot as a result of acceleration, or gravity, is described in units of acceleration equal to 'one G' (gravitational acceleration). Trials between a Messerschmitt Me 109 (captured before the Battle of Britain) and the Spitfire, revealed that the seat in the German aircraft was reclined further than in the British Fighter. This meant that the Luftwaffe pilot would be sat in a more horizontal position, and therefore able to pull more 'G' without blacking out. A simple solution was implemented, whereby Spitfires were fitted with modified two-step rudder pedals. The rationale being that the pilot would place his feet on the lower pedal during normal flight and raise them onto the higher pedal when about to engage the enemy, so he could execute higher 'G' manoeuvres.[20]

The exceptionality of Mitchell's creation allowed it to be developed and used for a variety of roles. One that is perhaps not so well known is the clandestine, although highly successful role performed by the Spitfire as an instrument for intelligence gathering. Here, the Royal Air Force adopted a policy of employing fighter prototypes, after removing their guns, leaving them with only their speed and height to evade enemy aircraft. The application of this approach was recorded in a narrative by the Air Ministry.[21] A special detachment was formed at RAF Heston in September 1939. Referred to as the Heston Flight, it was placed under 11 Group and administered by RAF Northolt until June of the following year, when it transferred to Coastal Command.

The detachment, which came to be known as the Photographic Development Unit from January 1940, continued to operate from Heston, as well as forward operating posts in France, where the aircraft were identified as 212 Squadron, to help mask the secretive nature of their work. All the Spitfires were 'cleaned up', their surfaces streamlined, and all non-essential equipment removed to increase their operating range and also their top speed, in the hope that this would give them the edge when being pursued by Luftwaffe fighters. Those aircraft required to fly high-altitude sorties were painted a shade of blue, to help hide them against a clear blue sky. Those that were required to fly low-level sorties were painted a shade of pink, as this was considered the best colour to protect them against ground fire as the pink blended well against low cloud, especially in the early morning or late evening sunlight.

The initial delivery of Spitfire Mk Is for photographic reconnaissance were designated Types 'A', 'B', and 'C'. Type 'A' had armaments removed and an F.24 camera with a 5-inch focal length mounted in each wing. Their range was found to be too restricted when operating from English

FIGHTER AIRCRAFT

bases, and the scale of photographs obtained varied between 1/70,000 and 1/80,000, when taken from normal operational heights. The type 'B', or medium-range photographic Spitfire arrived in January and was fitted with an additional twenty-nine to thirty gallon (132 to 136 litre) fuel tank behind the pilot, which extended its range at cruising speed to 750 miles (1,207 kilometres), making it practicable to initiate sorties from the south-east of England. The greater focal length of the lenses fitted to the cameras, 8 inch instead of 5 inch, meant that from a height of 32,000 ft (9,754 metres), photographs could be secured at a scale of 1/48,000, as against 1/76,800.

The type 'C', or long range photographic Spitfire, became available less than two months before Hitler's invasion of Western Europe. In addition to the fuel tank behind the pilot, it was fitted with a thirty gallon (114 litre) bulge tank in the port wing, increasing the plane's range at cruising speed to 900 miles (1,448 km), bringing Kiel, the Kriegsmarine's U-Boat Wolfpack lair, within the scope of reconnaissance. At the time of the fall of France, all of the Photographic Development Unit and 212 Squadron's Spitfires were type 'B' and 'C' photographic Spitfires. Indeed, it was one of these aerial scouts, which first spotted the Germans manoeuvring to outflank the Allied Armies by breaking through the Forest of Ardennes, and so forcing the British and French to retreat.

In considering the aircraft available to Fighter Command at the beginning of the Second World War, it is relevant to say something about the Rolls-Royce Merlin II engine that powered the Hurricane Mk I, Spitfire Mk IA, and Boulton Paul Defiant Mk I. Its pedigree can be traced back to the Napier Lion and Rolls-Royce R engines, which successfully powered the Supermarine Seaplanes, enabling them to win the Schneider Trophy on three successive occasions. Rolls-Royce recognised that only liquid cooled engines allowed the clean aerodynamic design required for fast planes, especially fighters, and that far greater power could be obtained from them than from any comparable air cooled types. Detailed work started on developing a new engine in 1932, the same year that Adolf Hitler became Chancellor of Germany.[22] The result was a powerful 27 litre capacity, 1,000 horsepower, liquid cooled engine, originally known as the PV-12, which indicated it was a 'private venture' with no government funding. It would come to be known formally as the 'Merlin', following Rolls-Royce's convention of naming its engines after birds of prey. The development of the Merlin came at the right time, as Mitchell and Camm's interceptor monoplane designs would both be based around this streamlined engine, resulting in the aerodynamic front profile of both the Spitfire and Hurricane.

ENEMY SIGHTED

For the sake of completeness, mention should be made of the Rolls-Royce Griffon engine, which was to power later marks of Spitfire. Work on designing the Griffon, named after the Griffon Vulture, had in fact commenced before war was declared, but was temporarily halted at the behest of the Minister for Aircraft Production, Lord Beaverbrook, in order to allow Rolls-Royce to focus on producing the Merlin powerplant. The Griffon 65 and 66 engines delivered over twice as much power, 2,220 horsepower as the Merlin II, and Griffon Spitfires were almost a third heavier than their Merlin powered predecessors.

So, which was the better fighter aircraft, the Royal Air Force's Supermarine Spitfire or the Luftwaffe's Messerschmitt Me 109? Well, it appears from a curious experiment performed by German engineers in 1942, that both were superior in certain aspects, and a composite of both performed better than either one individually.[23] The opportunity arose when a Spitfire Mk Vb, operating from RAF Westhampnett in 11 Group, was forced to land after being hit by flak over Normandy, and fell into enemy hands. The pilot, Lieutenant Bernard Scheidhauer of 131 Squadron, had become disorientated and mistook the Nazi Occupied Isle of Jersey, for the Isle of Wight, which had not been overrun. As a result, the aircraft was recovered to the Daimler Benz test facility at Echterdingen, Germany, where it was made airworthy. After initial flights as a Spitfire, the section to the front of the cockpit was replaced with that of a Messerschmitt Me 109, complete with a Daimler Benz engine. Flight tests of the 'Messer Spit', revealed that it was faster than the British fighter, more manoeuvrable than the German fighter, and could fly higher than both. As for Scheidhauer, he was captured and interned at the infamous Stalag Luft III prisoner of war camp, where he took part in the famous mass breakout. Lamentably, he was recaptured in Saarbrucken, along with his escape partner, Roger Bushell, 'Big X', and both were murdered by the Gestapo on direct orders from Adolf Hitler.

We have reflected on the potency of Fighter Command's two main day fighters, and the offering they both brought, but would they have been so successful without the other elements of Britain's air defence? The question can best be answered using the words of Winston Churchill, who surmised that:

> All the ascendancy of the Hurricanes and Spitfires would have been fruitless, but for the system which had been devised, and built before the war. It had been shaped and refined in constant action, and all was now fused together into a most elaborate instrument of war, the like of which existed nowhere in the world.[24]

Chapter 6

Fighter Command

'Capture Thread'

Fighter Command

Fighter Command, with its Sector and Satellite airfields and Operations Rooms at Headquarters, Group and Sector level, provided the necessary infrastructure for despatching the Royal Air Force's fighter aircraft. In September 1939, Headquarters Fighter Command was at Bentley Priory, Stanmore. The terms Bentley Priory and RAF Stanmore are synonymous, both having been used by historians when referring to Headquarters Fighter Command. Bentley Priory was located on a large estate in North London, which had previously served as a private home, hotel, and girls' school, before being purchased by the Air Ministry in 1926 to serve as part of the ADGB. This location had oversight of the 'recognised air picture' over the whole of the British Isles, and it was from here that the business of air defence was coordinated across a patchwork of Groups, which in turn controlled a myriad of Sectors and Satellites.

> The system dictated that the Command should be responsible for the identification of approaching formations, and for the allotment of enemy raids to Groups, where any doubt existed. Group Commanders decided which Sector should meet any specified raid, and the strength of the fighter force which should be employed. Sector Commanders detailed the fighter units to be employed and operated the machinery of interception.[1]

The Fighter Command Operations Room at Bentley Priory was in the ground floor ballroom, and there was a Filter Room below it, in the basement. The building did not afford protection against blast damage, and so Fighter Command's ability to operate effectively would have been severely diminished if Bentley Priory were to receive a direct hit during

ENEMY SIGHTED

a bombing raid. This vulnerability was recognised, but it was not until March 1940, a mere four months before the Battle of Britain began, that both Operations Room and Filter Room were relocated to a secure concrete underground bunker.

A general situation map on top of a plotting table was used to display aircraft tracks over the whole of the British Isles and its sea approaches. The Filter Room would receive information of radar plots from the Chain Home (CH) and Chain Home Low (CHL) Radar stations, detailing its position, strength, height and direction. A Filter Officer, representing each Radar station, would check, or 'filter', the information to determine whether the plot represented hostile or friendly aircraft. This was done by cross-referencing the plot with others, and against the 'Pip Squeak' signals sent by British fighters on their TR.9D radios, to the High Frequency (HF) Direction Finding (Huff Duff) receivers located on the Sector stations.

If the plot represented enemy aircraft, then it was given the designation 'H' for hostile. This plot would be allocated a raid number, such as 'Hostile One Four', and this number would continue to be used for that raid until it had left British airspace. If the plot represented friendly aircraft, then it was given the designation 'F' for friendly, and if the aircraft could not be identified, the plot would be designated 'X' for unknown. The plots were entered onto a crescent shaped filter table displaying the British Isles, the English Channel, North Sea and a large part of Northern France. Each filtered plot was then passed directly to the Fighter Command Operations Room upstairs, and the relevant Group Operations Room, in whose area the plot was entering. The Operations Room at Uxbridge would receive the majority of hostile plots, as most raids were targeting London and the south-east of England. As the plots progressed inland, they would continue to be followed by the Observer Corps and reported to Group Operations Rooms, who in turn relayed the information, and availability of their squadrons, back to the Fighter Command Operations Room. There, the WAAF Plotters and Tellers would update the general situation map, providing senior officers with a 'recognised air picture', a view of what was happening across the entire British Isles.[2]

The AOC Fighter Command had oversight of the Fighter Command Operations Room and was supported by senior representatives from the Observer Corps; anti-aircraft and searchlights; Bomber Command; Coastal Command; and the Ministry of Home Security. Balloon Command was accessible through Group Operations Rooms. This joined-up approach allowed vital information to be speedily sent, received and actioned by those who needed it, when they needed it. Everybody would have the same filtered view of what was happening, what Fighter Controllers today would call a 'recognised air picture'.

It is said that Dowding, as Head of Fighter Command, had day-to-day responsibility for the fighting over Northern France, and subsequently over Britain itself. Events would show that he was the right man to steer Fighter Command during the most crucial period in its history. He was the right man, in the main, because of his experience and his personality. First, as one of the main architects of the integrated air defence system, he possessed intimate and detailed knowledge of all its essential elements. This knowledge allowed him to deploy those essential elements in unison, to deadly effect. Second, Dowding's reserved but obstinate nature and reflective mind meant that decisions were made not to satisfy an overinflated ego, but rather, based on informed knowledge and need. Fortunately for the Royal Air Force, Dowding 'was the very antithesis of Goering',[3] whose constant interference, and showcasing was to cost the Luftwaffe dearly.

Group

At the time war was declared, there were three Groups within Fighter Command: Numbers 11, 12, and 13, protecting the British Isles. Responsibility for defending East Anglia and the industrial Midlands fell to 12 Group, with Headquarters at Watnall, in Nottinghamshire, under the Command of Air Vice-Marshal Sir Trafford Leigh-Mallory. The north of England, Scotland, and Northern Ireland were the responsibility of 13 Group, with Headquarters at Kenton, in Tyne and Wear, under the command of Air Vice-Marshal Richard Ernest Saul. The English Channel, south-east England, and the capital itself was defended by 11 Group, with Headquarters at Uxbridge, in Middlesex, under the command of New Zealander Air Vice-Marshal Sir Keith Rodney Park. A fourth Group, Number 10, which would have responsibility for defending the south-west of England, and Wales, would not be ready to begin operations until July the following year; its Headquarters were at Box, in Wiltshire, and the Commander was Air Vice-Marshal Sir Christopher Joseph Quintin Brand.

If Dowding had day-to-day responsibility for controlling the fighting over Northern France and Britain, then Park, had hour-to-hour responsibility for the fighting over south-east England and the English Channel. He had previously served as Dowding's Senior Air Staff Officer, and like him, had a thorough understanding of Fighter Command's integrated air defence system. As well as this understanding, he also had the benefit of having personally led others to fight against the same enemy, during the First World War. During a BBC interview in 1961, he remarked:

> My experience in 1917, 1918, in the Royal Flying Corps, was absolutely indispensable to me when, later in 1940, I was commanding the fighter defences in the south of England. First of all, covering the retreat from Dunkirk, and then throughout 1940, and especially during the Battle of Britain.[4]

Park understood that securing air superiority was an encumbrance to invasion, and this would be his strategic imperative, during both the Battle of Britain, and later in the war, the Battle for Malta. He was assisted in this goal by Dowding, who allowed his Commanders to determine individual tactics within their own Groups. This contrasted with the hindrance suffered by Park's Luftwaffe counterparts who, rather than being empowered to use operational discretion, were hampered by counterproductive orders, such as forcing German fighter escorts to fly alongside their bombers, and so losing any tactical advantage during dogfights with British fighters.

Each Group was equipped with its own Group Operations Room, but only those at Bentley Priory, Uxbridge and Box were given the protection afforded by being underground. The air defence over 12 and 13 Group would not be coordinated from a subterranean environment until the end of 1940, after the Battle of Britain.

Group Operations Rooms were configured in a similar way to that at Bentley Priory, except that the general situation map on the plotting table, showed only the area covered by the Group, and its surrounding vicinity. A board on the wall, called a 'totaliser' or 'tote' board, displayed the squadrons within the Group, and their status. Filtered information from Bentley Priory and reports from the Observer Corps were reconstructed onto detailed blocks, and moved into position on the general situation map, in croupier-like fashion, by female plotters. The Senior Group Controller would then determine which of his resources should engage with the raid and directed his Sector Controllers accordingly.

In its 1937 Battle Order, 11 Group declared that its wartime aim was 'to destroy enemy aircraft carrying out attacks on England, and to inflict such casualties as will force the enemy to desist from his attacks. In view of London's importance to the national existence, 11 Fighter Group has a special responsibility for its protection.'[5] Its raison d'etre, to shield Churchill's 'fat cow' from the Luftwaffe's aggression, is depicted on the 11 Group Fighter Command crest, whose Latin motto *tutela cordis*, translates into 'Defence of the Heart'. The crest depicts the clock tower of the Palace of Westminster, surrounded by an Astral crown incorporating a six pointed star between two wings. Astral crowns are used in heraldry to denote a connection with aviation. The tower represents London, the heart of the Empire, with whose safety the Group was charged. The hands of the clock are at eleven o'clock, to represent the Group's number.

Sector & Satellite

There were seven Sectors within 11 Group, all radiating out from London, and all had their own Sector Operations Room. From here, Sector Controllers, on instructions from Uxbridge, would direct the squadrons under their control to intercept German raids. Six of the Sectors within 11 Group also had Satellite airfields, which were to serve a very important function. When the German military overran Poland, Belgium, the Netherlands and France, they destroyed many of the opposing aircraft while they were still on the ground. This was largely because none of those countries possessed an effective air defence system capable of giving advance warning of an attack from the air. As events would show, the Luftwaffe's intention was to inflict the same devastation on Britain's Royal Air Force. Fighter Command, however, did have an effective air defence system and was prepared. The system had limitations and could not thwart every attack against the precious airfields, and so a tactic was employed whereby a squadron's aircraft would be dispersed across the Sector airfield, and across Satellite airfields. This meant that one Luftwaffe raid could not decimate an entire squadron, because the parked aircraft were too widely dispersed.

The possibility of the Luftwaffe delivering a coup de grace against a Sector was acknowledged, and planned for by 11 Group in its 1937 Battle Order, 'as a result of enemy action it may at times be necessary for squadrons to abandon their permanent aerodromes and operate from Satellite aerodromes'.[6] This was particularly the case when during a battle, fighter aircraft needed to land to rearm and refuel, before taking off again. The degree to which Satellite airfields were used during an aerial battle, varied from Sector to Sector, and was dependent on the 'air picture' at the time. However, it is clear that without them, Fighter Command would not

ENEMY SIGHTED

have had the operational flexibility, and resilience, desperately needed during the battles, first over France, and then Britain.

The Sectors within 11 Group, in anticlockwise order around London, were Sector 'A' at RAF Tangmere in Sussex, with its Satellite airfield at Westhampnett; Sector 'B', at RAF Kenley in Surrey, with its Satellite airfields at Redhill and Croydon; Sector 'C', at RAF Biggin Hill in Kent, with its Satellite airfields at Gravesend, West Malling, Detling and Lympne; Sector 'D', at RAF Hornchurch in Essex, with its Satellite airfields at Hawkinge, Manston, and Rochford; Sector 'E', at RAF North Weald in Essex, with its Satellite airfields at Martlesham Heath and Stapleford Tawney; Sector 'F', at RAF Debden in Essex, with no Satellite airfield; and lastly, Sector 'Z', at RAF Northolt in Middlesex, with its Satellite airfield at Hendon. Northolt is famous for the Polish Squadrons which operated from there, and its proximity to Uxbridge. Because of the role they played during the Second World War, and in particular the Battle of Britain, the names of many of these Sectors, and their Satellites, would enter the national psyche, becoming familiar not only to the Britons who lived during that conflict, but also to those who would come after them.

Sector Operations Rooms were located on the actual airfield or nearby, and unlike the underground Operations Room at Uxbridge, they were built above ground, which meant they were vulnerable to attack from the air. An illustration of this came on 18 August 1940, when 100 bombs were dropped on RAF Kenley. The raid resulted in ten people being killed, with many injured and widespread damage being caused, including to the direct telephone lines linking the Sector Operations Room and Uxbridge. There were clear instructions that in the event of this happening, communication between Sector and Group should, if possible, continue through radio transmissions. If there was a complete breakdown of communication with Uxbridge, then the Sector Controller was to assume control of all operations within his Sector, and to coordinate the response with adjoining Sectors.[7] On this occasion, a vacant butcher's shop in the nearby village of Caterham, at that time being used to train staff in Operations Room duties and procedures, was adapted to function as a temporary Sector Operations Room. The fact that telephone engineers, were able to restore 90 per cent of the telephone lines within two-and-a-half days, is testament to the sterling work undertaken by the General Post Office (GPO) during, and between, air raids. The same attack had also made the airfield at Kenley inoperable, and to underline the value of satellite sites, its fighters used the airfields at Croydon and Redhill to land and refuel, while their home airfield was temporarily out of action.[8]

FIGHTER COMMAND

There were two units within a Sector Operations Room, and both had a specific role to play. The first was the Direction Finding Room, which helped to inform the Sector Controller where his fighters were at any given time. The system was called 'Pip Squeak', named after a contemporary comic strip, 'Pip, Squeak and Wilfred'. British fighters were fitted with High Frequency (HF) Direction Finding (Huff Duff), and later, Very High Frequency (VHF) Direction Finding receivers, allowing information to be shared among pilots, or between pilots and the Sector Controller. The HF radio transmitter in each fighter was set to automatically transmit a signal to three Direction Finding stations located on every Sector, for a specified fourteen second period in any minute. The bearings from the three stations were then matched by the Direction Finding Room, and a unified bearing was plotted on the general situation map in the Sector Operations Room. The code word for the 'Pip Squeak' system was 'Cockerel', and if a pilot forgot to turn on his 'Pip Squeak', it would mean that his position was not revealed to the Sector Operations Room, leading the Controller to broadcast, 'is your cockerel crowing?'[9] 'Pip Squeak' meant that pilots could focus on air fighting, rather than concentrating on navigation and fixing their position. If an individual pilot needed help, then the Sector Controller could guide him back to an airfield. Importantly, because the system told the Sector Controller where his squadrons were, it allowed him to direct, or 'vector', them towards the enemy.

The second unit within the Sector Operations Room was Sector Ops. Plotters, positioned around the plotting table, would place tracks, raid plaques and other indicators on the general situation map, to display the position of friendly fighters based on information provided by 'Pip Squeak', and hostile raids based on filtered information from Bentley Priory, or from plots 'told on' by the Observer Corps. The Sector Controller, flanked by 'Ops A' and 'Ops B', would sit on a raised dais in front of the plotting table. 'Ops A' received instructions from the Group Operations Room, as to which hostile raid was to be intercepted, and whether at squadron or section strength. 'Ops B' were responsible for all lines of communication, including those to the airfield and its satellites. The Sector Controller would instruct 'Ops B' to 'scramble' aircraft, having assessed the squadron state board in front of him.

Ops Deputy Controllers, supported by dead reckoning navigators, would use the 'Principle of Equal Angles', to determine the compass heading British fighters needed to vector, to intercept the German raiders.[10] The methodology used here exemplified the brilliant, yet simple, solutions adopted by Fighter Command when addressing several significant challenges to its air defence capability. The 'Principle of Equal Angles' was also referred to as the 'Tizzy Angle', after the chairperson of the CSSAD committee, Henry T. Tizard, who stipulated its use. By drawing a line, from the raiders to the fighters, and making this the base of an isosceles triangle, with the fighter angle always equal to the raiders' angle, the two formations would meet at the apex of the triangle. If the raiders altered course, the Controller could visualise a new triangle on the general situation map and tell the fighters to alter their heading accordingly. If the fighters outpaced the raiders, and reached the apex first, they would be ordered to circle and wait. This simple system, which had evolved through improvisation, proved to be an extraordinary success.[11]

FIGHTER COMMAND

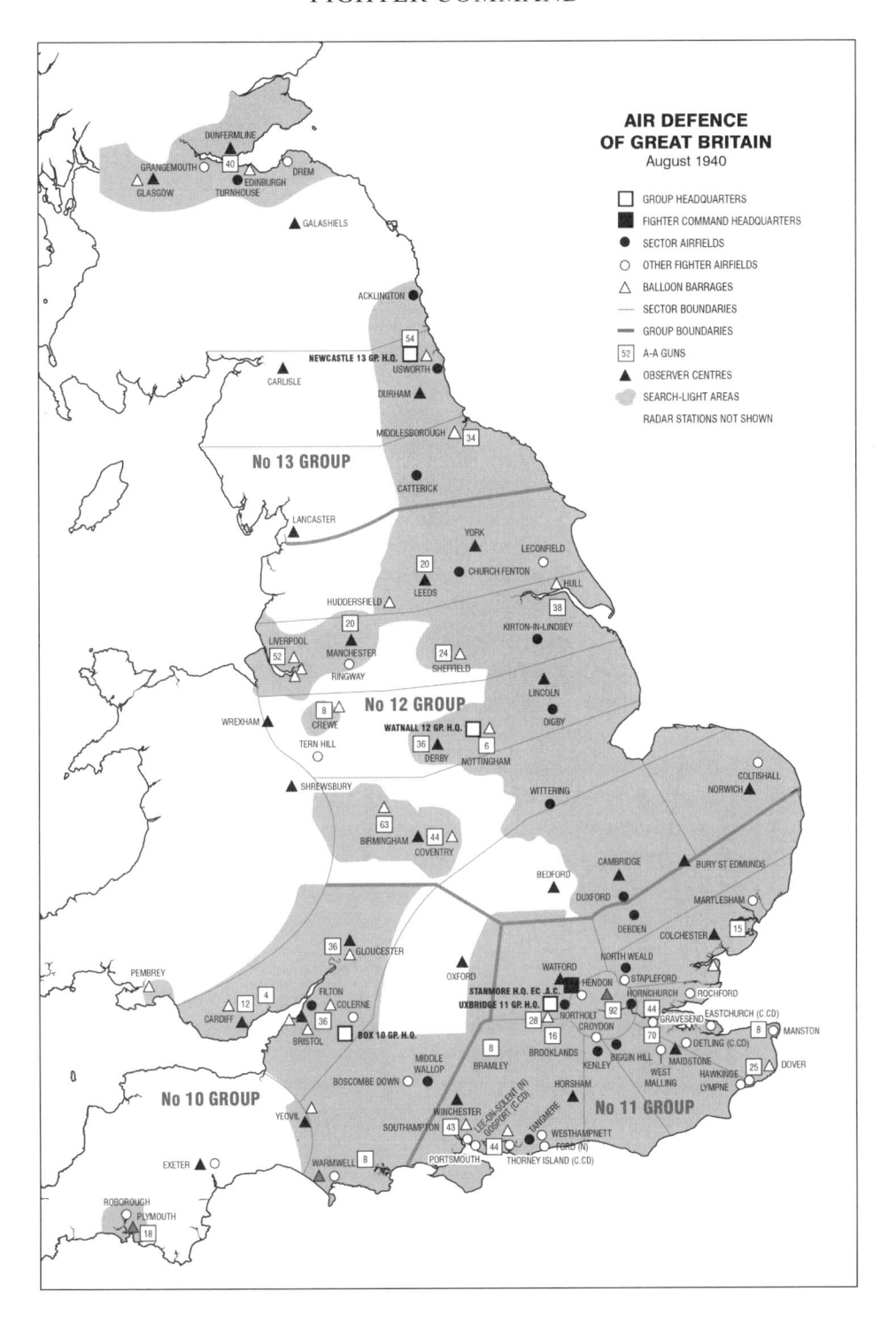

ENEMY SIGHTED

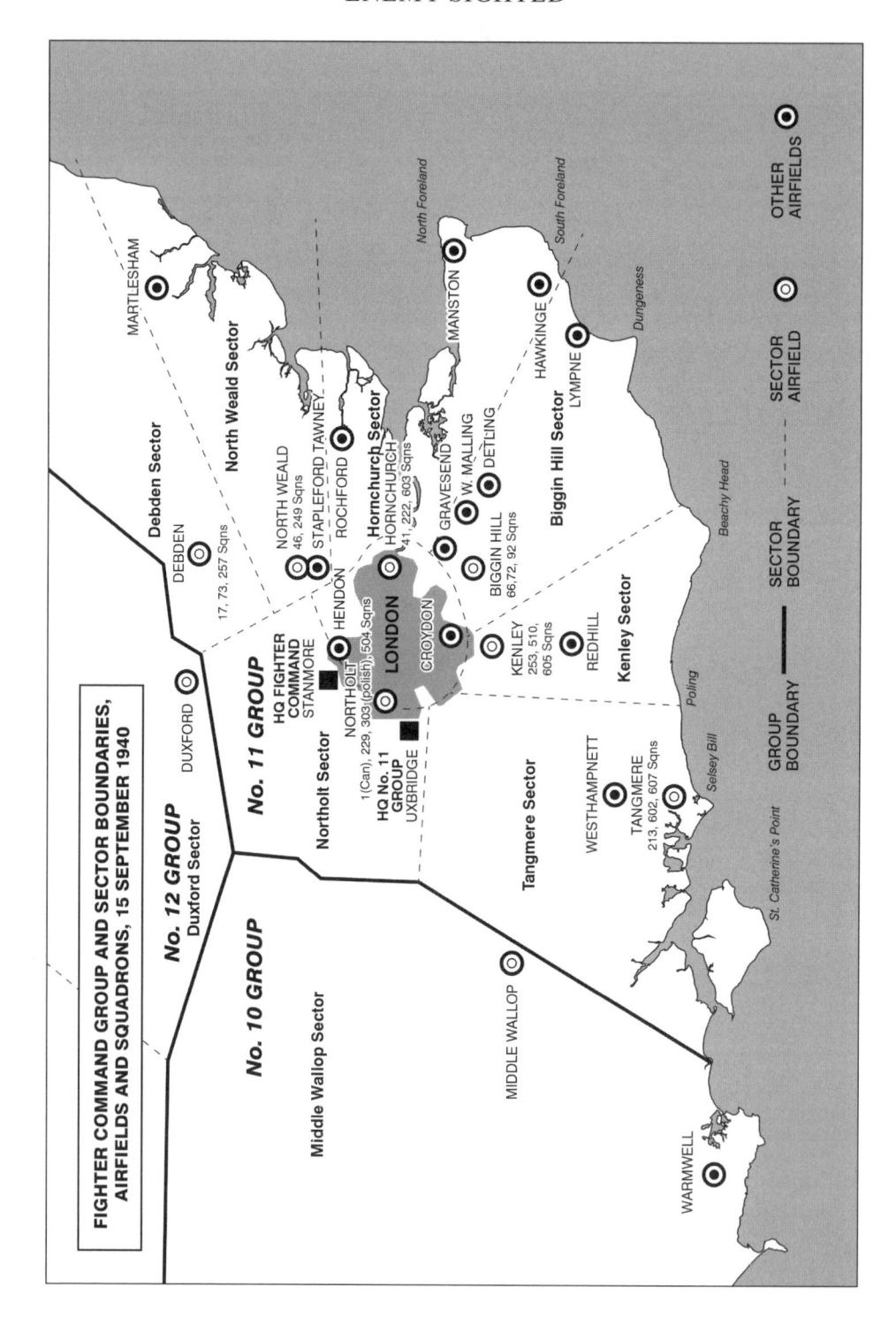

Chapter 7

Radio Detection and Ranging (Radar)
'Signal Thread'

Acoustic Detection

Before we explore radar it is worthwhile looking at what came before, to understand the colossal breakthrough achieved by using radio signals to detect approaching enemy aircraft. A key person in determining what preceded radar was Doctor William Sansome Tucker, a lecturer in Physics, at Imperial College, London. Tucker was posted to the Experimental Sound Ranging Station at Kemmel Hill in Belgium during the First World War, where he pioneered a methodology for locating enemy gun positions using a combination of mathematics and microphones. Importantly, the methodology was discovered also to be effective in detecting approaching enemy aircraft. After the war, Tucker was appointed Director of Acoustical Research at the Air Defence Experimental Establishment, Biggin Hill, where he conducted further research into 'sound ranging', using acoustic mirrors.

The mirrors, large parabolic reflectors constructed from concrete, were positioned along the coast, to detect approaching aircraft. The concept of using them for detecting aircraft acoustically was explained in a presentation on 'The World of Sound', by Sir William Bragg, at the 1919 Royal Institution Lectures for Children:

> It is obvious, of course, that there are ways of finding from what direction the sound of an aeroplane has come. We might, for example, make use of the power of a concave mirror to focus a sound ... the hum of an aeroplane is low in pitch, the sound waves are long, and therefore the mirror must be correspondingly large.[1]

ENEMY SIGHTED

It was found that as a mirror's size increased, so too did the distance over which it could detect an approaching aircraft. For this reason, the mirrors built along the east and south-east coast of England varied in size, with earlier versions being just under 15 ft (6 metres), and the final one at Romney Marsh, Kent, reaching 200 ft (61 metres) in length. However, sound ranging had several limitations, which would ultimately restrict its development. The first is that it was vulnerable to interference from temperature variations, or the sound of car engines, boats and even birds. The second was that while it could provide a bearing, it could not provide height or range. These shortcomings were laid bare during air exercises held five years before the declaration of war,[2] when no more than two in five 'hostile' bombers, were detected by the final mirror at Romney Marsh. The third limitation was its restricted range, even the large sound mirror at Romney Marsh had a maximum range of only eight miles (thirteen kilometres). The ponderous Vickers Virginia bombers, whose role it was during the air exercise to invade British airspace, had a sedate cruising speed of only 73 mph (117 kph). This meant that even if the bombers were detected eight miles out to sea, there was still less than seven minutes available for operators to alert the Operations Room at Uxbridge, and for fighters to be scrambled, before the 'enemy' reached land. This already inadequate short period of time in which to get fighters into a position where they could intercept the enemy, was further diminished with the introduction of the Luftwaffe's new, faster fighters and bombers. The Messerschmitt Me 109 and Me 110 fighters had a maximum speed around five times faster than the Vickers Virginia, and the Dornier Do 17 and Heinkel He 111 bombers were around three-and-a-half times faster. Sound location as a means of detecting approaching enemy aircraft had been made redundant. Britain would be dependent on radar. A sentiment echoed by the Dowding character in the 'trusting in God and praying for radar' scene of the 1969 Metro Goldwyn Mayer film, *The Battle of Britain*.

Radio Detection and Ranging (Radar) and Radio Direction Finding (RDF)

Churchill coined the term 'the Wizard's War',[3] to acknowledge the almost mystical role played by science and technology during the Second World War. Radar, alchemy-like, provided the means by which Fighter Command was able to repeatedly 'conjure up' defending fighters in the right place, and at the right time, to intercept their bewildered Luftwaffe adversaries.

RADIO DETECTION AND RANGING (RADAR)

Britain possessed 'Radio Direction Finding' technology, referred to widely as RDF, which enabled pilots to fix their position using a receiver in the aircraft, and radio beacons on the ground. It had also developed 'Radio Detection and Ranging' technology, or radar, to use its American acronym, which allowed operators on the ground to use beacons to find an aircraft's position, without the aircraft having a receiver onboard, or any assistance from the pilot.

In simple terms, RDF allowed an aircraft's location to become known to operators on the ground, only if a pilot willingly agreed. It could be used to direct lost pilots to an airfield, or show the location of friendly fighters on Sector and Group Operations Room situation maps.

Radar, on the other hand, enabled an aircraft's location to become known to those on the ground, without the pilot's approval, or even their knowledge. It informed the British of where, when, and how many enemy aircraft were approaching. This enabled them to make the most effective and efficient use of their finite resources, not least the precious fighters, which would otherwise have been compelled to conduct continuous standing patrols over the English Channel.

In today's parlance, radar was a 'game changer', and the British shrouded their radar programme in a cloak of secrecy, deliberately misusing the term RDF to describe their precious asset, and so concealing its true purpose from the enemy.[4] Indeed, clandestine measures would continue to be used even after it was operationally deployed.

When scientists huddled in the back of a Morris van near Daventry 'saw' Squadron Leader R.S. Buckle's Heyford bomber on their display screen, they realised that radio signals were the key to unlocking the interception puzzle. This offered hope of an antidote to the orthodoxy that 'the bomber would always get through'.[5] Indeed, it was the expectation of that hope being realised that led Britain to build its air defence system around radar.

The development of radar itself, training Filter Officers at Bentley Priory and Radar operators at the various Radar stations, was work in progress. A memorandum circulated by the Radio Research Station at Bawdsey a year before war noted that 'it is apparent that filtering is still an art, rather than a science'.[6]

Some steps in development were small, and some were huge, but they all shared the common attributes of being actionable, and innovational. A case in point was the challenge of converting the range and bearing of hostile aircraft seen on Radar screens into a position on the standard grid map used by Fighter Command. Speed was essential, because the quicker this was done, the quicker fighters could be scrambled. A mechanical converter was developed, but the time taken needed to be shortened still further if interceptions were to take place. An electrical calculator was developed, using rotary switches, and relays with metal fingers to 'wipe' over contact plates. This device, dubbed the 'fruit machine', greatly increased the efficiency and speed of radar operation.[7]

The development of radar itself continued apace, as Britain moved ever closer to hostilities with Nazi Germany. The edification of those whose task it would be to filter radar's illumined offerings, and those who would apply the knowledge to direct Britain's air defence, progressed unabated. In recognition of the fact that radar was, disconcertingly, yet unproven under battle conditions, Fighter Command conducted a number of air defence exercises to optimise the system. Reports on exercises conducted by 11 Group in early July 1939, revealed that a number of Radar stations were showing 'error in readings'.[8] A subsequent exercise in late July shows that the 'error' issue had been acknowledged, and was being addressed 'of a total of fifteen interceptions effected, it is interesting to note that eleven of these were carried out using the RDF method.' However, there was still 'much needed improvement in the future in the speedy identification of non-hostile aircraft as friendly'.[9]

Errors in readings undermined Fighter Command's ability to successfully engage the Luftwaffe. Not only had Radar to infallibly detect hostile aircraft, but it also had to provide a precise reading on distance, height and bearing. When a Radar station provided inaccurate readings, it was often attributable to geographical or aerial-related characteristics specific to that station. Readings had to be routinely calibrated and modified, especially following any recent adjustments to the radar system or its structure. To illustrate the point, in August 1940, during the height of the Battle of Britain, Radar stations on the south coast at Ventnor, Poling, and Pevensey, could not give accurate bearings, and Ventnor, Pevensey and Dover could not provide accurate height readings. If British fighters could not be vectored to an exact point, where the Luftwaffe's aircraft already were, or where the 'Tizzy Angle' determined they were heading towards, then they were unlikely to intercept and successfully engage with the enemy.

The calibration of Radar equipment required a target aircraft to be flown at a known distance, height and bearing from each Radar station. However, fighter aircraft could not be used for this task as their pilots had to remain available, or were already committed to operational sorties. Balloons, tethered to vessels were trialled, but proved to be unreliable, mainly

RADIO DETECTION AND RANGING (RADAR)

because the wind, or water, current would not allow them to maintain a constant position. The solution was found in the month after war was declared, when the Air Ministry contracted the task of calibration to the Cierva Company, who brought with them their unconventional autogyros, a hybrid between a fixed-wing aircraft and a helicopter. The aircraft were attached to 24 Squadron under scientific supervision, and initially operated three Cierva C.30s before re-equipping to Avro Rotas. Just over a year later the establishment increased to nine aircraft and operated as the Rota Calibration Flight from RAF Duxford in Fighter Command's 12 Group.[10] The Cierva aircraft, although unprotected and unarmed, continued to carry out their vital calibration work, while always remaining vulnerable to sudden attack from Luftwaffe fighters. If the means to calibrate radar equipment had not been available, then many vectors would have resulted in defending fighters being sent to barren locations, devoid of any German aircraft, and Fighter Command would have been severely hampered in its struggle against the Luftwaffe.

The comment within the 1939 air defence exercise report, highlighting the need for 'speedy identification of non-hostile aircraft as friendly', was made to avoid what today would be described as a 'blue on blue', or 'friendly fire' incident. Identifying aircraft in this way was crucial, to prevent enemy raiders getting through unchallenged, and friendly aircraft being brought down by mistake. Radar was able to announce the presence of aircraft, but it could not readily confirm whether they were friendly or hostile. Confirmation helped inform the recognised air picture, which Controllers on the ground and Squadron Leaders in the air relied upon, when making life and death decisions in a fast-moving, highly pressurised environment.

The much feared misreckoning occurred within a mere three days of war being declared, in what has come to be known as the 'Battle of Barking Creek'. On the early morning of 6 September, a searchlight battery in the Thames Estuary reported seeing what was thought to be enemy aircraft overhead. The 11 Group Operations Room at Uxbridge instructed the Sector Operations Room at North Weald to send two sections, comprising six Hurricanes, to investigate, but, inexplicably, the North Weald Controller chose to scramble fourteen Hurricanes – over twice the number instructed by Uxbridge. Another factor, unbeknown to operators at the Canewdon Radar Station, was that the screening to suppress back radiation echoes, reflected by the land to the west, was not working correctly, and so any aircraft approaching from that side would wrongly be presumed to be

ENEMY SIGHTED

coming from the sea, which was to the east. When the fourteen Hurricanes appeared on the radar screen, they were mistakenly identified as a large formation of hostile aircraft approaching from the sea, because of both the screening failure and their signature being much larger than that for six aircraft, the number presumed to have been scrambled from North Weald.

The entry in the 11 Group Operations Record for the incident provides an insight as to the confusion on that day: 'twenty raids were plotted from RDF and Observer Corps sources from 06.30 hours onwards giving indication of massed enemy attack on London up the Thames Estuary. Fighters were sent up to intercept, but it seems probable no enemy aircraft were present.'[11] More Fighter Command aircraft were despatched to intercept the 'hostile raids', and in the confusion, Spitfires from 74 Squadron shot down two Hurricanes from 56 Squadron, killing one of the pilots. It is an uncomfortable fact that the Hurricanes brought down by friendly fire on that September morning were the first aircraft to be shot down by Spitfires.

As with most Fighter Command aircraft at that time, none of the Spitfires or Hurricanes involved in the incident on 6 September had been fitted with Identification Friend or Foe, (IFF). As a result of the 'Battle of Barking Creek', the programme to equip all fighter aircraft with IFF, was accelerated and completed by June the following year.[12] IFF was a system invented by scientists at the Radar Research station at Bawdsey, in which a regenerative receiver on an aircraft reflected amplified signals back to British radar screens. The Radar operators could see these blips were brighter, and more elongated than those received from hostile aircraft, and so reported the plots as friendly. It is worth noting, however, that IFF had operational limitations as a result of its interdependency with radar. Notwithstanding the fault with the Radar station at Canewdon, Britain's Radar stations were arranged to only detect aircraft coming from the sea, and so IFF could only confirm aircraft as friendly if they were first detected on radar. As most fighting over Britain occurred over land, and not the sea, then IFF could not identify friendly fighters unless they were flown over the English Channel.

The availability of 'Pip Squeak' provided Controllers with a recognised air picture, showing the location of both hostile and friendly fighters, and so could reduce the risk of misidentification. On 6 September, 'Pip Squeak' would have merely confirmed what those on the ground already knew, that friendly aircraft were in air. Unfortunately, they also mistakenly thought many enemy aircraft were in the same area, and pilots sent to intercept them, having no technical means to differentiate between friend and foe, were left having to rely on the 'mark one eyeball'. A court martial held after the tragedy, ruled that the incident had been an unfortunate 'accident of war'. One of those who helped defend the Spitfire pilots at their court martial was Roger Bushell, who had been a barrister before the war and was now himself a fighter pilot. Bushell would later be shot down over Calais, while supporting the evacuation of British troops from France. He became a prisoner of war and, by a quirk of fate, was incarcerated in the infamous Stalag Luft III, along with one of the two pilots he had defended. He would go on to mastermind the largest mass breakout from a prisoner of war camp in Germany, in what was to become known as 'The Great Escape'. His pseudonym was 'Big X'. His exploits, and that of the other escapees, has come to be immortalised through the epic Hollywood film, *The Great Escape*.

AMES Type 1 Chain Home (CH) Radar Stations

Britain was to be shielded by a chain of Radar stations, located mainly along its eastern and southern coastline. They would be known as Chain Home (CH) stations, although the sites were officially designated Air Ministry Experimental Stations (AMES) to provide further subterfuge as to their real purpose. Eighteen CH stations were to be ready by April 1939, providing detection capability from Dundee in the north, to the Isle of Wight in the south. Authority to extend coverage by a further four CH stations was given by the Air Ministry seven months before the declaration of war, providing additional coverage to the Royal Navy's base at Scapa Flow in the extreme north, and Bristol and Wales in the south-west of the British Isles.[13]

Building CH stations necessitated assistance from industry, but this would also increase the risk of the secret work being either deliberately, or carelessly, disclosed to the enemy. Contracts were awarded to two British companies and the work was separated into distinct parts, so no one team of individuals, or company, had knowledge of the overall system. The responsibility for building transmitter equipment fell to Metropolitan Vickers Limited of Manchester, and supplying receiver equipment to A.C. Cossor of London. A small box, within the transmitter, was designed and built separately, to further mitigate against the risk of espionage. It is a testament to all those involved that no information surrounding the sensitive work was leaked to Nazi Germany.[14]

ENEMY SIGHTED

As Britain lurched towards war the programme to build CH Radar stations was accelerated, resulting in three types of Radar stations: 'Advance', 'Intermediate', and 'Final'. 'Advance' CH Radar stations could not read a plot's height. They had wooden huts, mobile or experimental equipment, and towers that were 70 ft (21 metres) and 90 ft (27 metres) high. 'Intermediate' CH Radar stations had improved aerials and were able to read a plot's height. Their equipment was similar to that of the 'Advance' stations, but their towers were taller, 240 ft (73 metres) in height. The aim was to improve all Radar stations until they configured to the standard of a 'Final' CH Radar station, which included the ability to read range, direction, and height.[15]

'Final CH', or to give them their official title, 'AMES Type 1 CH Radar stations', were also referred to as 'East Coast CH Radar Stations'. They had four steel transmitting towers, in line, 350 ft (107 metres) tall, spaced approximately 180 ft (55 metres) apart. Each tower was fitted with cantilevered platforms at 50, 200 and 350 ft (15, 61 and 107 metres). Dipoles, aerials consisting of a horizontal metal rod with a connecting wire at its centre, were configured in stacks of eight, to form nets, which were slung between the towers. These transmitter nets were connected to heavily protected transmitter buildings, housing two identical transmitters, capable of being changed over rapidly in the event of failure, or damage to one following an enemy attack.

There were also four, 240 ft (73 metres) tall receiving towers, usually placed in rhombic formation. Servicing platforms, accessed by a central ladder arrangement, were positioned at regular intervals on the towers, in order to reach pronged, trident-like, dipole stacks spaced one above the other at a height of 215, 95 and 45 ft (66, 29 and 14 metres). The towers were constructed from wood rather than steel to avoid influencing the balance and symmetry of the receiver dipole stacks by the proximity of any metallic parts. The receiving towers and the associated receiver building were located some hundreds of yards from the transmitter buildings, and in some cases in a separate compound.

The dipole antennas, perched on AMES Type 1 CH Radar towers, could not rotate, and remained fixed, looking out towards the sea and land mass beyond. CH worked like a 'floodlight', irradiating radio signals along 100 miles (161 km) of airspace within its 'line of shoot', in order to detect encroaching aircraft. Once a blip was seen, the Radar operator rapidly needed to determine whether it represented a genuine plot, or if it had been caused by any clutter on their Radar screen. They were assisted in

RADIO DETECTION AND RANGING (RADAR)

this task in two ways. First, CH employed a long interpulse period between signals, to reduce the amount of interference, or 'scatter', reflected from the ionosphere. Second, all CH stations were synchronised with the National Grid System in order to avoid mutual interference, or what was referred to as 'running rabbits'.[16]

The colossal transmitting and receiving towers stood facing the threat, like 'gladiatorial retiarius', armed with weighted nets and pointed tridents, ready to snare their enemy. Once snared, members of the Women's Auxiliary Air Force (WAAF) – most Radar operators were women – meticulously studied the patterns dancing on the screens of their fixed RF8 or mobile RF7 receivers, before attributing the signal's strength, range, direction and height.

If the Luftwaffe's attacks were to be repelled, then all parts of the air defence system needed to work to the same recognised air picture. This placed a great reliance on vital information being instantaneously and precisely communicated between all the essential elements. In this case, information would be sent by telephone to the Filter Room at Bentley Priory, where each CH Radar station was represented by a Filter Officer. This individual would then forward the filtered information, again by telephone, to both Fighter Command and Group Operations Rooms.

The rate that plots were 'told' from the Filter Room was intense, resulting in the standard number of thirty-six every ten minutes being routinely exceeded. There was, for obvious reasons, no attempt by 'Tellers' to conform to the standard, and Sector and Group Operations Rooms had to respond with additional staff and telephone lines.[17]

Telephone and teleprinter lines were the preferred means of communication. They were the arteries and veins, feeding the heart and limbs of Fighter Command. By the time war was declared, the General Post Office (GPO) had installed 500 long-distance emergency telephone circuits, and a much greater number of similar circuits of under twenty-five miles (forty kilometres) radius. The laying of additional lines, maintaining vital defence communications, and repairing sections damaged following air raids, was coordinated by the GPO through the Defence Telecommunications Control (DTC) organisation. In addition to the vast telephone communications network, the GPO also introduced the Defence Teleprinter Network (DTN), providing dedicated telegraph circuits. The DTN was to play an integral role in the transmission and receipt of important messages, combat reports, intelligence reports, pilot and aircraft replacement requirements and damage assessments during the turbulent period that was to follow.[18]

When the Battle of Britain began in July 1940, there were twenty-one CH stations available to defend the British Isles. Dowding described them as the 'backbone of the system', while also acknowledging their inability to provide total radar coverage, as 'they had the serious limitation that they failed altogether to give indications of aircraft flying below 1,000 ft (305 metres)'.[19]

Worryingly, this gap in coverage meant that Luftwaffe aircraft were able to infiltrate British airspace by flying below radar. While it was difficult for large raids to remain undetected, smaller formations and individual aircraft were able to routinely hoodwink CH's 'gladiatorial retiarius', and circumvent their ascending gaze. When referring to CH's limitation, Dowding was later to state that 'to overcome this disability, which was particularly hampering to operations against low-flying minelayers, smaller units called Chain Home Low stations were included in the protective line.'[20]

AMES Type 2 Chain Home Low (CHL) Radar Stations

The solution provided by Chain Home Low (CHL), which would come to be known formally as AMES Type 2 Chain Home Low (CHL), was perfected by scientists at the Bawdsey Radio Research Station. An examination of how CHL came to be also provides a fascinating insight into the development of other radar systems around the same time.

Scientists, led by Doctor Edward Bowen, had been developing Airborne Interception (AI) radar so that defending aircraft, regardless of visibility, could detect Luftwaffe night bombers, or Kriegsmarine ships and submarines on the water's surface.

Unlike the 'floodlighting' technique employed by CH, AI emitted a narrow beam of radio waves, like a 'search light', to 'illuminate' targets between three or four miles and 1,000 ft (five or six kilometres and 305 metres), the latter being the distance considered necessary for pilots to visually identify a target in darkness. The fact that it operated on a shorter wavelength meant it required shorter aerials, which was useful as it had to be carried by an aircraft. However, AI equipment also needed to be considerably lighter and smaller than CH. For AI to be successfully implemented, 'the key to progress were valves with greater power of amplification, that could function at even higher frequencies'.[21]

The answer lay with the British company Pye, which was about to launch a new television. Of great significance were its cathode-ray tube,

RADIO DETECTION AND RANGING (RADAR)

which was suitable for use with Radar; its small, light chassis, called the 'Pye strip'; and its ground-breaking EF50 high-performance valves. Bowen would later describe the EF50 as 'a valve which was destined to play almost as important a part in the Radar war as the magnetron'.[22]

Professor John Cockcroft from Cambridge was appointed as Assistant Director of Scientific Research by the Ministry of Supply at the outbreak of war, to develop the AI concept into a ground based Coastal Defence (CD) radar. The role of CD radar was to provide artillery guns covering the North Sea and English Channel, with information on a target ship's range and position. The decision to have Cockcroft lead in this important area was a productive one. He was a highly regarded physicist who, along with Doctor E. Walton, seven years earlier, had been the first to split the atom by artificial means, an achievement for which he was to receive the Nobel Prize for Physics in 1951.

As the first CD Radar stations were being built in the north of Scotland, to give protection to the British Fleet, at Scapa Flow, low flying German bombers were also evading CH radar, to lay magnetic mines around Britain's eastern coast, especially in the area of the Thames Estuary. Continuing to lose shipping and being denied access to the London Docks and other east coast ports would have a profound effect on the British war effort. The threat posed by the clandestine aerial intruders was real, a briefing to the War Cabinet stating, 'we have also suffered losses recently through mines and everything points to the enemy's mining campaign being intensified'.[23]

Cockcroft was immediately approached by Watson Watt, and asked to further develop AI, beyond CD, into what would come to be known as CHL. Pye were approached to supply aerials and receivers for an initial twenty-five sets, which were to be located at existing CH sites. There was a problem with the EF50 valves to be used in CHL, in that although a British design, the valves were in fact manufactured for Pye by Philips, a Dutch company. Arrangements were made for Philips to urgently deliver a large number of completed valves and manufacturing machinery so Pye could produce more themselves in Britain. Getting the equipment out of Holland was a close run thing. The country was invaded by the German Wehrmacht only hours after the crates had been loaded onto one of three ships leaving the port of Vlissingen. The Luftwaffe attacked the convoy as it sailed for England, badly damaging one of the ships and causing it to return. Miraculously, the ship carrying the EF50 valves and machinery was able to evade the bombers and deliver its precious cargo safely to the port of Harwich, on the east coast of England.[24]

ENEMY SIGHTED

CHL sets 'had a restricted range of about thirty miles (forty-eight kilometres), and were incapable of giving heights with any degree of accuracy. They were, however, extremely accurate in azimuth, and constituted an essential feature of the Defensive and Warning Systems.'[25] Aircraft as low as 500 ft (152 metres) could be detected by CHL, although this minimum height would to some extent depend on the geographical positioning of individual sites. Their accuracy in 'azimuth', which is the position of an object in the sky, expressed as an angle related to a distance on the horizon of the Earth, was pivotal in informing the recognised air picture.

The initial CHL sites required two aerials, one for transmitting, and one for receiving radio signals, each mounted on a 20 ft (6 metres) wooden gantry. The aerial equipment consisted of four stacked arrays of five dipoles, 'resembling a bedstead on its side'. Unlike CH, CHL aerials were not fixed, and indeed needed to move in order to sweep the sky for enemy aircraft. The first CHL aerials lacked any electrical means of being turned and so, remarkably, were turned manually by peddling an upturned bicycle frame, located in the wooden hut underneath the gantry.[26] Later versions of CHL were fitted with Caledon motorised turning gear and a shared transmitting and receiving aerial, mounted on either 20 or 185 ft (6 or 56 metres) towers, dependent on the nature and height of the site above sea level.[27]

When the Battle of Britain began in July 1940, there were thirty CHL stations available to defend the British Isles. Their existence, an embodiment of the innovation, adaptation and operationalisation which took place during the forging of Britain's air defence system. The development of Pye's ground-breaking EF50 high performance valves, used to amplify radio signals, proved to be innovative. The evolution of coastal defence radar to meet the grave threat from low-flying minelaying aircraft demonstrated an ability to adapt. If Luftwaffe aircraft had been allowed to fly to Britain undetected, then interceptions could not have taken place, and the battle would have been lost. Contriving a 'Heath Robinson' arrangement to manually turn CHL aerials until the automated Caledon turning gear became available, signalled arguably the greatest asset, the single-mindedness to not wait, but operationalise elements as they became available. It is said that the motto of the development team at Bawdsey Radio Research Station, was 'second best tomorrow'. They realised, that Britain was in peril and the country could not afford to wait for perfection. Time was at a premium, and they had to operationalise radar at the earliest opportunity, even if it was not, at that point, the best it could be.[28]

RADIO DETECTION AND RANGING (RADAR)

German Understanding of Britain's Radar Capability

Astonishingly, in October 1938, less than a year before the outbreak of war, the British reciprocated an earlier visit to Germany, and invited the Luftwaffe to reconnoitre the Royal Air Force. The German delegation was led by Field Marshal Erhard Milch, the man responsible for rearming the Luftwaffe. He is reported to have asked, 'How are you getting on with your experiments in the radio detection of aircraft approaching your shores? […] We have known for some time that you are developing a radar system. So are we, and we think we are a jump ahead of you.'[29] This account is not corroborated by British officers, who were present during the visit, but it does beg two questions: 'What did the Germans know about British radar?', and 'Why was it not taken more seriously by them?'

Regardless of the veracity of what is alleged to have been said by Milch when he visited Britain, it is clear that the vast latticed towers springing up across the eastern and southern coast of Britain had not gone unnoticed. In early 1939, General Martini, the Director of Luftwaffe Signals, despatched Germany's last airship, *Graf Zeppelin II*, to investigate the exact nature and capability of the newly erected towers. Germany was also developing radar and would go on to successfully deploy its *Freya* early warning, and *Würzburg* anti-aircraft systems against the Allies. However, there was a crucial difference in the approach adopted by both countries. German radar, operated on a relatively high frequency of around 200 megahertz, while British radar operated on a much lower frequency of around 20 megahertz. As a result, scientists onboard the airship had monitored the wrong frequency, and so failed to detect radio transmissions emanating from the towers. They incorrectly formed the view that British radar was both ineffective and non-operational. Unbeknown to *Graf Zeppelin's* crew, the Radar operators who were located beneath the towers had in fact been plotting the track taken by the Zeppelin throughout its surveillance flight, around the eastern edge of England, and up along the coast of Scotland.[30]

General Martini's Luftwaffe Signals Directorate submitted the inaccurate information on the latticed towers as part of their regular intelligence summaries to the 5th *Abteilung*. This was the intelligence arm of the Luftwaffe General Staff, responsible for collating information about foreign air forces, and preparing target information for an air war. The intelligence was then forwarded to the German High Command, with the observation that, 'British air defence is still weak'. Later the same year, the 5th *Abteilung* prepared a document titled, 'Proposal for the Conduct of

ENEMY SIGHTED

Air Warfare Against Britain', but there was no mention of British radar.[31] These grave miscalculations were to have catastrophic repercussions for German military ambition during the Battle of Britain.

The French military had showed interest in acquiring Britain's CH radar, just three months before war was declared. French officers were sent to visit the Filter Room at Bentley Priory, and to attend courses on radar. Arrangements were made for Radar stations to be situated in France, and contrary to British requests, the French shared details on radar with their own manufacturers. In any event, the mercurial speed with which the German military overran France, meant that the project was ended before any work had commenced.[32] If CH Radar stations had been built on French soil, or if the Germans had coerced French manufacturers into revealing the information their government had perilously shared with them, then Britain's secret detection capability would have been laid bare before the enemy, and the technical advantage afforded by radar compromised.

Another opportunity to gain some insight into Britain's radar capability was squandered, when German scientists examined a mobile radar unit, abandoned by the British Expeditionary Force in France, only to dismiss it as being inferior to their own equipment. Arrogance, and a lack of specific intelligence, contributed to a culture of complacency among the German High Command, who underestimated just how vital radar was. This weakness was espoused by the Luftwaffe's Commander in Chief, Herman Goring, who 'loathed technicalities of any sort and was totally unable to understand them'.[33]

The culture of complacency and arrogance did not, however, permeate to those leading the Luftwaffe in the air. Adolf Galland, a Luftwaffe Major during the Battle of Britain, understood the significance of Britain's radar capability:

> From the very beginning, the English had an extraordinary advantage, which we could never overcome throughout the entire war: Radar and fighter control. For us, and for our Command, this was a surprise, and a very bitter one. England possessed a closely knit radar network conforming to the highest technical standards of the day, which provided Fighter Command with the most detailed data imaginable. Thus, the British fighter was guided all the way from take-off to his correct position for attack on the German formations. We had nothing of the kind. In the application of radio-location technique the

RADIO DETECTION AND RANGING (RADAR)

enemy was far in advance of us ... For us there was only a frontal attack against the superbly organised defence of the British Isles, conducted with great determination.[34]

There is an old Maltese saying, that 'to destroy the spider you have to destroy the cobweb'. The inability or unwillingness of Goring and those at the highest echelons of the Luftwaffe to understand the absolute necessity for destroying the 'web' that Radar provided, ultimately meant that it remained intact, to be used to lead the defending spider to its prey.

Fortunately for Britain, it had in Dowding the very antithesis of Goring. Fighter Command's leader proved to be an analytical and apprised opponent, who understood how technology could aid the defence of this country, and so propelled its implementation. Dowding would later state that, 'the system operated effectively, and it is not too much to say that the warnings which it gave could have been obtained by no other means and constituted a vital factor in the Air Defence of Great Britain.'[35]

The development of Radar for Airborne Interception

Britain's integrated air defence system was expected to provide early warning of enemy raids, throughout both day and night. It was the reason why Chain Home and Chain Home Low Radar stations maintained a round the clock vigil, ensuring Fighter Command's constant state of preparedness. Once alerted of a likely incursion over 11 Group, the Operations Room at Uxbridge would scramble aircraft. The chances of a successful interception during daylight were high, as the raiders were visible to both pilots in the air and observers on the ground. However, spotting, and therefore successfully intercepting, raiders during night time was a much more challenging prospect. It would have remained so, if it were not for a remarkable British invention: the cavity magnetron.

Chain Home radar operated using radio wavelengths of between 15 and 30 metres, and this meant the aerials had to be large, thus the very tall transmitting and receiving towers. Their size precluded the system from being fitted in aircraft, or even ships. But, if the radio wavelength could be reduced, then so too could the corresponding aerials. The challenge therefore for an airborne interception radar system, was to create a radio valve capable of transmitting powerful emissions at a wavelength of around 10 cm, as opposed to 15 or 30 metres. Magnetrons, vacuum tubes employing powerful magnets and resonant cavities to produce oscillating radio waves, offered a solution. They were known not only to Britain and her American ally, but also to Soviet Russia, Nazi Germany and the Empire of Japan. Which, if any, would be first to produce a magnetron capable of emitting microwaves? Whoever it was would be able to exploit the technical and military possibilities that it offered. Thankfully, it was a British team at Birmingham University who, in 1940, first developed such a device, capable of operating at wavelengths of 9.8 cm. The invention was downsized and adapted by the GEC Research Laboratory, at Wembley, so it could be fitted into aircraft and ships. The Airborne Interception (AI) radar was born.

Initially fitted to Fighter Command's current night fighter, the Bristol Blenheim Mk IF, and then the Bristol Beaufighter, airborne radar mitigated the deficiency of not being able to see raiding aircraft during the night, by instead revealing their presence on a radar screen. Dowding commented:

> It became necessary to develop at high pressure, a system of operation which should enable night fighters to make interceptions even against targets that are not illuminated. The difficulty of this task will be realised when it is considered that it became necessary to put the fighter within 100 or 200 yards (91 to 183 metres) of the enemy, and on the same course, instead of the four or five miles (six to eight kilometres), which were adequate against an illuminated target.

The 'system of operation' continued to be developed, much of it during the night when radar-equipped Blenheims were deployed against Luftwaffe bombers. Dowding felt that the results, 'though disappointing, were not entirely negligible; several bombers were shot down in this area during the experimental period, and many discovered that they were pursued and turned back before reaching their objectives'.[36]

A case in point was on the night of 22–23 July 1940,[37] when a Blenheim Mk IF, serial number L6836, flown by Flying Officer Glyn 'Jumbo' Ashfield, of the Fighter Interception Unit at Tangmere, was directed by Uxbridge to intercept a possible raider. With assistance from the Tangmere Sector Operations Room and the Radar station at Poling, Ashfield manoeuvred his aircraft to intercept an aircraft near Selsey Bill. He recorded,

> At 23.00 we were told to patrol in line eight. At 23.30, a vector of 180 degrees from Selsey Bill was given with instructions

Right: **Louis Blériot crossing the Channel**
Louis Blériot seen here during the final stretch of his historic flight on 25 July 1909, approaching the famous White Cliffs of Dover. Britain would now have to guard against invasion, not only from the sea, but also the air. (Library of Congress)

Below: **Hillingdon House**
Hillingdon House in the inter-war period. Note the wooden huts to the south, one of which would have housed the original Operations Room. (Dilip Amin)

Left: **Hugh Dowding**
Air Chief Marshal Sir Hugh Caswall Tremenheere Dowding guided development of the world's first integrated air defence system, and then oversaw its use, leading Fighter Command during an epoch moment in its history. (Public Domain)

Below: **Keith Park in Hurricane**
Air Vice-Marshal Sir Keith Rodney Park, the 'Defender of London', seen here sat in the cockpit of his personal Hurricane on 15 September 1941, one year after the Battle of Britain, which he was instrumental in winning. (Historic Military Press)

Chain Home Radar Station
The Chain Home Radar Station at Poling in 11 Group circa 1945. The heavily protected transmitter building can be seen on the left, in front of three of the four in-line 360-foot steel towers used to hang the transmitter aerials. The receiver building is to the right, situated in the middle of four 240-foot wooden receiver towers, placed in rhombic formation. Poling was badly damaged by Ju 87 'Stuka' dive bombers on 18 August 1940, necessitating the placement of temporary radar equipment to fill the gap in Fighter Command's shield. (Historic Military Press)

Chain Home Radar Station visible from France
The distance between Nazi Occupied Europe and Britain really was very small. Seen here is a view of the transmitter and receiver towers at Swingate Radar Station, near Dover in 11 Group. This picture was taken in the summer of 1940 by a German propaganda photographer using a long-range lens, while stood across the English Channel on the cliff top at Cap Gris-Nez. (National Museum of Denmark)

Radio Operator at Poling Radar Station
WAAF Radar Operator, Dorothy Merwood, seen here at Poling Radar Station in 11 Group. The operators, most of whom were women, meticulously studied the patterns dancing on the screens of their fixed RF8, or mobile RF7 receivers, before attributing the signal's strength, range, direction, and height. Radar was Britain's all-seeing eye and gave Fighter Command vital minutes to scramble its fighters. (Historic Military Press)

Bentley Priory internal view of plotting room
WAAF Plotters and Tellers at work in the underground Operations Room at Fighter Command's Headquarters at Stanmore, also known as Bentley Priory. The Headquarters Controller is sat above them, watching the plots being laid out and alerting the relevant Group Controller in whose area the raid is entering. (© MoD/Crown Copyright 2023)

Sector Operations Room, Duxford
The Sector Operations Room at Duxford in 12 Group during the Battle of Britain. The Sector Controller, fourth from left holding telephone, was responsible for accurately plotting, collating, and disseminating information between Group and his fighter Squadrons. He would give verbal instructions to the pilots in their aircraft, directing or 'vectoring' them towards the enemy. He was assisted in this vital and complex task by an array of Radio Operators, Clerks, and Liaison staff. (© MoD/Crown Copyright 2023)

Observer Corps Post
An Observer Corps Post during the Battle of Britain. Note the Observer Post Instrument being used in the centre of the dugout to provide information on the position, height, and direction of travel of Luftwaffe aircraft. The Corps was a crucial element within the integrated air defence system, continuing to report on enemy raids after Radar was no longer able to 'see' them. (Public Domain)

Barrage Balloon being raised
Designed to protect vital sites from bombing raids carried out by low flying enemy aircraft, balloons could be launched over water, as well as over land. The original caption, dated early 1940, states: 'A balloon going up from an anchored barge at the Thames Estuary floating balloon barrage station recently. The balloons are part of the British defence against Nazi planes and are aimed especially at planes which might be headed for London. Passed by British sensor.' (Historic Military Press)

Barrage Balloon attacked by Luftwaffe fighter
Balloon barrages were a hindrance to bombing raids and were therefore frequently targeted by Luftwaffe fighters during the Battle of Britain. Here a balloon is seen falling to the ground in flames after being shot down by a Messerschmitt Me 109 during an aerial attack over the Kent coast on 30 August 1940. (Historic Military Press)

Anti-aircraft gun 1940
Anti-aircraft guns were used to provide a defensive belt along the approaches to and around cities, including London. They were also positioned to protect places of strategic importance, such as Fighter Command Stations. Seen here is a 40mm Bofors anti-aircraft gun and its crew, pictured in an emplacement at Stanmore, London, on 28 June 1940. (Historic Military Press)

Searchlight 1940
Searchlights were operated in direct partnership with anti-aircraft guns to illuminate Luftwaffe bombers as they carried out night raids over Britain. Seen here is a 90cm searchlight, or projector anti-aircraft, and its crew in position at the Royal Hospital, Chelsea, London, on 17 April 1940. (Public Domain)

Bristol Blenheim Mk IF
The Bristol Blenheim was withdrawn as a day fighter as it could not engage on equal terms with the Luftwaffe's Messerschmitt 109 and 110 fighters. It would go on to prove more successful in the night fighter role against German bombers. (Historic Military Press)

Boulton Paul Defiant Mk I
Seen here in July 1940, the Defiant was highly successful during its initial engagements with Luftwaffe fighters, who were unaware that it was equipped with a rear firing turret. However, Defiants became vulnerable during subsequent encounters, once German pilots realised that they lacked any forward firing guns. They were reassigned to a night fighter role and proved more successful against Luftwaffe bombers. (Public Domain)

Hawker Hurricane Mk I
Seen here are two Hurricanes of 17 Squadron, pictured on the ground at Debden in 11 Group during the Battle of Britain in July 1940. Note the parachute on the tail of the aircraft in the foreground, deliberately placed for a rapid scramble. A third Hurricane can be seen about to land. (Public Domain)

Supermarine Spitfire Mk I
Pilot Officer David Moore Crook of 609 (West Riding) Squadron scrambling to intercept enemy aircraft in September 1940. The image has the following handwritten caption: 'Taking off for one of the London battles, September 1940'. (Public Domain)

Messerschmitt BF 109
The designation 'Bf' and 'Me' were interchangeable. The Messerschmitt Me 109 was the Luftwaffe's main day fighter and proved a capable adversary to Fighter Command's Hurricanes and Spitfires. Seen here in the foreground are a pair of Messerschmitt Me 109s with their ward, a Heinkel He 111, pictured on a Luftwaffe airfield in Occupied Europe. (National Museum of Denmark)

Messerschmitt Me 110
Named the 'Destroyer', this twin engine Luftwaffe fighter proved inferior to Fighter Command's Hurricanes and Spitfires, and on occasions they themselves had to be protected by the single engine Me 109. This aircraft, coded 2S+-H, of 1/ZG 2, was brought down during the Battle of Britain, crashing at Beaties Farm, North Baddesley, Hampshire, at 16.00 hours on 13 August 1940. (Historic Military Press)

Junkers Ju 87
The 'Stuka', much feared by those on the ground during the Blitzkrieg offensive in Europe, was withdrawn from operations against Britain after suffering unacceptable losses following encounters with Hurricanes and Spitfires. Seen here are Luftwaffe aircrew resting beside their Junkers Ju 87s, at their base in France in the summer of 1940. (National Museum of Denmark)

Heinkel He 111
One of the main Luftwaffe bombers during the Battle of Britain. According to the original caption, these Heinkel He 111s were pictured 'heading to England' during 1940. (National Museum of Denmark)

Dornier Do 17
Called 'the flying pencil' due to its narrow fuselage, the Do 17 was commonly seen during enemy raids over Britain in 1940. It is the German bomber represented on the front cover of this book. Seen here are Luftwaffe ground crew and armourers bombing up a Do 17 in preparation for a mission during the Battle of Britain. (National Museum of Denmark)

Neville Chamberlain at Heston
'Peace in our time'. Waving the piece of paper that resulted from the Munich Agreement signed the day before, Prime Minister Chamberlain speaks to the crowd that had gathered at Heston Aerodrome on his return on 30 September 1938. Although there would be no peace, the agreement brought precious time for Fighter Command to prepare for the aerial fighting that lay ahead. (Polish National Archives)

Churchill becomes Prime Minister
After the declaration of war, Neville Chamberlain resigned and was replaced by Winston Churchill on 10 May 1940. Churchill is photographed here, raising his hat in salute, acknowledging those Londoners who had gathered to greet him soon after he became Prime Minister. (National Museum of Denmark)

BEF arrives in France
On declaring war, Britain sent much of her professional army, the British Expeditionary Force (BEF) and its equipment to France. Photographed here is the BEF arriving on the continent. Men of the Manchester Regiment are making their way along a sandy track near the quayside at Cherbourg, after arriving in France in September 1939. In the background is HMS *Express*. (Historic Military Press)

The evacuation from France; Operation *Dynamo*
Defeat in France was strategically catastrophic for the British, but Churchill called the return of so many men to England 'a miracle of deliverance', and he praised the Royal Air Force for its role in that achievement. Seen here on one of the beaches near Dunkirk are Allied troops who have formed long winding queues, ready to take their turn to board small boats which took them to larger vessels during Operation *Dynamo*. (Historic Military Press)

Spitfire Supermarine lost during Operation *Dynamo*
The wreckage of Spitfire serial number K9912 and squadron code letters YT-O, flown by Pilot Officer Kenneth Hart of 65 Squadron, based at Hornchurch in 11 Group. On 26 May 1940, Hart shot down an Me 109 but was brought down himself by Hauptmann Wilhelm Balthasar of 1./JG 1. Having managed to get his crippled aircraft down onto the beach at Dunkirk, Hart set fire to it before subsequently joining one of the evacuation vessels heading to England. A handwritten note on the rear of the photograph, written by the German soldier who took it, states that it was taken on 5 June 1940. (Historic Military Press)

Hawker Hurricane lost during Operation *Dynamo*
This is believed to be the wreckage of Hurricane serial number P2902 and squadron code letters RD-X, flown by Pilot Officer Ken McGlashan of 245 Squadron, which had operated as a detachment from Hawkinge in 11 Group during Operation *Dynamo*. The squadron had been ordered to 'counter German bombing activity over Dunkirk' on 31 May 1940. McGlashan was shot down during combat with Me 109s. He eventually made it to the Mole at Dunkirk from where he was evacuated to England on board the Thames paddle steamer *Golden Eagle*, still lugging his torn parachute saturated in oil and glycol. P2902 was eventually recovered and has since been returned to airworthiness. (Historic Military Press)

Churchill, the wartime leader
Winston Churchill, pictured looking out across the English Channel from an observation post at Dover Castle on 24 August 1940. A source states: 'Enemy air attacks were in progress at the time, and two German bombers were seen to crash into the sea.' (Polish National Archives)

Goring, Head of the Luftwaffe
The Luftwaffe's Commander, Hermann Göring, centre, seen observing the south coast of England through high-powered binoculars, during a visit to the front in France in September 1940. (Polish National Archives)

Luftwaffe raid on England; Messerschmitt Me 110s
Messerschmitt Me 110s flying in formation to their target over England. (National Museum of Denmark)

RADIO DETECTION AND RANGING (RADAR)

to 'flash weapon'.[38] After two to three minutes, contact was obtained by Sergeant Leyland. Correction of height from 10,000 ft to 6,000 ft (3,048 to 1,829 metres), and flew course five degree course correction. After about six minutes, enemy aircraft sighted by observer, Pilot Officer Morris, to port and just below. A little height was lost, placing enemy aircraft between the Moon and ourselves. By fuselage silhouetted against Moon, aircraft identified as Do 17. No challenge signal given by us. I took station astern and although unable to see rudder characteristic, the type of exhaust flame distribution from enemy aircraft confirmed to my mind that aircraft was not British. We flew full throttle until inside minimum AI range and at about 400 to 500 ft (122 or 152 metres) I opened fire. As I could not see my foresight, I closed with continuous fire and by the huge firework display which resulted from bullets making contact around his engines, I knew the aim to be okay. I continued to fire until, with enemy aircraft looking the size of a house, it gave a lurch to starboard, and nose fell. I attempted to follow while firing, when the whole of the cabin Perspex was covered with oil from the enemy aircraft. In the next few seconds we were on our back and recovery was not made until 700 ft (213 metres) by which time we had lost contact with the enemy. We were given a vector home of 30 degrees by Poling and after five to six minutes, crossed the coast, east of Bognor. As the coast was crossed, my observer Pilot Officer Norris reported a huge blaze behind and slightly to port and gave a bearing position of contact, as five miles (eight kilometres) south of Bognor. This blaze lasted for about five to ten minutes ... Pilot Officer Carey of 43 Squadron, who was on patrol at the time, saw the fire and resultant blaze in the water.[39]

Ashfield had just provided an account of what is thought to be the world's first aerial victory achieved using airborne radar.

The cavity magnetron was to play an even greater role still. In September 1940, Churchill sent a mission to America. It was led by Henry Tizard, chairman of the Committee for the Scientific Survey of Air Defence (CSSAD). Known as the Tizard Mission, its members took with them a collection of Britain's most guarded scientific secrets. It was a gift, a gesture of trust and faith, that the United States would use its vast manufacturing might to support an embattled Britain. The gift included designs for proximity fuses, plastic explosive, self-sealing fuel tanks, rockets, gunsights, Frank Whittle's jet engine, and even papers detailing the feasibility of a nuclear fission bomb. It also included a prototype cavity magnetron, prompting the official historian of America's wartime Office of Scientific Research and Development to record, 'When the members of the Tizard Mission brought one to America in 1940, they carried the most valuable cargo ever brought to our shores. It sparked the whole development of microwave Radar and constituted the most important item in reverse Lease-Lend.'[40]

Today, the cavity magnetron is a common feature, used routinely across many homes for an unremarkable purpose, it is the device that powers our microwave oven to heat our food. However, this device has served a much more redoubtable purpose. The exchange of secrets and collaborative working not only precipitated an Anglo-American Alliance for the remainder of the Second World War, but it also served as a catalyst for 'the special relationship', which is still consequential today.

Chapter 8

Observer Corps
'Signal Thread'

Radar's invaluable contribution towards defending Britain's airspace is unequivocal. However, radar's Achilles Heel during the early part of the Second World War was its inability to look behind once German raiders had flown overhead. This meant it was unable to provide the over-land, recognised air picture necessary for Fighter Command to direct its aircraft and anti-aircraft guns. The Observer Corps, another 'signal thread' element within the spider's web, would serve to address this weakness. It was a view endorsed by Dowding, who stated in his Despatch: 'It is important to note that, at this time, they constituted the sole means of tracking enemy raids once they had crossed the coastline.'[1]

Churchill would later write of radar: 'a weak point in this wonderful development is of course, that when the raider crosses the coast it leaves the RDF, and we become dependent upon the Observer Corps'. He readily acknowledged the contribution made by members of the Observer Corps, while at the same time lamenting the observation process' lack of sophistication:

> this would seem transition from the middle of the twentieth century, to the Early Stone Age. Although I hear that good results are obtained from the Observer Corps, we must regard following the raider inland by some application of RDF as most urgently needed. It will be some time before the RDF stations can look back inland, and then only upon a crowded and confused air theatre.[2]

The Air Ministry understood the enormity of the role soon to be played by the Observer Corps, and the volunteer organisation was formalised into a paid service, under the direction and control of Dowding's Fighter Command, in August 1939. The structure of Observation Posts, Centres and

ENEMY SIGHTED

Areas was formally integrated within the air defence system. Raid reporting procedures were standardised, and then continually improved across the country. The Observer Corps would go on to be granted the title 'Royal Observer Corps' some twenty months after it was formalised, in recognition of the unfaltering contribution made by its members during the lead up to, and throughout, the Battle of Britain.

The Observer Corps was mobilised on 24 August 1939, ten days before the declaration of war with Germany and, coincidently, on the same day that the underground Bunker at Uxbridge became operational. Around 30,000 observers occupied around 1,050 Observer Posts, over an area of 60,000 square miles (some 96,561 square kilometres) across the country. While the areas under greatest threat from aerial attack, London, south-east England, the east coast, and most of the south coast, were covered by Observation Posts every six to ten miles (ten to sixteen kilometres), north-west Scotland, West Wales and Cornwall, were not protected until the following year.[3]

By the time the Battle of Britain began, some ten months after war was declared, Britain was divided into three Observer Corps Areas, with thirty-one Observer Corps Groups, each typically with between thirty and fifty Observer Posts.

The territory controlled by the 11 Group Operations Room at Uxbridge was covered by the Southern Observer Corps Area, from its Headquarters at Bentley Priory, RAF Stanmore. Many of its Groups, namely Number 1 Maidstone, Number 2 Horsham, Number 3 Winchester, Number 17 Watford, Number 18 Colchester and Number 19 Bromley, bore the brunt of the Luftwaffe raids during the Battle of Britain, leading to some Posts becoming 'saturated'.[4] Their dogged resilience in the face of unrelenting daylight and night-time attacks is well documented.

In August 1940, when the Luftwaffe attempted to knock out Fighter Command by carrying out daylight raids against its airfields in the south-east, these Groups remained viable, and tracked in the region of 8,000 enemy sorties over a tumultuous two weeks.[5] Four months later, on the night of 30 December, the Bromley Centre alone plotted 240 tracks, in just under four hours.

> At the height of the raid the confusion of sound was so great that it became almost impossible to separate the tracks. Furthermore, owing to cable breakages, communications between Posts and Centre were severely dislocated. By late

evening, thirty-three lines were out of action. Nevertheless, 160 hostile tracks were duly and correctly told to Uxbridge and Sectors.[6]

The role of the Observer Corps was to aid, in both passive and active defence, against attacks by the Luftwaffe. Its contribution to passive defence, as part of the raid warning system, centred on the reporting of enemy aircraft overhead, so air raid warnings could be given. Its involvement in active defence, tracking and reporting hostile raids, was crucial for Sector Controllers to direct their fighter aircraft to intercept the enemy.[7]

Dowding observed that, 'it was impossible for an enemy raid to originate in this country',[8] and the factuality of this statement meant the Observer Corps, whether supporting passive or active defence, were reliant on radar to provide initial reports of aircraft approaching over water. Plots identified by radar were sent to the Filter Room at Bentley Priory, where 'Tellers' 'told' the plots on to the Fighter Command Operations Room. From here, 'Sea Tellers' 'retold' the information to the Coastal Observer Centres.[9] 'Sea Tellers and Plotters were not supposed to know anything about radar, but somehow an awful lot of them did; very funny memos appeared on occasions, making rude remarks about radar, but the secret was never let out.'[10] Once a raid was picked up as it made landfall in the south-east of England, Observer Posts would track its progress, and relay details to Bentley Priory, 11 Group Sector Operations Rooms, and the Bunker at Uxbridge.

The way in which the Observer Corps contributed to raid reporting, was for Posts to tell enemy raids to Centres, and Centres then to retell reports to Sector Operations Rooms and Uxbridge. The information was then relayed by Uxbridge to the Headquarters Operations Room at Bentley Priory, which was responsible for coordinating the air raid warning system nationally. A large map, detailing around 130 'warning districts', coterminous with the layout of the public telephone system, was used to show the position and progress of tracks reported as hostile raids over Britain.

Three telephone operators were in continuous communication with the Trunk Exchanges in London, Liverpool and Glasgow, and when a raid was within twenty minutes flying distance of, for example, a warning district covering Dover, the Air Raid Warning officer would send a 'Yellow Warning' message. The telephone operator would transmit this to the London Trunk Exchange, and the London operator would immediately retransmit it to Dover, where other operators would pass it on to approved recipients in the Warning District. This was a preliminary caution for the information of police and fire services and involved no public warning. The running commentary provided by the Observer Corps was essential to determining the likely target, and gauging the risk to infrastructure and people. 'About five minutes later, if the same District were still threatened, a "Red Warning" would be given. This was the signal for the sirens to sound.' Again, the Observer Corps was able to report when raids had left the Warning District, and a 'Green' signal would be given to indicate that the raiders had passed, and the sirens would sound the 'All Clear'.[11]

The need to strike a balance between warning people in sufficient time, and not issue false warnings, was made more difficult by raids frequently changing direction while being tracked, and this had a demoralising effect on the public and adverse impact on the war effort. In an attempt to address this, a Subsidiary Air Raid Scheme was introduced, whereby a second warning, an 'alarm message', would be given when an attack was actually developing. On hearing the first 'Red Warning', people in selected buildings would not leave to take shelter, but rather carry on working until, and if, a telephone call were received ordering them to evacuate the building. The call was made by Observers from the Southern Observer Corps Area, who were located at good vantage points in London, such as the roof of the Air Ministry, and above St James' Park Underground Station. The scheme provided secondary warning across twelve square miles (nineteen square kilometres) of London to over 400 buildings, including Buckingham Palace. It was so successful at being able to precisely track hostile raids that the scheme was extended to cover other important factories elsewhere in the country.[12]

In considering the Observer Corps contribution towards active defence, it is clear that without a reporting and tracking capability over land, Fighter Command could not have known where the raiders were, and therefore successful interception would have been near impossible. Posts would report to their Centre, and the raid would be 'retold' on to Fighter Command Groups and Sectors, who would scramble and direct their fighters. The 'Tizzy Angle' methodology was particularly successful in bringing hostile and friendly aircraft together, but it was not infallible. Human error, and a time lag between receiving and processing information told by the Observer Corps or obtained from 'Pip Squeak' direction finding, could lead to miscalculations.

The fact that Observer Posts were deliberately sited to offer excellent views of the aerial theatre overhead, meant Observers could provide

OBSERVER CORPS

'running commentaries', when dealing with a single intruder, or a small raiding group. This was a pragmatic solution to the problem caused by time lag, and all that was required was sufficient visibility, provided by either daylight or moonlight. As approaching British fighters flew within ten miles (sixteen kilometres) of the enemy, the Duty Controller in the Observer Corps Centre would phone the relevant Sector Controller with the message, 'Urgent Running Commentary'. He would then relay information provided by the Observation Post on relative position, course, height, whether enemy aircraft were making for, or entering, cloud banks, and their position relative to any observed anti-aircraft shell bursts. The Sector Controller would then use this vital information to position his fighters into the most advantageous position possible to engage the enemy.[13]

The south-east of England experienced the greatest number of Luftwaffe incursions and failing to track large raids accurately risked presenting a confused air picture on the general situation map at Uxbridge. An unwelcome consequence was that this could hinder Controllers from orchestrating successful interceptions, and fatally delay the issuing of air raid warnings. The difficulty in tracking large raids presented in a number of scenarios. The first was when large raids split up towards different targets, or as evasive action after being attacked by defending fighters. The second was when large numbers of enemy aircraft were approaching, either in close succession within a narrow corridor – 'Crocodile Raids', in formation – 'Mass Raids', or flying at random – 'Random Activity'.

In relation to the first scenario, the method of 'telling' was revised so that the main portion of the enemy formation shown on the general situation map at Uxbridge retained the original raid number, and smaller elements were denoted by a suffix letter added to the original raid number. However, the high volume of plots being 'told' during periods of intensive enemy action still saturated the system, and it was determined that 'telling' must be selective, and the 'Teller' must understand the point of view of the Operations Room. To facilitate this, an RAF officer was appointed to act as Observer in the Operations Room at Uxbridge, and two members of Fighter Command's Operational Research Section were assigned to work with the Observer Corps Centres.[14]

The second scenario, involving plotting large numbers of enemy aircraft, was addressed by showing 'Area Raids', 'Battle Zones', or 'Sweeps', on the general situation map. When the density of aircraft approaching from the sea was so great that the raid reporting system could not continue to differentiate separate tracks, the area covered was 'told' by an 'Area Raid'. The corners of a quadrilateral, numbered one to four, were plotted by triangular corners facing outwards and 'told' clockwise from the north-east corner. As the raid made landfall, the Observer Corps would 'tell' individual formations. If this was still not possible, then the 'Air Raid' would become a 'Battle Zone'. All previous raid blocks would be removed and an annular counter placed over the centre of the area. If the raid was 'told' as heard, then the plain underside of the counter was displayed. There were two sizes of counter available, a 'Small Battle Zone', indicating an area of ten miles (sixteen kilometres) diameter or less, and a 'Large Battle Zone', indicating an area of more than ten miles diameter. Where the raid was progressing along a broad 'Sweep', the centre would be 'told' with the length of front. A red strip of approximate length to the general situation map was placed with its centre at the position 'told' and at right angles to the direction of flight, which was indicated by an arrow counter.[15]

The main role of enemy fighters operating over Britain was to provide a chaperone to the large bomber formations over London and the south-east. A secondary role, as the battle progressed, was for fighters and fighter bombers to carry out large raids without bombers. The Luftwaffe wanted to entice Hurricanes and Spitfires into the air and into a war of attrition with their Messerschmitt Me 109 fighters, which they believed the British, numerically, could not win. The Germans' hope was that their fighters would decimate Fighter Command and reduce Britain's capacity to resist invasion. Park realised this and gave a clear instruction to his Controllers at Uxbridge, that the 'main object is to engage enemy bombers, particularly those approaching under the lowest cloud layer'.[16]

To carry out the instruction, Controllers needed to discern whether the aircraft within a raid were bombers, fighters, or both. A new system of 'telling' was introduced, first in 11 Group, and then across Fighter Command. When the Observer Corps was able to, a raid was 'told' in the normal manner by teleprinter, adding the letters 'ZF' for enemy fighters, and 'ZB' for enemy bombers. When the raid consisted of both, then the letters 'ZB' were given, and if a raid split of its own accord, or was forced to as a result of being attacked by British fighters, then the raid would be told as a 'Split Raid', using the identification 'ZB' or 'ZF', as appropriate.[17] Identifying whether aircraft in a raid were fighters or bombers also allowed Controllers to tactically deploy their fighters, and comply with another of Park's instructions. 'Some Spitfire squadrons are to be detailed to engage the enemy fighter screen at 20,000 or more feet (6,096 or more metres). The Hurricanes, because of their inferior performance, should normally be put in against the enemy bombers, which were rarely above 16,000 ft (4,877 metres) by day.[18]

Raids by low-flying Luftwaffe fighters and bombers against southern coastal targets presented another problem for Fighter Command. Sightings had to be quickly communicated if the RAF was to intercept the enemy before they reached their objective. In late 1942, Operation *Totter* saw Observation Posts, including a number within the area covered by Uxbridge, issued with pyrotechnic rockets. The rockets were fired when the enemy was sighted, alerting fighters who were flying standing patrols and poised to intercept the raiders. An additional measure, Operation *Rats*, was introduced to speed up the actual telephone reporting of sightings. On seeing an intruder, the Post would immediately pass the word 'Rats' to the Observer Centre, before passing any plot. This was then immediately passed to the Sector Controller, who would scramble aircraft or direct those already airborne towards the Post. In spite of these measures, it was found that the spacing between Posts still allowed enemy aircraft to fly without their tracks being maintained with the continuity required for controlled interception by fighters, and the issue of air raid warnings. The deficiency was mitigated by building around 150 'Satellite Posts', which were connected by telephone to the nearest existing Post or Centre, thereby increasing the existing coverage.[19]

It merits saying something about the significant, but lesser-known, role played by Group Operations Rooms like that at Uxbridge and the Observer Corps in assisting friendly aircraft in distress. Observers, on seeing or hearing an aircraft in trouble, reported the position and course to their Observer Centre, who forwarded it to the Group Operations Room. The Flying Control Liaison Officer there, who was responsible for initiating action to recover lost or damaged aircraft, worked closely with the Observer Corps Liaison Officer, also in the Group Operations Room. Some Observer Posts in areas near to Bomber Command bases were equipped with searchlights that Observer Posts shone, to indicate the direction friendly aircraft needed to take to reach safety. Some were equipped with radio sets, codenamed 'Darky', which were used to give an aircraft its position and course to set for the nearest airfield. Others, in hilly or mountainous locations, were provided with red flares, codenamed 'Granite', which were lit when an aircraft was in danger of flying into high ground or approaching high ground at an unsafe height.[20]

ENEMY SIGHTED

Observer Posts

Observers maintained a constant vigil from a network of Observation Posts, which were augmented and improved throughout the war. While a 'standard pattern hut' had been designed, it was difficult to acquire, and the majority of Posts were simple constructions, affording some type of protection against the weather. A Post could be a trench, surrounded by sandbags in the open countryside, or a hut on top of a tall building in a city location, as long as it was able to provide optimum surveillance of the surrounding airspace. This criterion is exemplified by Easy Four Windsor Post, which came within Number 17 Watford Group, and therefore the Operations Room at Uxbridge. Easy Four Windsor Post was located on the top of the Brunswick Tower at Windsor Castle, affording commanding views to not only the Observers, but also to King George VI, Queen Elizabeth and the then Princess Elizabeth, who in 1944 climbed the steep ladder to join them during a V1 'Doodle Bug' rocket attack on London.[21]

Each post was equipped with a number of essential items to enable constant surveillance and consistent reporting. A field telephone, considered a more secure method of communication than radio, was provided to 'tell' information on to the local Observer Corps Centre. Binoculars were provided to aid viewing distant aircraft. A logbook was used to record all observations throughout a tour of duty, and, of course, tea-making facilities were available to brew the quintessential 'cuppa'.

A mechanical sighting instrument, called an 'Observer Post Instrument', with an attached height corrector, called a 'Micklethwait', after the Observer who developed it, was used to fix an aircraft's position over land, by gauging its horizontal bearing and vertical angle. The device, resembling a surveyor's theodolite, was mounted over a circular gridded map, often attached to a tripod. The map covered a ten mile (sixteen kilometres) radius around the particular post, plus five mile (eight kilometres) circles around others in its cluster. One observer would set the instrument with an estimate of an aircraft's height and align a sighting bar with it. This bar was mechanically connected to a vertical pointer, which would indicate the position of the aircraft on the map. A second observer reported the map coordinates, height, and number of aircraft for each sighting to the local Observer Corps Centre. Estimating an aircraft's height using the human eye was difficult, and yet the first observer was expected to do this when setting the Observer Post Instrument. The degree of accuracy to which this was done affected the accuracy of an aircraft's reported position. To compensate for this, where possible, the initial height estimation would be triangulated with information from other posts in the same 'cluster', in order to determine height more accurately.[22]

Telling height accurately was important, because Group and Sector Controllers needed to position their fighters above the enemy to give them the tactical advantage. Height was all important because it allowed the interceptors to see the enemy first, take the initiative, and convert their height into speed as they dived down to attack. Information from the Observer Corps, and indeed radar, would often tell height incorrectly, sometimes by several thousand feet. This was the primary cause for intercepting fighters finding themselves underneath enemy formations, and therefore vulnerable to being 'bounced'. 'Many pilots complained bitterly of these inaccuracies, but it was miraculous that they were not more frequent, or that the system, strained to the utmost, could work at all.'[23]

Observer Posts had to rely on tracking aircraft by sound during the night, or when adverse weather restricted visibility. They were reluctant to tell information on an aural track's height, strength, or direction, 'owing to the possibility of considerable error'. However, Fighter Command's Operational Research Section, which had come from the Bawdsey Radio Research Station, recommended that estimates of height and strength be provided as 'the average observer was able, with experience, to estimate strength and height, with an accuracy and reliability worth having.' Height was subsequently told to the nearest 500 ft, or 152 metres. An estimation at war's end, concluded that height told visually had an average 10 per cent error rate, and was less reliable above 20,000 ft (6,096 metres), while that told by sound had an average 20 per cent error rate.[24]

Observer Centres

The role of an Observer Corps Centre was to inform the 'recognised air picture', so that the necessary action could be taken to support passive and active defence against aerial attacks. This was achieved by filtering reports from Observer Posts within the Centre's area, and 'telling' the tracks of friendly and hostile aircraft simultaneously to Sector and Group Operations Rooms. Centres also played a key role in reporting aircraft that were in distress, those that had crashed, and where aircrew had baled out. Many rescue attempts were initiated, and lives saved, as a result of Observer Posts reporting to Centres on the position of aircraft going into the sea, or

ENEMY SIGHTED

crashing on land, and where parachutes were seen to fall. An instance of this occurring was during the Battle of Britain when Squadron Leader Tom Gleave's Hurricane, operating from the Biggin Hill Sector in 11 Group, was struck by cannon fire during an engagement with enemy aircraft. His machine was set ablaze and the starboard wing fell away. Gleave was seen to bale out by observers from 19 Group at Bromley, and they reported: 'Hurricane and hostile bomber crashed Q8779. Hurricane pilot bailed [*sic*] out in approximately Q9577.' Gleave was rescued, injured and badly burnt, and became one of plastic surgeon Archie McIndoe's first 'guinea pigs'.[25]

The Duty Controller at the Centre was responsible for the efficient working of that Centre, which involved the input of information received from Posts, and the output of information to Group and Sector Operations Rooms. He had responsibility for working with the Observer Corps Liaison Officer on duty at the Group Operations Room, and for carrying out the instructions passed to him by the Controller in the Group Operations Room, through the Observer Corps Liaison Officer. The Duty Controller was supported by a number of assistants, whose roles were refined as the war progressed and lessons were learnt.

The Post Controller, previously known as the Duty Controller's Assistant, supported the Duty Controller by overseeing the input of information from Posts to the Centre. The Assistant Duty Controller, previously known as the Sector Liaison Teller, supported the Duty Controller by overseeing the output of information from the Centre to the Group and Sector Operations Rooms. He was responsible for the efficient working of the Tellers in the Centre, and for liaising with Observer Corps Liaison Tellers in the Sector Operations Rooms. This individual would also work with the Observer Corps Liaison Officer in the Group Operations Room and would assume the responsibilities of the Duty Controller in his absence. The Floor Supervisor, previously known as the Table Supervisor, reported to the Duty Controller and Post Controller. It was this individual's role to ensure that the Plotters worked efficiently, and to supervise arrangements for the provision of raid plaques, counters and other equipment.

The Observer Corps system for reporting and plotting was, paradoxically, simple and yet sophisticated. As Churchill had observed, it did not have recourse to the technological wizardry that was available to the process of tracking over sea. Unlike radar, Observers relied on the 'mark one eyeball', and in this sense it was 'Early Stone Age'. However, the highly organised structure, clearly defined methodology and fast-tracked communication was in itself highly developed and sophisticated. 'It provided the fastest

OBSERVER CORPS

flow of accurate information obtainable. Reports of plots from the Posts to the Observer Corps network often reached over 1 million in twenty-four hours. A plot obtained by even the most remote Post could be transmitted to Fighter Command in less than forty seconds.'[26] The fact that the Observer Corps' role in defeating the Luftwaffe is not as widely recognised as that of other essential elements appears not only unjust, but also serves to provide an incomplete understanding of the integrated air defence system. Without it, successful interceptions would have been near impossible; the bomber would have got through, and invasion would have been likely. To return to our analogy of a spider catching a fly in a room, radar tells the spider when and where the fly enters the room, but it is the Observer Corps that tells the spider where its prey is, so that it can be caught.

Chapter 9

Anti-Aircraft Guns & Searchlights

'Signal & Capture Threads'

Air Defence on the Ground

The great aerial battle being fought over Britain in 1940 would determine which side was to have air superiority over the other. If Fighter Command could outlast the Luftwaffe, then they would deny Germany the conditions necessary for invasion. If the Luftwaffe was to endure, then without Fighter Command, Britain would be severely weakened and left vulnerable to attack from the sea as well as the air. It was, in the main, a war of attrition, in which the defending force had to bring down more enemy aircraft than they themselves were losing.

The major burden for downing the Luftwaffe's machines fell to the Hurricanes and Spitfires of Fighter Command; they were not alone in this task however. Anti-aircraft guns, searchlights and balloons formed the final essential elements within the integrated air defence system. It was recognised within official circles that each of these defensive measures on the ground would 'contribute to the total defence' of the country, and each needed to be 'developed to the highest degree of efficiency possible'.[1] These 'signal' and 'capture' threads, constructed to ambush and snare German aircraft, were a critical part of the 'spider's web' woven to defend key locations across Britain.

The main focus for German raiders, notwithstanding August 1940 when their attention turned to 11 Group's airfields, was on aircraft factories and cities, especially London. As part of the integrated air defence system, air and ground defences were positioned in concentric layers, to prevent the enemy reaching their targets. The area around the cities, and between them and the coast was, therefore, made an Air Fighting Zone in which Fighter Command's aircraft would operate, assisted at night by searchlights. To this end, there was a continuous searchlight belt 30 miles (48 kilometres) deep, stretching from the Solent, east of London, north to the Humber, and then north-west to the Tyne Tees area. A further belt ran between the Forth and the Clyde. Important cities were surrounded by Gun Defended Areas where raiders who managed to penetrate the Air Fighting Zone were met by a barrage of shells from heavy anti-aircraft guns supported by searchlights during darkness. As more equipment became available, more cities were defended, the defences of others increased, and searchlight cover was extended to the greater part of the country.[2]

Vital locations within the 11 Group area, such as the Hawker Hurricane factories at Langley and Brooklands, and Supermarine Spitfire factory at Southampton, received additional cover in the form of light anti-aircraft guns, to repulse low-level precision strikes by the Luftwaffe. The importance of these sites, and their vulnerability to attack, was made clear by Churchill who wrote in May 1940, 'the utmost available AA (Anti-Aircraft) strength should be concentrated on the aircraft factories. These are more important than anything else at the moment.'[3]

Anti-Aircraft Command

At the outset of war, anti-aircraft guns and searchlights were organised into a unified Command under General Sir Fredrick Pile, whose Headquarters, like that of Balloon Command, was located adjacent to Fighter Command's at Stanmore. It is noteworthy that Pile was the only British General to retain the same command throughout the war. Although he had responsibility for the operational deployment of these defences, as an integral part of the air defence system, Anti-Aircraft Command reported ultimately to Hugh Dowding, the AOC Fighter Command. Such an arrangement, without close liaison and willing cooperation, had potential to compromise air defence, and so it is a testament to effective collaboration that Pile recorded in his despatch, 'relations were always most cordial'.[4] Had the working relationship been fractious, as was the case in Fighter Command between Keith Park, the AOC 11 Group and Lee-Mallory, AOC 12 Group,[5] then the potency of fighter aircraft and anti-aircraft guns working together would have been diminished, to the detriment of Britain's air defence.

The Anti-Aircraft Command was arranged into seven Divisions across the country. The 1st Division operated across Churchill's 'fat cow', London, and shared a land boundary with the 6th Division, which operated across south-east England and southern East Anglia, stretching from Lowestoft on the east coast to Worthing on the south coast. Both shared their areas with

ENEMY SIGHTED

Fighter Command's 11 Group Operations Room at Uxbridge. The 1st Anti-Aircraft Division incorporated the 11 Group Sector station at Northolt, and the 6th Anti-Aircraft Division's geography meant it shared responsibility for guarding the approaches to the capital, with five of the remaining six Sector stations controlled by 11 Group, namely Debden, North Weald, Hornchurch, Biggin Hill and Kenley.

There were four main Gun Defended Areas at Harwich, Dover and Folkestone, the North Bank of the Thames Estuary, covering the Thames and Medway North, and the South Bank of the Thames Estuary, covering Medway South, Rochester and Chatham. A number of 11 Group Sector airfields considered vulnerable to air attack were also protected by heavy anti-aircraft guns positioned in the vicinity. Each Gun Defended Area was controlled by a Gun Operations Room, based locally at either Felixstowe, Dover, Vange and Chatham respectively. Each Gun Operations Room was connected directly to the 11 Group Operations Room at Uxbridge, from where plots of enemy raids were sent, and these were in turn passed down to all gun sites.[6] Searchlights in the Air Fighting Zone were connected to the respective 11 Group Sector Operations Room, so that information and orders could be relayed in order to coordinate action against enemy aircraft.

When formed, Anti-Aircraft Command[7] was equipped with only 695 heavy anti-aircraft guns, many of which were old and obsolescent, or on loan from the Royal Navy. The recommended total at this time was a staggering 2,232 guns. The number of light anti-aircraft guns was also woefully short, with only 253 available, against a much larger recommended number of 1,200, and again some were on loan from the Royal Navy. The fact that seventy-six of these were of the new, highly effective Bofors 40 mm type was to be welcomed, but, in truth, Britain's position was far worse than even their enemy realised. German intelligence reported[8] that, 'in view of the island's extreme vulnerability to air attack and the comparatively limited amount of modern equipment, the number of heavy (1,194) and light (1,114) AA guns available is by no means adequate to ensure the protection of the island by ground defences.'

The assessment also overestimated how many searchlights were available to the British, reporting that 'the large number of efficient searchlights available, 3,200, constitutes an advantageous factor in defence at night'. In fact, the actual number of searchlights deployed was 2,700, a significant shortfall against both what the Germans thought, and the Air Ministry recommendation of 4,700.[9] The German battle plan was based on an inflated estimation of the strength of Britain's ground defences, which they still considered to be inadequate. How much more emboldened would they have been had they known the true level of deficiency?

At the time of the Battle of Britain, Anti-Aircraft Command fielded five types of guns, classified as either light or heavy anti-aircraft. The Bofors 40 mm, and Vickers Two Pounder fell into the former, and both fired a 2 lb (1 kg) high explosive round, primarily against low-flying raiders. The Bofors was a Swedish design, and those built under licence in Britain were equipped with an electrohydraulic automatic gun laying capability, whereby the target was tracked using a telescope. It 'proved to be versatile, reliable and robust and was responsible for shooting down a number of low-flying enemy aircraft'. The Vickers, also known as the 'Pom-Pom', was a British design inferior to the Bofors, which had in the main replaced it by 1940. The Chief of Imperial Staff had initially refused to sanction the development of any light anti-aircraft weapon above half the size of the Bofors or Vickers, and they may never have entered service at all, were it not for the tenacity of army officers, who persevered with trials showing that 2 lb of high explosives was the minimum quantity required to immediately destroy a targeted aircraft.[10] This near miss is a further example of fate intervening to mitigate against a flawed decision, that otherwise would likely have undermined the effectiveness of an essential element within Britain's integrated air defence system.

There were three weapons in service, which were classified as heavy anti-aircraft guns. These were the Vickers 3.7 inch (94 mm), QF 3 inch (76 mm), and QF 4.5 inch (114 mm). The Vickers 3.7 inch was one of the most widely deployed guns, originally built to be mobile, and later mounted on static sites. Its 28 lb (13 kg) high explosive round, could be fired at raiding aircraft flying up to 35,000 ft (10,668 metres). The actual height of detonation was determined by inserting the fuse in a machine beforehand, to correspond with the height of the enemy aircraft. The QF 3 inch, like the Vickers Two Pounder, was obsolete, and mainly replaced by the Vickers 3.7 inch by 1940. The QF 3 inch fired a 16 lb (7 kg) high explosive round up to a height of 22,000 ft (6,706 metres), although its effective range was nearer 16,000 ft (4,877 metres). It was obsolete by 1940, and was mainly replaced by the Vickers 3.7 inch. Interestingly, senior officers in the British Expeditionary Force preferred them over the Vickers 3.7 inch guns, and so decided to take forty-eight of them to France. Much of the heavy artillery was left behind during the evacuation from the Continent, and so it was fortuitous that the 3.7 inch guns, more effective in the anti-aircraft role, had been preserved in Britain for the battle that was to follow. The QF 4.5 inch, was the largest anti-aircraft gun in Britain's armoury, firing a 55 lb (25 kg) high explosive round up to a height of 42,000 ft (12,802 metres), although its normal operating ceiling was between 22,000 and 28,000 ft (6,706 and 8,534 metres). The QF 4.5 inch gun, like the QF 3 inch, had naval origins, and was readily identifiable by its armoured gun shield turret.[11]

Searchlights were manned by the Royal Artillery, and the main type in use at the onset of war was the 35-inch, or 90 cm projector, fitted with a high density arc lamp and a sound locator. Sound locators had proved to be effective in the previous war but were less so in the subsequent one. The reason for this was that they registered the apparent position of the source of sound, lagging behind the target to the extent of the time taken by sound to travel from the target to the sound locator. When the speed of the target was low it was comparatively easy to allow for this lag, but modern bombers were now travelling around three times the speed of those in the previous conflict, resulting in the searchlights generally being defeated.[12] An improved searchlight, the 59 inch (150 cm), entered service from the summer of 1940. It was equipped with a high density carbon arc lamp and large reflector, producing an intensely bright narrow beam, capable of penetrating mist and low cloud, to expose aircraft up to 20,000 ft (6,096 metres).

Searchlights made it dangerous for German pilots to carry out a steady and level approach to their intended target, making accurate bombing difficult. Bombers were forced to fly higher in the night sky, so as not to get caught in their penetrating glare, and they would often carry out evasive manoeuvres, such as frequently changing height and speed, in order to avoid detection. If caught in a searchlight's beam, a bomber was vulnerable to both anti-aircraft guns and night fighters. Dowding reported on the latter that:

> We relied on daytime interception methods, and on the searchlights to illuminate and hold the bombers. If they were capable of doing this, all would be well, since the distance at which an illuminated bomber can be seen by night is comparable with the range of visibility by daylight.[13]

This was the case on the night of 14 September 1940, when a Blenheim from 25 Squadron at North Weald, 'shot down a He. 111 after a chase of twenty minutes, during which time the searchlight held the enemy aircraft'.[14]

The 6th Anti-Aircraft Division, covering the approaches to London, would experience the largest number of incursions by the Luftwaffe, which, like ethereal beings, visited the capital on fifty-seven consecutive nights during the Blitz. Searchlights were deployed throughout in single light stations. Most were spaced at around 18,000 ft (5,486 metres) intervals, but those located along the coast, and in 'gun defended areas' were sited more closely at around 10,500 ft (3,200 metres).

In July 1940, the area covered by the Operations Room at Uxbridge would have appeared to Luftwaffe crews to be bristling with anti-aircraft guns. There were 316 heavy anti-aircraft guns, 135 light anti-aircraft guns, and 620 Lewis .303 inch (7.69 mm), and Hispano 20 mm (.787 inch) anti-aircraft light machine-guns, located across the 1st and 6th Anti-Aircraft Divisions.[15]

The heavy anti-aircraft guns were deployed, in the main, around the larger conurbations, ports and estuaries. Some were also used to defend 11 Group's airfields, and the Hawker Hurricane factory at Langley. The light anti-aircraft guns were deployed to protect specific vulnerable points against low-flying raids. There were forty-five such sites within the 6th Anti-Aircraft Division, and these included a combination of Chain Home Radar stations, Sector stations, dockyards, oil depots, ammunition stores, industrial complexes, and vital factories.[16]

A report, incorporated within Dowding's despatch on the Battle of Britain, indicated that between the onset of war and the end of the Battle of Britain, 219 enemy aircraft, flying over 11 Group's area, fell to the 6th Anti-Aircraft Division's heavy and light anti-aircraft guns.[17] This figure is likely to have been unwittingly inflated by claims from multiple guns firing at the same target, and by gunners believing they had downed aircraft that had in fact already been fatally damaged by defending fighters. But even though the final tally may be in doubt, the contribution made by the guns is not.

As well as destroying and damaging enemy aircraft, the guns broke up the large 'herd like' formations, in which bombers sought mutual protection, exposing isolated individuals to attack from defending fighters. The guns also served a revelatory purpose, their shell bursts functioning as fingers, to point in the direction of enemy aircraft, and help lead Fighter Command's predators towards their prey. A case in point was on the morning of 18 September 1940, when enemy raiders were split up over Maidstone, and one machine was shot down by anti-aircraft fire. Later the same day, anti-aircraft guns 'betrayed' a further raid to Spitfires stalking over Hornchurch.[18]

Not unlike the balloon barrage, shell bursts had an unsettling effect on Luftwaffe aircrew, forcing them to take avoiding action by flying higher, or

ENEMY SIGHTED

zig-zagging. Either manoeuvre was likely to result in the bombing being less accurate. Seeing and hearing anti-aircraft guns being used against enemy aircraft also had a positive effect on the morale of those who were at that moment being bombed. The feeling of 'hitting back' galvanised a beleaguered population, but in truth this was imprecise technology, requiring many rounds to be fired to bring down an aircraft, especially during the hours of darkness. This imperfection was illustrated, during the night of 7 September 1940, when the guns fired at streams of enemy aircraft over London for six hours, resulting in the loss of just one bomber.[19]

Chapter 10

Balloon Command

'Capture Thread'

Balloons, which had been used to good effect during the First World War, were again raised above aircraft factories and other vital locations, such as cities and ports. Their purpose was to provide an additional layer of defence, against low-level attacks by German raiders.

Balloon Command was formed less than a year before Britain declared war on Nazi Germany, and its first AOC-in-C was Air Vice-Marshal Owen Boyd, a determined individual who had flown and fought on the Western Front in the previous war. As AOC-in-C, he had responsibility for operational deployment of the balloon barrage, but as balloons were an integral part of the air defence system, Boyd and his Command ultimately reported to Hugh Dowding. To aid collaborative working, its Headquarters were located adjacent to Fighter Command's at Stanmore. Boyd provided energetic leadership to the Command throughout the Battle of Britain, after which time he was promoted to Air Marshal, Deputy to AOC-in-C Middle East, where his tenacious character would once again be evident. While en route to take up his post in Egypt, Boyd's Wellington aircraft was forced down by Italian fighter planes over Sicily, where he was captured and imprisoned in Vincigliata Castle, dubbed 'Mussolini's Colditz'.[1] His first attempt to escape, using a tunnel, resulted in him being recaptured, but a subsequent attempt saw him successfully return to England. Boyd's replacement at Balloon Command was Air Vice-Marshal Leslie Gossage, who had previously commanded Fighter Command's 11 Group, at Uxbridge.

The number of establishments approved for balloons by the Air Ministry was 1,455,[2] but on the eve of war, Balloon Command was able to deploy only 444 balloons over London, and a further 180 elsewhere. This left the Command unable to meet its defensive responsibility across many vital points, leaving numerous areas across the country unguarded against low-level attacks. However, as British industry adjusted to wartime demand,

ENEMY SIGHTED

a new balloon factory, Kelvin Hall (KH) in Glasgow, was soon able to increase production,[3] ensuring that around 2,000 KH balloons would always be available throughout the remainder of the war.

The Command was divided into five Balloon Groups covering Britain, and these were further segmented into Balloon Centres, each of which contained a number of Balloon Squadrons. At the commencement of hostilities, and throughout the Battle of Britain, the area covered by the 11 Group Operations Room at Uxbridge fell within 30 and 32 Balloon Groups, based at Chessington and Ramsey. Balloon Centres, number 1 at Kidbrooke, 2 at Hook, 3 at Stanmore, and 4 at Chigwell, came within the control of the former, and number 12 at Fareham within the latter. During the height of the Battle of Britain, they fielded an establishment of 692 balloons, of which 630, were tethered to the ground or vehicles, and sixty were waterborne to protect shipping and deter aerial minelaying.[4]

The standard barrage balloon flown during the Battle of Britain was kept aloft by around 20,000 cubic ft (6,096 cubic metres) of hydrogen gas. Balloons were fitted with steel cabling, and tethered to winch-equipped lorries for mobile deployment, or to screw pickets, railway sleepers or sandbags, in the case of permanent sites. Waterborne moorings were used to position balloons protecting against attacks on shipping and harbours, and to deter low-level minelaying of estuaries.[5]

There were two methods for deploying balloons over vulnerable sites. One was 'perimeter siting', in which they were moored equidistantly along only the circumference of the site, and the other was 'field siting', where they were moored equidistantly over the whole circular area being defended. The latter method increased the probability of impact by two to three times,[6] and again, even if enemy aircraft did not collide with the balloons or their steel cables, the prospect of it happening was sufficient to discourage them from flying through the barrage.

It is evident, at a tactical level at least, that the Luftwaffe viewed the balloon barrage as an obstacle to be removed prior to bombing raids taking place. This view is borne out by enemy action, conducted over five separate days during the Battle of Britain, when Me 109s targeted barrage balloons over the fiercely contested channel port of Dover.[7]

Balloons posed a significant threat to any low-flying aircraft, regardless of whether they were friendly or hostile. An unwelcome fact is that because there were more friendly aircraft than hostile ones flying over Britain, a greater number of them, 310, would collide with balloons or their cables, causing ninety-one to crash.[8]

BALLOON COMMAND

Dowding, although alarmed at the loss of friendly aircraft, considered that from an air defence perspective, the presence of the balloon barrage served to 'exercise a very salutary moral effect upon the Germans'.[9]

German Intelligence reported on 16 July 1940 that 'only limited importance should be attributed to the numerous barrage balloons, as these can be used only at low altitudes, 1,000 to 2,000 metres, owing to the medium wind velocities prevailing over the island. The balloons cannot be raised at all at appreciable wind velocities.'[10]

The Germans were correct in that balloons could only be raised to a maximum altitude of around 4,921 ft (1,500 metres), but wind was not the only constraining factor in their deployment. On 27 July 1940, nine balloons raised over the Thames were struck by lightning, and replacements needed to be hoisted over the London skyline to fill the void that had been created.[11] However, German Intelligence had failed to fully understand what the British expected from their balloon barrage. The intention was to make it difficult for the Luftwaffe to carry out low-level bombing against Britain, and not that enemy aircraft would become ensnared. Boyd did not deploy his balloons in the expectation that large numbers of enemy aircraft would be destroyed after colliding with them. His presupposition is borne out by post-war research which shows that throughout the Second World War, only fifty-four enemy aircraft are confirmed to have struck balloons or their steel cables over Britain, and of these, only twenty-five are confirmed to have been brought down as a result. One lucky machine, which avoided being brought down by a balloon, was a Ju 88 bomber whose pilot stalled while attempting to avoid it, and actually landed on top of it. Fortunately for him, the propellers did not puncture the hydrogen filled envelope and the bomber slid off, albeit with no forward speed. The good luck continued, as the pilot regained control just as the crew were preparing to bale out.[12]

Dowding's assessment was 'that the heavy cost of their installation and maintenance, and their drain on manpower, were on the whole justified. It is true that their material results, in terms of enemy air craft destroyed, were not impressive, they suffered staggering casualties in electric storms, and had brought down a number of our own aircraft; on the other hand, they ... protected the vital objectives, which they surrounded, against low-altitude attacks and dive-bombing.'[13]

The relatively low number of hostile aircraft known to have collided with balloons or their cables, despite intense enemy activity, serves to vindicate Dowding's belief that barrage balloons deterred conventional low-level bombing by Heinkel He 111s and Dornier Do 17s, and dive bombing by

ENEMY SIGHTED

Junker Ju 87 Stukas. They forced the enemy to fly higher, and therefore operate within a more restricted vertical space, between the barrage balloons and the bombers' operational ceiling height. The consequence of them being squeezed into this area was twofold. The first is that they then became vulnerable to being spotted by searchlights during night raids, and attack round the clock from Fighter Command's aircraft and anti-aircraft guns. The second consequence, well understood by the Air Staff, is that the raids would be less effective as 'further inaccuracy in aim would result if the defences forced the attackers to fly high or to attack more by night'.[14]

Chapter 11

The Underground Operations Room

'Down the Spider Hole'
Part One

We have likened Britain's integrated air defence system to a 'spider's web', with 'signal' and 'capture' threads. 'Signal threads', represented by Chain Home Radar stations, the Observer Corps, searchlights and teleprinter and telephone communications, detected the presence of intruding 'flies' – the Luftwaffe. 'Capture threads', represented by fighter aircraft, anti-aircraft guns and balloons, engaged with and incapacitated their prey.

We now turn our attention to the Bunker, 11 Group's subterranean Operations Room, where information provided remotely by 'signal threads' was received and relayed to the 'capture threads'. The Operations Room, colloquially referred to by those who worked there as 'the Hole', can, for the purpose of our 'spider's web' analogy, be viewed as 'the spider hole'. A 'spider hole' is described as a trench or indentation, used by a spider for rest or ambush, or a small rough excavation for concealing a person, as from an enemy. The Operations Room was the place from which the 'spider' was despatched to attack the 'fly'.

Hidden from view, and protected from aerial bombardment, the Operations Room, deep below RAF Uxbridge, was the place from where senior officers directed and coordinated the fierce aerial battles fought over London, southeast England, the English Channel, and north-west France. The decisions made in that room would help determine the outcome of major campaigns throughout the Second World War. They helped to slow down the Nazi invasion of France and the Low Countries; protect the troops being evacuated from Dunkirk; deny the Luftwaffe the air superiority needed to invade Britain; support the exploratory raid on Dieppe; shield the troops landing in Normandy; and defend against Hitler's *Vergeltungswaffen*, the V1 and V2. These engagements would influence not only British, but world history.

Uxbridge's location, just outside and to the west of London, meant it was near enough to the capital and the rest of 11 Group to accommodate logistical needs and facilitate effective communication, but far enough to make it more difficult for the enemy to reach unhindered. If the defences were breached, then precise bombing would still be challenging for the raiders, as Uxbridge did not have the same number of readily discernible landmarks as London, necessary for them to fix their position in relation to the bombing target. This was therefore considered to be a suitable site from which to evaluate raid intelligence, and launch a systematic response, in defence of the capital, and the approaches leading to it.

The underground Operations Room, which can be seen today, is the final embodiment of a series of Operations Rooms used at Uxbridge following the First World War.[1] In 1925, the Operations Room was located within a wooden building to the south of Hillingdon House, then the Headquarters for ADGB. Three years later, it moved to the Conference Room within Hillingdon House itself, but the need to accommodate a growing number of Headquarters' staff within that building meant it was to move again. The AOC ADGB prophesied that, 'the final model of the Fighting Area Headquarters Operations Room will take the form of an underground room in the vicinity of Hillingdon House'. This, however, would not come to fruition until several years later, and the Operations Room would in the meantime relocate in 1933 to 'Baghdad Block', where the concept of isolating the control dais, to afford a degree of quietude for the Controller, was first introduced. The Room then moved to its penultimate location, Building 76. This building, constructed as a First World War Cadet Officers' Mess, and then used as a Sergeants' Mess, proved unsuitable for all-year-round operation, as damp conditions during winter months adversely affected the electrical equipment within the Operations Room.

In 1933, Wing Commander Modin, a staff officer at ADGB, expressed concern that the Operations Room's geographic location would not, in itself, guarantee protection against aerial attack. He wrote:

> Uxbridge Royal Air Force buildings would provide an easy bombing target from all points of view. I feel that our Operations Room at least must go underground ... and the sooner it is put there the better, as not only will the reinstallation of communications and apparatus generally take time, but if that machinery is to function smoothly in a sudden emergency, installation must have been completed and the whole layout repeatedly worked and tried out before the danger of such emergency arises.

THE UNDERGROUND OPERATIONS ROOM

As the threat of war with Nazi Germany increased, so too did the impetus for a new underground Operations Room. The Deputy Chief of Air Staff, Air Vice-Marshal Courtney, wrote in July 1936 that:

> As regards the Operations Room, it is so small that the chances of it getting a direct hit are not large, provided it is kept reasonably inconspicuous from the air. I think it would be reasonably safe to place it somewhere on the Uxbridge estate provided it is kept away from the main block of the Headquarters building and is not placed adjacent to any other conspicuous landmark. It certainly ought to go underground.

The Headquarters building referred to by Courtney was Hillingdon House, a splendid white mansion, still visible today when approaching the present Operations Room. It functioned as a Headquarters for 11 Group from 1936, when Fighter Command was created, and for Bomber Command, until its relocation to RAF High Wycombe in 1940.

In December 1936, Dowding wrote to the Director of Organisation, Air Commodore Welsh:

> I have discussed this matter with Gossage, and we have come to the conclusion that the best place for the underground Operations Room will be inside the grounds at Uxbridge, and between the existing Operations Room and the Golf Links. I enclose a rough sketch to enable the site to be identified.

'Gossage' was Air Vice-Marshal Ernest Gossage, the then AOC 11 Group. It was he who, during the Battle of Britain, would wisely support the building of duplicate Sector Operations Rooms, a decision which proved to be invaluable following the Luftwaffe's devastating raids on Sector stations. Gossage was subsequently replaced as AOC 11 Group by William Welsh, on his promotion to Air Vice-Marshal, and Welsh would in turn hand over the reigns of 11 Group to the 'Defender of London', Keith Park.

A copy of Dowding's memo and sketch can be seen today, on display in the underground bunker.[2] Hillingdon House is clearly illustrated in the sketch, its location helping to show where Building 76, the then above-ground Operations Room, was situated. This building would be used for training purposes after the present underground Operations Room was completed, and it was retained as a contingency in case its replacement became unavailable for any reason. Building 76 was demolished in 2016, to make way for the new Battle of Britain Bunker Exhibition and Visitor Centre. The sketch shows that Dowding thought the underground Operations Room should be located below where the Hawker Hurricane is now displayed outside. It was, in fact, built adjacent to the old Operations Room, Building 76, on the opposite side of the road to where it is shown in the sketch.

In September 1938, the then Prime Minister, Neville Chamberlain, visited Germany on three occasions to meet the leaders of Nazi Germany and Fascist Italy. He pursued a policy of appeasement in the hope of averting a war, which many felt was now inevitable. As the world careered towards global conflict, the urgency to build an underground Operations Room gathered pace. On the 28th of that month, Britain declared a state of emergency, and the Operations Room in Building 76 was fully manned on a watch basis. The final act of appeasement was carried out in Munich two days later, on the 30th, when Great Britain and France signed an agreement with Hitler, acquiescing to the German annexation of the Sudetenland in Western Czechoslovakia.

Chamberlain returned the same day to Heston Aerodrome. Waving a piece of paper before a cheering crowd, he said,

> This morning I had another talk with the German Chancellor, Herr Hitler, and here is the paper which bears his name upon it, as well as mine ... We the German Führer and Chancellor and The British Prime Minister have had a further meeting today and are agreed in recognising that the question of Anglo-German relations is of the first importance for the two countries, and for Europe. We regard the agreement signed last night, and the Anglo-German naval agreement, as symbolic of the desire of our two peoples never to go to war with one another again.[3]

Later that evening he would stand outside 10 Downing Street and describe what many hoped had been achieved. Using the words of another British Prime Minister, Benjamin Disraeli, on his return from the Congress of Berlin sixty years earlier, Chamberlain wished for 'peace for our time'.

Many were sceptical on hearing Chamberlain's claim that he had secured 'peace for our time', but although he had not secured peace at this time, he had indeed secured time: time to prepare for war. The Royal Air Force

THE UNDERGROUND OPERATIONS ROOM

understood this and made good use of the time that was available. It moved rapidly to a wartime footing, and within that footing was the priority to relocate its command and control capability for London and the south-east of England, below ground, 'down the spider hole'.

The Operations Room was to play a vital role in the forthcoming conflict, and so it was classified as 'Top Secret' to prevent the enemy from learning of its existence or location. A veil of secrecy shrouded the Air Ministry's tendering process to build the underground complex, and the contract was ultimately awarded to Sir Robert McAlpine's construction company. The work itself was coordinated by the Air Ministry Works Directorate, which was a technical branch of the Civil Service, and led by Robert Mason Creer, a civilian who would later be commissioned in 1943 to the rank of Squadron Leader. A picture of Creer in uniform, and a subsequent one taken many years later showing him sitting in the Senior Controller's chair, is on display in the Bunker.[4]

Planning and excavation work, carried out in 1938, highlighted problems with the replete London clay that would surround the underground cavity. It had initially been intended to build the Operations Room 66 ft (20 metres) below ground, to afford protection against aerial attack, but this was reduced to 60 ft (18 metres), to mitigate against the likelihood of the building flooding. Building the two-storey subterranean structure would be challenging, it had to be done secretly, and yet speedily, if Fighter Command was to be ready to meet the imminent onslaught. The pace at which it needed to be planned and carried out, was astonishingly rapid. Time was at a premium, and this is evident from the minutes of a conference held in 1938, to determine the 'lay out, equipment, procedure, and manning of Operations Rooms'. Astonishingly, with only ten months remaining before the declaration of war, Air Commodore Saul of 11 Group was forced to state the Group had not yet received plans of the future Operations Room. Arrangements were hurriedly made for staff from Uxbridge to visit Headquarters Fighter Command, and inspect the plan that was available there.[5]

Construction work on the underground Operations Room was carried out at mercurial speed, beginning in February 1939, and finishing an astonishing seven months later, in August of that same year. This was completed just in the nick of time, as the new Operations Room was up and running by 25 August, a mere nine days before Britain declared war on Nazi Germany. The build time is not only remarkable for its exiguous nature, but also because of what was provided in that short time: a state-of-the-art, modern command centre from which 11 Group could coordinate the fight against its aerial nemesis, the Luftwaffe.

ENEMY SIGHTED

The Bunker has a footprint of approximately 42 ft by 116 ft (12.5 metres by 35.5 metres), plus related infrastructure. The floor of the lower storey is approximately 60 ft (18 metres) below ground level. It has substantial walls and ceilings, constructed from almost 3 ft (1 metre) of concrete, reinforced with rolled steel joists. The building is further protected by a covering of over 30 ft (9 metres) of earth above its roof, this exteriority being designed to withstand a direct hit from the heaviest munition capable of being delivered by a bomber of the time, a 500 lb (227 kg) all-purpose bomb. The concerns aired by Modin, Courtney, Welsh, Gossage and Dowding had been heeded by the Air Ministry.

Above ground, the Operations Room is hidden from view by an obscuration of grass, undergrowth and trees. There is little to betray what lies underneath, other than a few minor protrusions, necessary for access, egress and ventilation. A Luftwaffe wartime reconnaissance picture of RAF Uxbridge, now on display in the Bunker,[6] confirms that it was indeed imperceptible to the gaze of German aviators. The photograph, taken on 8 October 1940, towards the end of the Battle of Britain, has been annotated by Luftwaffe intelligence staff, highlighting several points considered to be of military interest, 'numerous sturdy buildings and some wooden barracks' and 'wireless station', but it offers no clue as to the existence of the Operations Room.

The two main protrusions above ground, the entrance and emergency exit points, are each sealed by a heavy blast-proof metal door, designed to shield the Operations Room from a bomb burst, or against a ground assault. Each opening has an airlock and stairwell attached to one of two underground Plant Rooms, X and Y, from where exhaust and air vents connect to the surface, rising above the grass like prodigious mushrooms.

The electrical generators in Plant Rooms X and Y are no longer operating, but the air ventilation units, built at the Portsmouth Royal Naval Dockyard, are both still functioning. It is worth noting that while they lack the modernity of today's air conditioning units, they do, nonetheless, represent advanced engineering for their time. The Porton Air Filtration Unit was capable of filtering 2,500 cubic feet (almost 80 cubic metres) of air per minute and would ensure a fresh supply of air was circulating from the surface, through the vents and into the Bunker. The unit in Plant Room X was modified by the Chemical Defence Experimental Station (CDES) at Porton Down, to provide a gas filtration capability. The ingenious adaptation resulted in the air pressure below ground being greater than that above ground, so the air inside was heavier than the air outside. This meant that in the event

THE UNDERGROUND OPERATIONS ROOM

of a gas attack, the heavier air below ground would prevent the lighter, hazardous, chemical-laden air above ground from entering, and so the vital work of the Operations Room could continue unhindered. CDES is better known today as the UK government's Defence Science and Technology Laboratory (DSTL). The DSTL's secretive work has more recently come to public notice after its scientists confirmed, in 2018, that Novichok nerve agent, developed by Russia, had indeed been used to poison former Russian double agent, Sergei Skripal, and his daughter, Yulia, in Salisbury.

The exit and entrance, situated at either end, are connected to the main block by 53 ft (16 metres) long corridors, which are aligned in opposite directions. Visitors to the site today can visualise this labyrinthine chamber's complexity, thanks to a three dimensional model on display in the new Battle of Britain Bunker Exhibition and Visitor Centre.[7]

The emergency exit, located on the surface to the rear of the Operations Room, is protected by a rectangular brick pillbox situated on the raised ground behind it. This fortified structure was designed to provide defending troops with a commanding view over the Bunker's access and egress points, should it ever be attacked from the ground. There are two ventilator stacks in the immediate vicinity of the emergency exit, and a further two near to the entrance. One stack in each pair serves as an inlet, and the other an outlet, for the Bunker's two Plant Rooms.

To reach the ground floor of the Bunker, visitors must walk down, and back up, a total of seventy-eight steps. A photograph displayed in the Bunker, showing notable guests as they start their descent, is of particular interest.[8] It merits reflection, not only because it captures some of the leading figures within Fighter Command, but also because among them is Group Captain Douglas Bader. Bader had a well-deserved reputation for being tenacious and single minded. What is remarkable here, as he starts walking down the seventy-eight steps, is that Bader had no legs, having lost both in a flying accident. Astonishingly, he walked down the steps, and back up, on his prosthetic legs. The Bunker was not built with a mechanical lift, and one cannot be added to the infrastructure retrospectively as the building is now listed and therefore protected from any structural alterations. Assailing the steps requires a general level of mobility, and for those for whom this is not possible, the Exhibition and Visitor Centre provides an excellent virtual tour of the underground Operations Room.

Entrance to the building is accessed by negotiating a small set of external steps leading to a sturdy wooden door, positioned immediately behind the metal blast-proof exterior door. The passage of time, and wear, has resulted in minor movement within the wooden door's structure, creating a small gap. By placing a hand over the gap, it is possible to feel, and hear, the air whistling out as it is expelled from inside, demonstrating that the air pressure below ground is, indeed, greater than that above.

The wooden door leads to a small guardroom, separated by a counter and framed by a metal mesh screen and metal mesh door. In wartime, visitors would have been challenged by a Royal Air Force Policeman, standing behind the counter and armed with a handgun. There is still a rifle rack attached to the rear wall, now readied with decommissioned Lee Enfield .303 inch bolt-action rifles. These magazine-fed, repeating rifles were the mainstay for British, Commonwealth and Empire troops throughout the first half of the twentieth century. They could fire off twenty to thirty aimed rounds in sixty seconds, a feat known as 'the mad minute', and so would have been formidable defensive weapons if the Germans had ever attempted to storm the Bunker. It is interesting to note that the ammunition used by the Lee Enfield rifle was the same as that used by both the Spitfire and Hurricane, which were originally armed with wing-mounted .303 inch, or 7.69 mm rifle calibre machine-guns.

Anyone seeking entry beyond the metal mesh screening would have had to satisfy the guard, and present an official pass, authorising them to enter one of Fighter Command's most secretive establishments. Visitors today walk through the guardroom and descend the steep staircase, which halfway down leads to an 'L' shaped landing, providing access to the first of two plant rooms. The pale cream walls on either side of the staircase are superimposed with the original black trunking, cables, and pipes, installed over eighty years ago. Like darkened arteries, they serve as conduits, pumping electricity, telephony, water and sewage, some 60 ft (18 metres), between the Operations Room and 'terra firma'.

As you walk along these steep steps, there is a realisation that you are not only walking through history, but also walking in the footsteps of some of history's iconic individuals. As you descend into the Bunker, holding on to the wooden hand rail, it is awe-inspiring to reflect that famous figures, notably King George VI, and his consort Queen Elizabeth; Sir Winston Churchill, and his wife Lady Clementine; General Bernard Montgomery, the British commander who defeated the Germans in North Africa; General Charles de Gaulle, leader of the French government in exile; and General Dwight Eisenhower, the Supreme American and Allied Commander, who would lead the invasion of Europe, have all walked down these same steps, and would likely have held on to the same handrail. These esteemed

THE UNDERGROUND OPERATIONS ROOM

individuals, all visited the Bunker because they understood that the decisions made there, and their ramifications, would influence not only the course of the war, but also the world, after it had been lost or won.

Descending further, beyond the 'L' shaped landing, leads to the bottom of the staircase, where a handwritten notation can be seen on the doorframe leading to the ring corridor. The words, 'Flood Level. July 14', are inscribed, roughly at the height of a person's head. Heavy rain, on 28 July 2014, had led to widespread flooding in the Uxbridge area, causing a deluge of water to cascade down the staircase, into the underground cavity. Fortunately, the door at the bottom of the staircase, designed to keep smoke and fire out, also kept much of the water at bay. However, a substantial amount did enter the lower floor, coursing along the rectangular ring corridor linking the main staircase and staircase leading to the emergency exit.

The ring corridor, radiating like the spiral thread on a spider's web, provides access to a further two sets of stairs, leading from the lower floor to the mezzanine floor area containing the Senior Controller's Cabin. An exploration of the ring corridor reveals further chambers on the ground floor. Here you find a second plant room; an ejector room, in which an air compression system removes sewage from the Bunker; a General Post Office (GPO) Room, with its original 1939 telephony equipment still intact; a Fuse Room, containing fuse boxes for the ventilation system, lighting system, teleprinters, GPO power and small power; a large Message Room, which would have housed a large group of WAAF operators, communicating through telephones, teleprinters and Lampson voice tubes.

Telephones and teleprinters were key to the Operations Room. If staff in the Bunker were unable to communicate with others working elsewhere across the network, then the system of integrated air defence could not function. The process, which in real time, provided the Senior Controller at Uxbridge with a recognised air picture, operated very much like a computer, in that all the information was calculated and laid out in front of him. The process by which the Operations Room was able to receive information and send it, very often to multiple locations simultaneously, operated very much like an internet.

The maintenance of the telephone and teleprinter network was therefore considered to be of the utmost priority, and resources were made permanently available to safeguard this precious asset. Three senior Post Office officials were appointed, so that one would be always on duty in the Bunker. That individual was responsible for all land line communications and Post Office equipment linking the Bunker and all its Sector Operations Rooms. Three

ENEMY SIGHTED

Post Office skilled workmen were appointed at Uxbridge and three more at each of 11 Group's Sector Operations Rooms, so that one was always on duty at each location to support the senior Post Office official.[9]

Direct communication between Sector stations and the 11 Group Operations Room was key to the whole system of integrated air defence. Park considered that, 'without signals, the only thing I commanded was my desk at Uxbridge.'[10]

In truth, being able to share vital information with Sector stations allowed the 11 Group Operations Room to be an underground communications hub. Without this ability, the 'Hole' was simply that, a hole in the ground.

Chapter 12

The Underground Operations Room
'Down the Spider Hole'
Part Two

Finally, at the very heart of the complex, is the Plotting Room itself, separated from the ring corridor by a white sliding door on which the words, 'Room 2, Plotting Room' are painted in large black letters. The floor is built on two levels, the uppermost being a raised wooden stage, accommodating a wooden dais overlooking a plotting table on the same level, which is used to display a general situation map. Fortuitously, this elevated position served to protect the table and map from water damage when the Bunker was flooded in 2014. The sliding door leads immediately to a small cubbyhole on the lower floor, situated underneath the raised wooden dais. There is a small wooden ladder, providing access to the dais overhead. The cubbyhole would have housed three members of the 'Ops B' team, who were responsible for operating a small telephone switchboard, teleprinter machine and a panel used to control the wall of indicator lights, or tote board, on the opposite side of the room. It was the responsibility of the 'Ops B' team to maintain communication with their counterparts on 11 Group's Sector stations, and to operate the portion of the tote board showing that the Group Controller's orders had been received by the Sector and had been complied with.

The raised wooden dais accommodated Operations Clerks, Intelligence Clerks and Liaison Officers, whose role it was to relay the information being displayed in front of them, to various arms of the government and military. The seat furthest away from the sliding door was where the Bomber Command Liaison Officer sat. He was responsible for coordinating the movement of friendly bombers over 11 Group and ensuring their whereabouts were known to the Operations Room. So, for example, if a flight of Blenheim aircraft were returning from a bombing raid over enemy territory, it was vital that the Operations Room recognised them as being friendly, and not hostile. One Bomber Command Liaison Officer during the

ENEMY SIGHTED

war was Flight Lieutenant Rex Harrison, a renowned actor of both stage and screen, who is most notably remembered for his role as 'Professor Henry Higgins', in *My Fair Lady*. His showbiz connections meant he was able to supply the Operations Room WAAFs with many complimentary tickets for shows in the West End, which they could enjoy when not working in the Bunker.[1]

A wall of curved glass overhangs the wooden dais and stretches across the entire length of the room. It is there to shield those working behind it in the gallery, from the incessant noise of frenetic activity below. The window, another example of clever engineering, is bowed, designed to prevent reflection. As if by magic, the glass appears to vanish when looking down from the gallery, allowing a perfectly clear view of the information being displayed. Both glass and gallery are partitioned into three separate areas, the largest being in the middle.

As viewed from the floor of the Operations Room, the left hand-side gallery accommodated Liaison Officers from the British Army and the Royal Navy. The Army was responsible for coordinating the anti-aircraft guns and searchlights. It was crucial to synchronise the use of anti-aircraft guns within the defensive network. The Army Liaison Officer was responsible for ensuring that gun batteries knew when to fire against enemy raiders, and when not to, because friendly aircraft were operating in the area. This was especially the case during the hours of darkness, when Fighter Command's night fighters were operating over 11 Group. The Liaison Officer needed to also maintain communication with the searchlights, so that they could illuminate enemy aircraft for the anti-aircraft guns and night fighters who were searching for them.

Fighter Command was responsible for the air defence of all sea approaches to the United Kingdom, and this included the provision of air defence for shipping within forty miles of the coast. The Command was also expected to inform the Admiralty of the activities and movements of enemy aircraft, especially those directed against dockyards and ports, and those engaged in minelaying. The Navy, that is the Admiralty, was required to provide Fighter Command with information regarding all convoy and shipping positions around the coast. Requests for the protection of shipping originated from the Naval Command from whose area the shipping sailed, and were addressed to the Fighter Command Group in whose area the shipping was to sail. The degree of air protection to be provided was decided by the Senior Controller, according to the importance of the shipping, and the potential threat of enemy air attack.[2] The majority of vital ports and busy shipping channels around the coast of south and south-east England came within 11 Group. The Navy Liaison Officer sitting behind the curved glass was key to effective communication, keeping the Admiralty informed, and ensuring the Senior Controller at Uxbridge was provided with a recognised air picture, in relation to convoy and shipping positions in the sea around 11 Group.

It appears the Group was busy over water, even before fighting intensified during the Battle for France and Battle of Britain, when it came to be known as 'Hell Fire Corner'. A note recorded under the heading 'The Phoney War', in a report outlining the first ten years of 11 Group, reads:

> Until the Battle of France took place, little of a spectacular nature took place for our aircraft. However, the resources of the Group were fully committed on standing patrols and convoy patrols. Protection was also given by 'Kipper Kites', as the fighters became to be known, which were detailed to protect our fishing fleets and light ships which were being subjected to enemy attack.[3]

The gallery on the right-hand side is where the Observer Corps Liaison Officer and Map Drawer were located. It was the Observer Corps Posts who assumed responsibility for raid reporting once Radar stations could no longer 'see' enemy aircraft. The information provided by them was crucial in apprising the Plotters and Tellers, who in turn updated the general situation map. The Observer Corps Liaison Officer was the conduit for ensuring effective, ongoing communication with the various Observer Corps Centres and the Observer Corps' southern Headquarters at Bentley Priory. The Map Drawer was tasked with tracing the routes flown by the enemy raiders, and one such map, for 14 September 1940, can be seen today, displayed in the Observer Corps Gallery.[4] Several maps could be drawn within every twenty-four hours to show that day's movements, enabling them to be used for raid intelligence purposes and inform defensive tactics. The ability to analyse records of previously flown routes was beneficial, particularly when dealing with the challenge of intercepting high-flying enemy aircraft, which could only be achieved if the Senior Controller was able to predict where the raid would be at a given point in the future. This was the case at the outbreak of war, when high-flying Luftwaffe reconnaissance aircraft, which had hereto proven to be elusive, were finally intercepted over 11 Group. An examination of previous maps revealed that the usual course flown during

ENEMY SIGHTED

these missions had been from Ostend, in Belgium, to Bury St Edmunds, and then across London, re-crossing the coast near Beachy Head. The Senior Controller at Uxbridge decided that for interception to take place, fighters based in London needed to be scrambled in advance while the raid was approaching the coast, and to Beachy Head when the raid was over Bury St Edmunds. An organisation known as Raid Intelligence was set up with the sole purpose of studying and analysing enemy raids. 'Their work proved effective when the solution to the problem of dealing with high-altitude fighter and fighter bomber attacks in October 1940, was only found by this Department after very careful study.'[5]

The central gallery with its row of telephones was the belvedere from which the Senior Controller, supported by his Assistant Controller and Operations Officer, observed the events unfolding in front of him. It is from this vantage point that fast time, life, and death decisions were made. The Senior Controller ordered the disposition of fighter aircraft on the ground and their states of preparedness; estimated the scale and probable objectives of enemy air attacks; ordered fighter aircraft off the ground in sufficient strength and in time to meet them; gave broad objectives as to the control of aircraft while airborne; and generally coordinated and supervised the control action of Sectors across 11 Group; as well as coordinating all the air defences within the Group.[6]

The Senior Controller had before him an abundance of information. What he did not have, was a plentiful amount of time in which to intercept enemy bombers and fighters. The challenge was to carry out interceptions early enough, and high enough, on formations of bombers operating with or without fighter escort, or fighters on their own. Information on an enemy raid would take on average four minutes to reach the Senior Controller at Uxbridge. In this short space of time, Radar operators at CH Radar stations had to detect a raid developing over the French coastline and send notification to Bentley Priory, where Filter Officers speedily eliminated the surplus information and relayed the filtered product to Uxbridge. Formations of enemy fighters, some carrying bombs, proved especially problematic. They could be over London within twenty minutes of their first being picked up by British Radar stations, and on some occasions had dropped bombs on south-east London seventeen minutes after the first radar plots were given. The only squadrons able to intercept the enemy fighters before they reached London, or 11 Group's precious airfields, were those already in the air on 'Readiness' patrol, or remaining in the air after an attack, plus one or two squadrons at 'Standby' on the east and south-east of

THE UNDERGROUND OPERATIONS ROOM

London. This was why Senior Controllers at Uxbridge had to be mindful of the time it took squadrons and other formations to climb from ground level to the required operating height.

A squadron operating Spitfire Mk Is required on average, around thirteen minutes to reach an altitude of 20,000 ft (6,096 metres), and they would perhaps need to climb higher, to 25,000 ft (7,620 metres), to have the tactical advantage over enemy fighters, in which case it would take around eighteen minutes. A squadron of Hurricane Mk Is, being somewhat slower, would take around sixteen minutes or twenty-one minutes respectively. The rate of climb was extended further by 10 to 12 per cent, when squadrons operated in pairs, and by 15 to 18 per cent when operating as a Wing of three squadrons. Controllers would therefore order squadrons to rendezvous over a point at operating height in order that they could climb quickly, singly, and not hold one another back by trying to climb in an unwieldy mass. It was better for a squadron to intercept the enemy with one squadron already above them, than by a whole Wing crawling up below, probably after the enemy had dropped their bombs.[7]

It was considered essential that Controllers possessed several vital attributes; the ability to command respect, both in aircrew to be controlled and in those working for them; and the ability to understand and appreciate the point of view of the aircrew being controlled, their difficulties, and the limitations and possibilities of the aircraft in which they were flying. Recent flying experience on current modern types, particularly in a fighter squadron, while not essential, was certainly valuable and therefore desirable.[8]

Park possessed these necessary attributes and demonstrated them by his actions. He was familiar with the characteristics of Fighter Command's modern fighters, routinely flying his personal Hurricane to visit fighter squadrons across 11 Group. At 48 he was considerably older than the pilots he led, and yet put himself at risk of attack from marauding Luftwaffe fighters, leaving the office chair he called his 'mahogany bomber', to fly his Hurricane on sixty-one occasions between 3 May and 24 November 1940.[9]

He was ultimately accountable for operational control of the integrated air defence system across his Group, maintaining oversight by delegating authority to his three Senior Controllers, Wing Commanders Lord Willoughby de Broke, Thomas Lang and Eric Douglas-Jones. It was they who controlled operations from the Bunker, in watches of four hours on and eight hours off, throughout the Battle of Britain. This allowed Park to take over control in the Operations Room at times of concentrated activity, while at the same time leaving him free to perform other necessary tasks.

ENEMY SIGHTED

All three of Park's Senior Controllers had recent flying experience, although only two had flown Fighter Command's new monoplane interceptors. John Verney, 20th Baron Willoughby de Broke, was a peer of the realm. He had previously served as Commanding Officer of 605 (County of Warwick) Squadron at RAF Tangmere in 11 Group, where he had overseen the squadron's transition from the ageing Gloster Gladiator biplane to its successor, the Hawker Hurricane. Thomas Lang did not have experience of flying a modern monoplane fighter. He had previously served as a Flight Commander with 610 (County of Chester) Squadron, which was equipped with Hawker Biplanes at the time, but would later receive Spitfires and then Hurricanes. Eric Douglas-Jones was posted to 11 Group Headquarters as Squadron Leader Operations, where he participated in planning the layout of the underground Operations Room, as it was being built. He performed the role of Operations Room Controller at the commencement of war, but by the beginning of 1940, had taken up the role of Commanding Officer for 54 Squadron, equipped with Spitfires at RAF Hornchurch in 11 Group. Here he led patrols and saw action over Northern France during the evacuation from Dunkirk. After Dunkirk, Douglas-Jones returned to Uxbridge and resumed the role of a Senior Controller in the Operations Room.

Park understood the need to strike a balance in how he controlled operations. On the one hand, he had to demonstrate around the clock tactical control over all his defensive assets. On the other, he had to place trust in the abilities and judgement of his Group and Sector Controllers. Dowding, his commanding officer, clearly felt he had been able to achieve this, writing:

> I must pay a very sincere tribute ... for the way in which he adjusted his tactics and interception methods to meet each new development as it occurred. Tactical control was ... devolved to the Groups; but tactical methods were normally laid down by Command Headquarters. During periods of intense fighting, however, there was no time for consultation, and Air Vice-Marshal Park acted from day to day on his own initiative. We discussed matters as opportunity offered.[10]

The trick was to develop a shared understanding, so that Park and his Controllers were all sighted on the same issues, and importantly, would adopt a common approach in dealing with them. 'His watchwords were

THE UNDERGROUND OPERATIONS ROOM

speedy challenge, repeatedly offered.'[11] Park's understanding of the situation was continuously enriched whenever he presided over the Operations Room, maintaining an appreciation of its workings and nuances. This he did routinely, as his house, now demolished, occupied land immediately behind the brick wall situated opposite the Bunker's entrance. The blue-green wooden door set within the wall is an original feature. Each morning, Park would walk through the opening and either turn right towards his office, Hillingdon House, or walk straight ahead and down the stairway leading to the Operations Room. Another way of raising his understanding of what was happening was through the routine interaction Park had with the fighter pilots dispersed across his Group, who were more than willing to share with him their thoughts on the challenges they were experiencing.

After reflecting on what was happening, and what he had seen and heard in both the Operations Room and elsewhere, Park would, when necessary, disseminate his latest 'Instructions to Controllers'. In this way, lessons learnt during aerial fighting, and subsequent adaptations to raid interception, were shared across 11 Group. This approach to controlling operations is illustrated through Instruction No.8, which Park issued on 2 September 1940, to clarify the use of reinforcements from a neighbouring Group:

> Whenever circumstances warrant asking for support, Controllers should request No.10 Group to patrol into No.11 Group area to westward of the north and south line through Brooklands-Maidenhead. No.10 Group squadrons may also be used to cover No.11 Group aerodromes within the area mentioned. No.10 Group has agreed to provide up to two squadrons whenever possible for this purpose.[12]

The situation that had necessitated Instruction No.8, was considered by Park, and Dowding, to have worsened and so, three days later, was followed by Instruction No.10:

> The Commander in Chief has directed that the following aircraft factories shall be given the maximum fighter cover, (not necessarily close patrols), during the next week: Hawkers, Kingston on Thames; Langley; Brooklands; Southampton aircraft factories. As the enemy bombing attacks on our fighter aerodromes during the past three weeks have not outwardly reduced the fighter defence, he is now directing some of

his main attacks against aircraft factories, especially in the west and south-west of London. The only direct protection that we can at present afford is to obtain from 10 Group two squadrons to patrol the lines, (a) Brooklands-Croydon, and (b) Brooklands-Windsor, whenever there is a heavy attack south of the Thames River. The task of these squadrons is to intercept bomber formations that may elude 11 Group fighters that are despatched to engage the enemy well forward of the factories and Sector aerodromes. The Southampton factories are of vital importance to the RAF, and 10 Group have agreed to reinforce the Tangmere Sector by up to three or four squadrons whenever a mass attack approaches the Southampton-Portsmouth area from the south. Whenever time permits, these two squadrons (Hawkinge and Manston or Rochford) are to rendezvous over Canterbury, and then be detailed to engage the enemy. The enemy's main attack must be met in maximum strength between the coast and our line of Sector aerodromes. Whenever time permits, squadrons are to be put into the battle in pairs. Some Spitfire squadrons are to be detailed to engage the enemy fighter screen at 20,000 or more feet. The Hurricanes, because of their inferior performance, should normally be put in against the enemy bombers, which are rarely above 16,000 ft by day. North of the Thames, 12 Group squadrons are to be requested, via Command, to cover North Weald, Stapleford, Hornchurch, also Debden. Pending arrival of 12 Group squadrons, the Group Controller should cover our Sector aerodromes by one or two squadrons. These must, however, be sent forward into the main battle immediately 12 Group squadrons arrive. The aerodromes west and south-west of London can be covered by 10 Group squadrons. Biggin Hill, Kenley and Croydon aerodromes can be covered by a maximum of two squadron; normally one flight should be adequate for each aerodrome, because the enemy should already have been engaged before he reaches the line of these stations.[13]

Returning to the Bunker, looking out from the gallery into the room below, a large flat window can be seen set within the wall on the right. Behind the glass is the 'Royal Box', built for the visit by King George VI and

THE UNDERGROUND OPERATIONS ROOM

his consort, Queen Elizabeth, in February 1941. The small room provides a discreet viewing gallery from which VIPs could observe proceedings, without impeding the normal functioning of the Operations Room.

The plotting table, centred on the raised wooden stage, is an irregular hexagon shape wooden construction. Its upper surface had been flat during the Battle of Britain, but was tilted afterwards, at the request of the Senior Controller. It now leans towards the viewing gallery, so that the information presented on it, can be more easily viewed from above. The paper general situation map displayed on top of the plotting table is of the same shape and size as the table itself, and is today covered by a Perspex sheet to preserve its delicate texture.

It is stirring to reflect that this was the actual map on the table at the time the Battle of Britain was being fought. It was also in use in the period immediately before then, when the Battle of France had been lost and troops were being evacuated from Dunkirk. A closer examination of the map, in the area to the east of Dunkirk, reveals several worn patches, inconspicuous reminders of the map's role during that monumental event. The scuffing was caused by wooden blocks being repeatedly pushed there, to represent the hordes of German aircraft on their way to attack the troops being evacuated, and the British fighters sent to stop them.

The map, albeit now somewhat faded, was originally drawn to show land areas in grey and all sea areas in green. It was treated with a benzine and wax solution to afford a degree of protection, and a matt surface to prevent it reflecting light.[14] The mapping outlines the two landmasses of southern England and north-western France, along with the Low Countries. They are separated by the waters of the English Channel, the Strait of Dover and the North Sea.

Black dots depict towns and cities to provide the map with definition when communicating information and actions. A prominent black line, stretching from the Isle of Wight in the south, to Buckingham in the north, and Great Yarmouth in the north-east, delineates the area falling within 11 Group. This is the area controlled from the Operations Room at Uxbridge, whereas the areas to the west and north of the black line showing parts of 10 Group and 12 Group, were under the direction of the Operations Rooms at Box and Watnall, respectively. It was necessary to include these adjoining areas on the map, in case the Bunker was required to direct its fighters to enter the neighbouring Groups. Red lines shown on land depict Sector boundaries within each Group, and in the case of 11 Group, shows the seven Sectors radiating out of London. Red circles within the 11 Group

ENEMY SIGHTED

area reveal the location of thirteen airfields from which fighter aircraft were scrambled to intercept German raids. A network of interlinking green lines stretching across the map show the boundaries of adjoining Observer Corps Groups, and the green triangle within each represents the regional Observer Corps Centre, which would have received information from individual Observer Corps Posts and relayed it to the Operations Room at Uxbridge.

This map, along with others across the United Kingdom's integrated air defence system, used a standardised map reference system, the British Modified Grid, to ensure accuracy and speed in 'telling' and 'plotting'. The system was based on a 'grid' rather than on the 'graticule'. Grid utilises uniform squares superimposed on a map, and numbered east and north from a selected point of origin. A grid of true squares on a map, which is flat, can only represent true squares on the Earth, which is a sphere, if it is assumed that the Earth is flat over the grid area. Limited areas at a time can be assumed flat, like the facets of a diamond. Graticule, on the other hand, is a network formed by the parallels of Latitude and Longitude, which follow the curvature of the Earth. Maps using graticule would have provided advantages for navigation over long sea and air distances, but the truth is that the distances over which Fighter Command's aircraft operated, while under control from the ground, were so small that navigational errors resulting from using a grid system were negligible. The grid system also offered several unique advantages, which at the time justified its use within air defence. First, cooperation with land forces had to be immediate and exact, and the only available large scale maps, covering areas where British land forces would operate, were those printed with a grid. Second, Operations Room staff across Fighter Command, including those at Uxbridge, had been trained to use, and had become experienced in, a grid reference system. The 'telling' and 'plotting' procedure was based on it, and now was not the time to introduce something different.

The British Modified Grid used on the map is a reference system of 'primary squares', 'secondary squares', and 'grid coordinates'. Primary squares, with sides of 311 miles (500 kilometres) are those established over the entire British Isles and surrounding sea, providing 'primary grid letters'. The primary square covering almost all of 11 Group in its entirety is the one identified by the primary grid letter 'W', and this can be seen on the map as a prefix to the letters identifying secondary squares. Secondary squares, with sides of sixty-two miles (100 kilometres), were established within each primary square. The Operations Room at Uxbridge had total responsibility for secondary squares identified by the secondary grid letters

THE UNDERGROUND OPERATIONS ROOM

'Q' and 'R', and a partial responsibility for segments of secondary squares identified by the secondary grid letters 'U', 'Z', 'L', 'M', and 'G'. Together, the area incorporated most of the airspace over London and the south-east of England, that was so fiercely contested during the summer of 1940.

Each secondary square is delineated along both vertical and horizontal sides into ten smaller squares. Each of these smaller squares is numbered and measures 6.2 miles (ten kilometres) across. The position of an aircraft or a specific location was given by telling grid coordinates, which consisted of six figures or four figures, in accordance with operational needs. Six figure grid coordinates determined position to within 109 yards (100 metres), whereas four figure grid coordinates determined position to within 0.62 miles (1 kilometre). For air defence purposes, an accuracy of one kilometre was considered sufficient, and therefore 'plotting' and 'telling' procedures provided for map references comprising one or two grid letters, followed up by a four figure grid coordinate.[15]

Like some giant chess board, the general situation map presented vital information, allowing the Senior Controller to visualise the threat and decide how best to move his exhaustible pieces. Responsibility for ensuring that the information was accurately depicted on the map, fell to the agile female Tellers and Plotters working systematically around the plotting table.

There would, during busy periods, have been around twenty to thirty Plotters and Tellers working unabatedly around the plotting table deep inside the Operations Room. They were part of the Bunker's establishment of around 280 staff, 80 per cent of whom were women. The contingent was divided into four teams, or 'watches', of seventy staff each, with three watches working eight hour shifts to cover each twenty-four hour period, and one watch, nominally, resting. The reality of the situation meant that very often, rest days were cancelled to replace those absent due to illness, or shifts were extended, due to intensive enemy action at the time when a handover was to take place.

The stoicism displayed by the Plotters and Tellers while working under tremendous pressure, is worthy of admiration and gratitude. If they had misplaced the plots, then British fighters would not have been sent to where the enemy were, would not have seen them, and interception would not have taken place. If the raid's height had not been shown accurately, then British fighters would have been directed to fly at the wrong altitude, and failed to intercept the raid, or more perilously, find themselves flying lower than the enemy and so likely to be 'bounced' by German fighters. If the enemy's strength was shown inaccurately, then either too many defending fighters would be sent, wasting precious resources, or too few, placing them at a tactical disadvantage and in grave danger.

Reflecting today, it is incongruous to imagine that in 1939, the widely held perception was that women were physically and emotionally unsuitable to perform such roles. Indeed, there were no women employed within the raid reporting system before the outbreak of the Second World War. Then, on 28 June 1939, King George VI established the Women's Auxiliary Air Force (WAAF), for duty with the RAF in time of war. It was not independent of the RAF, but rather, went on to replace men who were being readied or had already been sent to fight abroad.

In December 1939, the Air Ministry advised Park that it was considering using women from the WAAF, instead of men, in Operations Rooms below ground, but not those above ground. They thought women performed the duties of Plotters and Tellers admirably and would be properly protected in underground rooms. This affirmative view did not extend to women working in above ground Sector Operations Rooms, where they would be required to remain on duty and work with extreme accuracy during action, and so be unable to take cover during a raid. The Air Ministry also considered that watches, or shifts, working underground should be composed entirely of women, otherwise they would think they were being supervised as potentially unreliable. Park agreed with the Air Ministry that WAAFs were able to carry out plotting and telling roles to a satisfactory standard. He disagreed with their views on women not being able to work in above ground Operations Rooms, and that those in underground Operations Rooms working in mixed-sex watches would feel they were being monitored. He was, however, concerned that if women were permitted to resign, or be transferred out of Operations Rooms whenever they chose, then continuity of routine would be broken and security jeopardised. Park also stated that he did not know how women would react to air attack, and that the presence of men would give them confidence. This, perhaps, speaks more of the social attitude held by many men at that time, who considered women to be less resilient and in need of protection. Indeed, Park wanted three women to replace every two men lost, because he considered women were less able to stand up to the physical strain than airmen.[16]

Women would, out of necessity, be accepted into a variety of roles, including the raid reporting system, and their contribution was to be substantial. The trade of Clerk Special Duties (SD) was introduced in June 1940. At that time, it was intended to cover all personnel employed in Operations Rooms, irrespective of Command, and also personnel

THE UNDERGROUND OPERATIONS ROOM

employed in Filter Rooms. By 1942, it was recognised that procedures in Operations Rooms in different Commands varied considerably. Because of the specialisation required and the lack of opportunity and time for universal training and interchange of duties, it would have a serious effect on efficiency if Clerks SD trained for work in a Bomber Command environment were posted to work in a Fighter Command environment. This was particularly the case with supervisors and Non-Commissioned Officers (NCOs) upon whose knowledge, experience and ability so much depended. As a result, the Air Ministry introduced sub-classifications, with those assigned to Fighter Command Operations Rooms designated as Clerk SD (O) and those in Fighter Command Filter Rooms as Clerk SD (F).[17]

As war progressed, women were able to demonstrate their aptitude for the roles they were performing and the formerly held negative view shifted to a more informed and enlightened view of women's ability. This change was exemplified during a broadcast by the BBC in 1941, where a Sector Station Commander recognised the contribution made by the women on his station: 'The Royal Air Force is proud of its WAAFs. Each one of them does the work of one man and does it darn well. They helped us to win the Battle of Britain.'[18] The questionable supposition that women were unsuitable for such roles had been conclusively debunked.

Methods of telling and plotting were standardised across the integrated air defence system, with the expectation that information would be passed in approximately ten seconds. This length of time was shortened further during busy periods, only reverting to a normal pace once the situation allowed. Telling had to be controlled in this way, as the speed of aircraft and the number of plots, especially at Uxbridge, allowed no time for conversation or verification. The ability to annunciate clearly was part of the reason why both Plotters and Tellers were chosen, so that their words could be understood without misinterpretation. However, letters and numbers told normally could still be misunderstood and so a common phonetic alphabet and phonetic numbers were employed across the air defence network. It is interesting to note that of the letters spoken phonetically during the Second World War, only two, 'C for Charlie' and 'X for X-Ray' remain in use today by the British Military and British Police Service.

The standard for telling procedure stipulated that Plotters should always receive raid information in the same order and manner that they were expected to display it. For this reason, Tellers in the 11 Group Operations Room would first prefix the information with 'new raid', or 'standby' if the information was an update on an existing plot. They would then tell

ENEMY SIGHTED

the plot's direction of travel to the nearest eight point of the compass, in relation to the grid lines in use. So for example, North, North East, East, South East and so forth. If an aircraft was circling, then 'circling' would be told instead. The next piece of information to be given was the plot's position on the general situation map. The map reference letter was told followed by its phonetic word, for example, 'R for Robert'. If, when telling from the British Modified Grid, it was necessary to tell both letters of the two letter grid reference, the first letter was told by the phonetic alphabet word only. So for example, a plot approaching the Kent coast in grid square WQ, would be told as, 'William Q for Queen.'[19]

Once received, information was presented by sliding coloured counters onto the tilted side of angular wooden blocks. These were then placed on the general situation map to depict both enemy and friendly aircraft. The blocks were arranged so that the tilted side faced the gallery, making it more visible to the Senior Controller. This simple but effective idea was adopted following a visit in 1936 to the 11 Group Sector Operations Room at Kenley, where it was observed that 'small blocks were being used to tilt the height and strength of raid counters towards the Sector Commander and thus make the figures on these counters more easily read'.[20]

In the case of enemy aircraft, the uppermost counter was coloured yellow with black letters and numbers. The prefix 'H' meant 'Hostile' and the number represented the unique raid number. The counter below was coloured red with white numbers, to show how many enemy aircraft were estimated to be in the raid. So, for example, the block displaying a yellow counter 'H10' and red counter '40+' seen approaching the English Channel on the general situation map represents a raid, 'Hostile One Zero', which is estimated to be over forty enemy aircraft. The Senior Controller also needed to know where his airborne defending aircraft were at all times. These blocks also displayed two counters, red on top and blue below, and an additional third rectangular yellow counter, fixed above the wooden block by a pin. The red counter showed the number of friendly fighters in white numbers, and the blue counter, the height at which they were flying. The yellow counter identified the squadron number, or numbers, if they were operating in pairs, which was often the case. Again, returning to the map, looking at a block approaching the raiders with the red counter '21', blue counter '15', and yellow counters '229' and '303': this represents the twenty-one Hurricanes of 229 Squadron and 303 (Polish) Squadron from the Sector station at Northolt, flying at 15,000 ft (4,572 metres), to engage with the German bomber formation crossing the English coast.

THE UNDERGROUND OPERATIONS ROOM

Another block on the map, placed to the north of London, is of particular interest. It displays a red counter '55', with a blue counter '20', and a triangular yellow counter 'W', fixed above it. This depicts fifty-five Hurricanes and Spitfires, from the neighbouring 12 Group Sector station at Duxford. They were sent to protect the capital, flying as a 'Big Wing', a formation of five squadrons, three Hurricane squadrons, 242 (Canadian), 302 (Polish), and 310 (Czechoslovak), and two Spitfire squadrons, 19, and 611 (West Lancashire), thus the 'W' designation. The concept of whether to use small or large formations, or wings, of defensive fighters was mired in controversy, and seriously risked unsettling Fighter Command's efforts to resist the Luftwaffe offensive. The dispute was fuelled through a combination of frustration, and differing priorities.

The Commanding Officer of 12 Group, Trafford Lee-Mallory, felt that he should have been given responsibility for 11 Group, which was bearing the brunt of the aerial assault. One of his most outspoken Squadron Leaders was Douglas Bader, who led the 'Big Wing' over London on two occasions on 15 September. Bader, self-assured and forceful, led from the front, flying his Hurricane with great skill, despite having to rely on prosthetic legs following a pre-war air crash at Reading Aerodrome. Like Lee-Mallory, he too wanted to be more actively engaged in the fighting taking place over London and the south-east, and not merely act as a last line of defence protecting 11 Group's Sector Airfields, while others were sent further east to engage the enemy. Bader, supported by Lee-Mallory, advocated that defending Spitfires and Hurricanes could destroy more enemy aircraft if they operated in 'Big Wings' nearer the coast, and not over 11 Group's airfields. This less than harmonious state led to a dangerous situation in which Fighter Command's collective response was found to be wanting.

An unfortunate consequence of this tactic was that if enemy bombers were intercepted by the 'Big Wing', it was when they were on the homeward leg of their journey, after they had damaged 11 Group's Sector stations. This is because a 'Wing' required significantly longer to reach operating height, than a single or pair of squadrons.[21]

Park was forthright in his criticism of the lack of support from 12 Group, who he felt had:

> not shown the same desire to cooperate by despatching their squadrons to the places requested. The result of this attitude has been that on the two occasions recently when 12 Group offered assistance and were requested by us to patrol our aerodromes,

their squadrons did not in fact patrol over our aerodromes. On both these occasions our aerodromes were heavily bombed because our own patrols were not strong enough to turn all the enemy back before they reached their objective.

He felt it necessary to introduce a more circuitous process when deploying reinforcements from 12 Group. Senior Controllers at Uxbridge would now have to 'put their requests to Controller, Fighter Command, stating clearly when and where reinforcing squadrons from the North are required to patrol', recognising that 'such requests via Command will be a little slower in obtaining assistance but they should ensure that the reinforcing squadrons from the North are in fact placed where they can be of greatest assistance.'[22]

Framing the disunion, Dowding wrote:

> the problem arose, in an acute form, of the strength of fighter formations which we should employ. When time was the essence of the problem, two squadrons were generally used by Air Vice-Marshal Park in No.11 Group. He had the responsibility of meeting attacks as far to the Eastward as possible, and the building up of a four squadron formation involved the use of a rendezvous for aircraft from two or more aerodromes. This led to delay and lack of flexibility in leadership. On the other hand, when No.12 Group was asked to send down protective formations to guard the aerodromes on the eastern fringe of London, it was often possible to build up big formations, and these had great success on some occasions, though by no means always. A somewhat unfortunate controversy grew up round the two points of view, and Air Vice-Marshal Park was subjected to some external criticism with which I did not agree. Fortunately, however, the disagreement did not become acute until mid-October, when the battle had been virtually won.

He expressed his preference 'of using fighter formations in the greatest strength of which circumstances will permit', having employed this tactic to good effect over Dunkirk, but stressed that, 'during the attacks on London, the available strength of fighters did not admit of this policy, nor was time available'.[23]

In retrospect, history has shown Park's decision to deploy single, or pairs of squadrons, to have been the correct thing to do in the circumstances.

THE UNDERGROUND OPERATIONS ROOM

Had the Operations Room at Uxbridge deployed 'Big Wings' to defend the airspace over 11 Group, rather than smaller formations, then more raids would have got through, more of the Luftwaffe's objectives would have been achieved, and Britain would have been left in a more helpless and vulnerable position to resist invasion.

Returning to the information displayed on the general situation map, the wooden blocks were of limited use if they did not accurately represent the current position of hostile aircraft. This observation affirms the essential requirement to 'know the position of the enemy in space and time'.[24] The most prevalent bomber used by the Luftwaffe during the Battle of Britain was the Heinkel He 111. It had a top speed of 270 mph (435 kph), and could therefore travel over twenty miles (thirty-two kilometres) in five minutes. The Senior Controller had to know how old the information in front of him was, so that he could determine where the raiders were at any given time and then send his fighters to engage them. He was assisted in this task through the application of a simple but ingenious arrangement, commonly referred to as the 'Sector', or 'Colour Change Clock'.

Plotters arranged wooden blocks to represent enemy raids on the map. They then placed pointed counters immediately behind each block to indicate the raid's course and, crucially, the time when it was last known to be at that location. Where no course was given, the Plotter would place a round counter on the map. The colour of the counters, either red, yellow or blue, corresponded with coloured triangular segments on the Sector Clock, whose face was marked alternatively in the same colours for every five minutes. The minute hand on the clock determined which colour 'segment' was currently taking place. Counters were removed at five minute intervals, so that not more than two colours were on the map at the same time, and the colour of the counter closest to the wooden block would be that of the segment in which the minute hand was at the time when the plot was last known to be at that location. The information was therefore no more than ten minutes old,[25] and the procedure avoided what Dowding described as 'stale plots' being shown on the map.[26]

We can observe this methodology in action by examining the wooden raid blocks, Hostile 04, Hostile 06, and Hostile 10, shown on the general situation map. These depict the first raiders of the day after they had crossed the English Channel on the morning of Sunday 15 September 1940. The counters closest to the blocks are coloured blue, and the ones behind are coloured yellow. This corresponds with the minute hand being in the blue segment of the Sector Clock mounted on the adjacent wall. The Senior

ENEMY SIGHTED

Controller therefore understands that the information placed before him is no more than five minutes old. Our Heinkel He 111 bombers can be assumed to be no more than twenty miles (thirty-two kilometres) away from their last reported position and, if their course has remained the same, the Senior Controller will have a good idea as to their current location.

The Sector Clocks at Uxbridge were of the 'slave' type; that is, they were connected to and controlled by a 'master' clock in the local GPO telephone exchange. The 'master' clock also controlled an electronic colour-change apparatus installed on the plotting table. The colour-change apparatus received an electronic impulse from the telephone exchange every half minute which illuminated a coloured light commensurate with the colour of the segment occupied by the minute hand at that time. This device enabled Plotters to observe when to change the colours of the counters without lifting their eyes from the table.[27]

The dependency on all parts of the air defence organisation to share a coordinated time led to a procedure covering time signals and time checks. Every day, at 07.00 hours and 19.00 hours, a time signal was broadcasted by Headquarters Fighter Command at Bentley Priory to 11 Group at Uxbridge. This signal was received by the RDF plotter stood around the plotting table, who relayed it to the Floor Supervisor charged with ensuring that all Operations Room Sector Clocks were synchronised. As a 'belt and braces' approach, the Operations Room was also able to obtain a time check at any time of day or night by telephoning the GPO speaking clock at either the London or RAF Central GPO Exchanges.[28]

When viewing different Sector Clocks, it is noticeable that there is something dissimilar about them, but why is this? Both versions feature the familiar ring of red, yellow and blue triangular segments, and both are dissected to represent individual periods of five minutes. Well, prior to 1936, the base of the coloured triangles was near the centre of the clock face and the point was near the outer rim. Early in 1936, it was suggested that if the coloured triangles shown on the clocks were reversed to show the base of the triangle on the outer edge of the dial, it would then be easier to determine exactly when the colour of the counter should be changed. As an experiment, a ring with the colour triangles reversed was fitted to the clock face and proved superior to the previous method of indication. This new reversed indication of colour change was made standard, and all the operational clocks modified.[29] There are two Sector Clocks displayed in the Operations Room at Uxbridge. The one mounted near to the top left-hand side of the illuminated panel wall, displays triangular segments that point

THE UNDERGROUND OPERATIONS ROOM

outwards, and so is an earlier design. The one mounted lower, in the centre of the illuminated panel wall, has triangular segments that point inwards, and so can be identified as being of the revised type.

We now turn our attention to the information-laden wall facing the Senior Controller. During his visit on 15 September, Churchill likened sitting in the windowed gallery to being in 'the Dress Circle' of 'a small theatre', opposite which, 'covering the entire wall, where the theatre curtain would be, was a gigantic blackboard divided into six columns with electric bulbs, for the six fighter stations, each of their squadrons having a sub column of its own and divided by lateral lines.'[30] Churchill's locution, using mesmeric language, draws in his audience, so they too are sat alongside him, deep inside the Bunker. However, a comparison of what was said and what is, reveals some discrepancy in relation to the number of columns and fighter stations described by the great man. There are in fact twenty-six individual, or seven clusters of columns, or squadron indicator panels, and these are arranged under seven Sector stations, not six.

The designations above each cluster of squadron indicator panels read like a lexicon of iconic Battle of Britain airfields, now immortalised in history. They are 'Tangmere', quartering the Spitfires of 602 (City of Glasgow) Squadron, Blenheims of 23 Squadron, and Hurricanes of 213 and 607 (County of Durham) Squadrons; 'North Weald', quartering the Hurricanes of 46 and 249 Squadrons, and Blenheims of 25 Squadron; 'Hornchurch', quartering the Spitfires of 41, 603 (City of Edinburgh), and 222 Squadrons; 'Kenley', quartering the Hurricanes of 605 (County of Warwick), 253, and 501 (City of Bristol) Squadrons, and Blenheims of 600 (City of London) Squadron; 'Biggin Hill', quartering the Spitfires of 92, 72, and 66 Squadrons, and Boulton Paul Defiants of 141 Squadron; 'Debden', quartering the Hurricanes of 257, 17, and 73 Squadrons; and 'Northolt', quartering the Hurricanes of 1 (Canadian), 303 (Polish), 229, and 504 (County of Nottingham) Squadrons, and Boulton Paul Defiants of 264 Squadron. In total, the tote board shows that on 15 September, there were seven squadrons of Spitfires, fourteen squadrons of Hurricanes, three flights of Blenheims, and two flights of Boulton Paul Defiants, garrisoned across 11 Group.

The illuminated panels had their origins in a design submitted three years before the declaration of war, 'for a new type of electric squadron indicator panel to show by means of light spots, full particulars of the squadron, or flight, or individual aircraft of the squadron, at any given time throughout operational patrols.'[31] The 'light spots' signifying aircraft were presented as four colours, red, yellow, blue and green. A fighter squadron, before

ENEMY SIGHTED

attrition, was expected to field twelve aircraft. Each 'light spot' represented a 'section' of three aircraft, so for example, 'red section' or 'blue section'. Two 'sections' formed a 'flight' of six aircraft, 'A flight' and 'B flight', and both 'flights' operating together formed a squadron. This scheme can be seen in operation on the tote board, for example under the Northolt cluster of columns, where three Hurricane squadrons at full strength are represented by four lights each, while the flight of Boulton Paul Defiants is represented by only two.

The Senior Controller was responsible for the control of fighter aircraft, both on the ground[32] and in the air.[33] He also had 'to ensure that sufficient pilots were at hand and aircraft were serviceable to meet the current needs of defence'. This requirement to know how many air crews and aircraft were available for operations, was referred to as the serviceability rate. To assist in this task, Sector Operations Rooms across 11 Group reported to Uxbridge twice daily, and at all other times when there was a change in the number of operable resources. The available resources were shown on the tote board, below the squadron indicator panels, under the heading 'state of squadrons', 'P' relating to the number of pilots available and 'A' to the number of operationally available aircraft. It can be seen from observing the tote board, that on the morning of 15 September, a total of 375 pilots and 254 day fighters, of which eighty-four were Spitfires and 170 Hurricanes, were available to the Senior Controller at Uxbridge.

On the ground, the Senior Controller at Uxbridge had to ensure that the pilots and aircraft available to him were maintained 'in a state of preparedness', enabling them to be 'scrambled' to intercept an approaching enemy raid, if possible, before it was able to reach its objective. The degree of preparedness for each squadron or flight was communicated through the Sector Controller in the Sector Operations Room. He alone had direct communication with his pilots on the ground and in the air, and so it was important that all instructions from Uxbridge were transmitted through him.

The squadron indicator panel at Uxbridge operated like a ladder, which squadrons climbed down and then reappeared again at the top. The state or condition of each section within a squadron was shown by illuminated lights under the descriptors, 'Released'; 'Available 30 Minutes'; 'Available'; 'Ordered To Readiness'; 'At Readiness'; 'Ordered To Standby'; 'At Standby'; 'Ordered On 'I' Patrol'; 'Left Ground'; 'In Position'; 'Detailed To Raid'; 'Enemy Sighted'; 'Ordered To Land'; and 'Landed And Refuelling'.

The uppermost state, 'Released', indicated that the squadron was not expected to be required for duty until the end of the period specified in the

THE UNDERGROUND OPERATIONS ROOM

release order, when it would become 'Available'. This is demonstrated on the Uxbridge tote board by the Blenheims of 25 Squadron at North Weald, who, as night fighters, had been stood down during the hours of daylight, and so are shown as 'Released'. During periods of activity, a squadron on patrol that landed to refuel and rearm was automatically shown as 'Released', and, in the absence of further orders, would come to 'Readiness' as soon as its aircraft were replenished. Where possible, squadrons were 'Released' for meals, but this did not mean that individuals could leave the Sector station, unless specific permission had been given.

The next state on the squadron indicator panel is, 'Available 30 Minutes', where Pilots were not required to be in the immediate vicinity of their aircraft or the pilots' room, but the squadron had to be able to take off within thirty minutes of being ordered to do so. Continuing down, the next state is, 'Available'. Aircraft had to be ready to start up, and pilots had to be in the vicinity of the pilots' room, or aircraft, if dispersed around the airfield. Pilots did not need to be dressed in their flying kit when held at this state, but the squadron had to be available to take off within fifteen minutes.

Descending further still leads to the next states, 'Ordered to Readiness' and 'Readiness'. This is, perhaps, the picture that many have in their mind's eye, when visualising the Battle of Britain. The moment before Fighter Command's pilots took to the air. Aircraft positioned ready for take-off. Pilots in flying kit, close to the pilots' room or to their aircraft. Catching up on precious sleep. Reading magazines. Playing a game of chess or kicking a football. The foreboding ring of the telephone. The rallying cry, 'Squadron Scramble'! The exhilarating reverberation of the 'scramble bell'. Pilots running to waiting aircraft. Riggers assisting them into their parachutes, strapping them into their cockpit. Fitters starting engines. The deafening roar of Merlins bursting into life. Flames flickering and smoke billowing from now awakened and readied winged chariots. Chocks away. Moving into position. Twisting. Turning. Charging forward. Careering into the air. Airborne within five minutes. Then, when the urgency is even greater, there are the final states of preparedness on the ground, 'Ordered to Standby' and 'Standby'. The enemy is closing in, fast. Pilots sat in cockpits. Electric starters connected. Engines warm, but not running, too much risk of overheating. Again, the rallying cry, 'Squadron Scramble'! Merlins spurt flames and propellers spin furiously. A frantic race to get in formation. Wheels up. Airborne in less than two minutes.

The next state was, 'Ordered On 'I' Patrol', where the Senior Controller, seeing what was displayed in front of him on the plotting table and tote

ENEMY SIGHTED

board, would order named Sectors to despatch given units of fighters on interception patrol at specified heights and places, in time to intercept enemy raids. Patrol lines within Sectors were designated as 'front', for the outer boundary of the Aircraft Fighting Zone, or 'back', for the rear boundary of the Aircraft Fighting Zone. These were further delineated into left, centre and right, when facing outwards. The Sectors themselves were referred to by their phonetic alphabet lettering,[34] so 'A' Tangmere Sector was 'Ack'; 'B' Kenley Sector was 'Beer'; 'C' Biggin Hill Sector was 'Charlie'; 'D' Hornchurch Sector was 'Don'; 'E' North Weald Sector was 'Edward'; 'F' Debden Sector was 'Freddie'; and 'Z' Northolt Sector was 'Zulu'. The order was given a unique serial number, which ran consecutively throughout each twenty four hour period, a new series being commenced each night at 00.01 hours.[35] We can look to see how this worked by considering a likely scenario during the Battle of Britain. For the thirteenth time that day, the Operations Room at Uxbridge telephones the Sector Controller at Northolt, directing him to despatch the Hurricanes of 229 (Polish) Squadron to carry out an interception patrol, 15,000 ft (4,572 metres) over the Hornchurch Sector. Their objective is to prevent the enemy, which has been spotted over Dover, from bombing the Hornchurch airfield. This order will be given as, 'Serial One Three. Squadron Two Two Nine. Patrol Don. Right Back. Angels Fifteen. Enemy approaching from Dover.'

The operating height and speed of enemy bombers necessitated defending fighters be given interception patrol orders well in advance, if they were to be in a position and at a height to join battle. The order was given immediately a hostile or unidentified raid was told by the raid reporting system, while pilots were still on the ground, so they could take off and climb to height with a minimum of delay. While in the air, the interception patrol would be detailed to intercept a specified raid on the front line of the Aircraft Fighting Zone. Interception patrols not already detailed to specified raids were ordered to attack any enemy formations they saw that were not already engaged by a decisive number of fighters.[36]

Once the fighters had taken off, the Sector Operations Room would inform the Ops B staff in their cubbyhole at Uxbridge, who would then illuminate the 'Left Ground' state, alerting the Senior Controller that his instruction had been carried out. Control in the air would then transfer to the Sector Controller, who was responsible for keeping the patrol informed of the subsequent movement of the raiders and guide his aircraft into position to join battle with the enemy. The Senior Controller at Uxbridge took no further notice of the patrol, relying on the Sector Controller to keep him supplied

THE UNDERGROUND OPERATIONS ROOM

with relevant information. If it became clear to the Sector Controller that the patrol had failed to intercept the raid it had been detailed to, then he would report this fact on the 'I' line to Uxbridge and request instructions regarding the further movements of the patrol. Where a patrol had engaged a raid and subsequently lost it owing to bad weather conditions or other reasons, the patrol leader was expected to ask the Sector Controller, without delay, for further instructions. If the Sector Controller was in a position, from the plots on the table, to effect contact once more, he would order the patrol to do so, otherwise, he would order the patrol to land and refuel, and notify Uxbridge.[37]

The senior officer leading the formation would radio the Sector Controller when they had reached their specified place and height, and this was communicated to Uxbridge where staff updated the formation's state to show 'In Position', lying in wait until ordered to engage a particular enemy grouping, when 'Detailed to Raid' would be shown. On spotting the enemy, it was crucial to alert other defending fighters in the vicinity, and the Sector Controller on the ground. The old English hunting cry, 'Tally Ho!' would be broadcast by the fighter formation leader, announcing that the enemy had been intercepted and were being engaged. They had been instructed, 'where humanly possible', to also send details of the enemy's strength, location, and direction of travel, for example, 'Tally Ho! Fifty bombers. Thirty fighters. Angels Two Zero. Proceeding North Maidstone.'[38] On receiving the message, the information was immediately relayed by the Sector Operations Room to Uxbridge, where the 'Enemy Sighted' state would be illuminated, the different coloured bulbs being replaced by all red lights, informing the Senior Controller that contact had been made with the enemy.

The duration of a patrol during daytime, the period between when a formation took off, to when it left its patrol line, was stated to be one hour.[39] Having relatively small fuel tanks meant that fuel, or more specifically the lack of it, was a very serious issue for fighter aircraft, and so had to be carefully managed during operations. As a rule of thumb, therefore, fighters had to land after one hour of flying time to refuel. It was important for the Senior Controller at Uxbridge, and Sector Controllers who were in direct contact with their formations, to know the state of squadrons in this respect. The Sector Controller needed to know whether a particular squadron had sufficient fuel remaining to be directed to intercept a raid, or whether it had to land and refuel. Again, the simplistic brilliance, so typical of Britain's integrated air defence system, came into play to assist Controllers in their decision making.

On each squadron indicator panel, between the 'In Position' and 'Detailed To Raid' states, there were four coloured bars: white, blue, yellow and red.

Each would light up with white bulbs to indicate the time elapsed, in fifteen minute periods, since the formation took to the air. So, for example, when illuminated, the white bar showed the Senior Controller at Uxbridge that a squadron had been up for fifteen minutes; blue, that it had been up for thirty minutes; yellow, that it had been up for forty-five minutes; and, red, that it had been up for sixty minutes and should be ordered by the Sector Controller to return, if the decision had not already been made by the senior formation leader. Aircraft were instructed to return, and the 'Ordered To Land' state was lit up, after they had engaged with the enemy, had lost contact with them, or they were running low on fuel.

Once formations had landed, the 'Landed And Refuelling' state was illuminated on the squadron indicator panel. It was at this point that the fighters were vulnerable to attack from the air. This fragility was understood by 11 Group's Commanding Officer, who during the height of the Battle of Britain, instructed his Controllers that the Northolt based '303 (Polish) Squadron provide two sections for patrol of inland aerodromes, especially while the older squadrons are on the ground refuelling, when enemy formations are flying overland'.[40] A squadron or flight on landing from patrol was automatically at 'Released' while refuelling and rearming, but in the absence of further orders, it was expected to be at 'Readiness' as soon as these operations were completed. Being refuelled and rearmed, the Sector Controller would notify the Senior Controller that his aircraft were ready once again to enter the fray, and the 'Readiness' state at Uxbridge would be shown.[41]

The Senior Controller at Uxbridge always had to be sighted on the present meteorological condition of those areas over which his fighters might fly, and a forecast of what those present conditions may become. Air Ministry meteorological staff were responsible for providing this information. They were not, however, responsible for stating whether conditions were, or would be, fit for flying. Normally, forecasts were provided by meteorological staff at the Group level, and observations on present conditions were provided by others at Sector Operations Rooms and pilots in the air.[42] The information received on cloud condition was required to be displayed by Group Operations Rooms, under the heading of each Sector station.[43]

The weather on the morning of 15 September 1940, over each of 11 Group's airfields, is shown on the tote board at Uxbridge, under 'Weather States'. Thermometer-like scales indicate whether there is any cloud present, and if so, the height of the cloud base. The cloud density is given in simple fractional form; for example, over Debden, there was two-tenths

THE UNDERGROUND OPERATIONS ROOM

cloud cover. The overall visibility is indicated, again in a visually simplistic form, by a coloured disc above the scales below each airfield. Red informs the Senior Controller that flying is not possible from that airfield, and so he is unable to deploy his fighters from there. Fortunately, no airfields were unavailable to him on that day. Green informs the Senior Controller that visibility is clear, and the fighters there are available to him. This is the case for Debden, where visibility was two miles (three kilometres). The visibility over Hendon was borderline, at a mere 1,000 yards (914 metres), and so the disc is shown as being half red and half green, Again, there is evidence of granularity in the information available to the Senior Controller, even though it is presented in a visually simplistic form.

Balloon barrages posed as much a threat to defending aircraft as they did to the enemy. It was therefore necessary at Group level for the Senior Controller to know the height of a balloon barrage in the areas where fighters under his control may be deployed. Operational control of those balloons in a balloon-defended area that endangered fighter aircraft flying from a Sector aerodrome near them, was vested at Sector level in the Sector Controller.[44] The lower part of the tote board at Uxbridge displays four large white coloured vertical scales, each sub-divided into gradients of 1,000 ft (305 metres), with a balloon-shaped pointer indicating the height of a particular balloon barrage. From right to left, they are marked 'Dover', 'Tilbury', 'Gravesend' and 'London'. Balloons are shown as raised over Dover at 4,000 ft (1,220 metres), as the coastal town was bitterly contested and subjected to daily attacks from the Luftwaffe. They are raised over Gravesend, also at 4,000 ft. Gravesend, located on the River Thames to the south of London, lies directly in the path taken by German bombers targeting the London dockyards. Tilbury, home of some of the country's largest warehouses, was a prime target. The balloons had been raised even higher here, at 6,000 ft (1,829 metres), the logic being that the raiders would have to fly higher, so their bombing may be less precise, and they might – just might – miss the vital warehouses storing much of Britain's supplies. Being forced to fly higher would also bring them into the operational range of the anti-aircraft guns and defending aircraft. Finally, there is London, where at 3,000 ft (914 metres), the balloons are somewhat lower than elsewhere. This is because Fighter Command's aircraft would always engage the enemy over the nation's capital.

Chapter 13

The Locus Above

'Over the Spider Hole'

On leaving the Bunker through the main stairway, two replica aircraft can be seen on display nearby. They have been there since September and October 2010, when they were unveiled to represent Fighter Command's pre-eminent chargers: the Spitfire and Hurricane. Both are mounted on plinths, giving the illusion of being caught in mid-flight. The aircraft to the right is a Spitfire Mk IX, which had previously performed gate guardian duty at the main entrance to RAF Uxbridge until its closure in March 2010. It has the serial number BS239 and squadron code letters 5R-E. Initially this aircraft was flown by 341 (Free French) Squadron where it was involved in coastal artillery cooperation over France. Its current markings depict a later incarnation with 33 Squadron, which in June 1944 was based at RAF Lympne, a satellite airfield within the Biggin Hill Sector. The squadron was one of many across 11 Group which provided fighter support over the Normandy beachheads on 6 June 1944. This Spitfire was involved in a flying accident two weeks after invasion had begun and it was eventually struck off charge.[1] However, its replication at the Bunker serves to show not only that Spitfires were controlled from here throughout the Second World War, but also that all Allied aerial activity in support of the D-Day landings was coordinated from the hidden labyrinth below.

Looking ahead, across the road from the Bunker, is a Hurricane Mk I, replicating an aircraft flown in 1940 during the Battle of Britain. It has the serial number P3901 and squadron code letters RF-E. The markings are that of a fighter flown by 303 (Polish) Squadron, which in 1940, was based at RAF Northolt, the nearest Sector station to Uxbridge. This Hurricane is depicted in the personal livery of Squadron Leader Witold Urbanowicz, who is credited with fifteen confirmed kills during the Battle of Britain, nine while flying P3901.[2] Urbanowicz had been Deputy Commander of the Polish Air Force's 111 Fighter 'Kościuszko' Squadron in Warsaw, when the country was invaded. The Squadron's Commanding Officer at the time, Zdzisław Krasnodębski, would go on to reinstitute 111 'Kościuszko' traditions and unit marking in the Royal Air Force's 303 (Polish) Squadron at Northolt. It is interesting to note that the squadron name 'Kościuszko' was given in honour of Tadeusz Kościuszko, a national hero of Poland who, in 1792, fought against the Russian army of Empress Catherine II, after it had invaded Poland to end Polish internal reforms designed to liberate the nation from Russian influence. In 1939, Poland was again invaded by Russia, this time in a cartel of aggression with Germany. Polish patriots were again called upon to protect Polska's sovereignty. History was indeed repeating itself. Urbanowicz was one such patriot, fighting the Russians as they invaded his homeland, and successfully downing a Russian R 5 reconnaissance aircraft over Poland. He was later captured by the advancing Soviet Army but managed to escape and made his way to England to carry on the fight.

Commissioned in the Royal Air Force Reserve, Urbanowicz received his first posting on 4 August 1939 to 145 Squadron, flying Hurricanes from Westhampnett, a satellite airfield within 11 Group's Tangmere Sector. While with 145 Squadron, he honed his aerial combat skills still further, destroying a Messerschmitt Me 109 on 11 August, and a Ju 88 one day later. Bloodied in the fighting over Britain, Urbanowicz then joined 303 (Polish) Squadron at Northolt as a Flight Commander on 21 August, where he became reacquainted with his former Commanding Officer, Zdzisław Krasnodębski. Many of the Polish pilots had combat experience gained over their homeland, France, and for some, over England; but 303 (Polish) Squadron was still not considered operational, due to language difficulties and differences between the tactics used by both air forces.

This position changed on 30 August, while 303 (Polish) Squadron's 'B' flight was on a training exercise. Lieutenant Ludwik Paszkiewicz records:

> I was Green One flying Hurricane 'RF.V'. I took off at 16.15 and I flew with five others of 'B' flight to St Albans at 9,000 ft [2,743 metres], on exercise to intercept six Blenheims. At about 16.35, I saw fire on the ground and shells bursting at my altitude, and a strong enemy formation in two tiers in echelon at about 14,000 ft [4,267 metres], flying from starboard. I saw some of our fighters among them. I said to Apany[3] Leader 'Bandits 10 o'clock' but received no reply. I made towards the enemy. The flight remained behind me. I waggled my wings, and then saw at the same altitude as myself an enemy aircraft

banking towards me. When he was almost head on, he saw me and went into a steep dive. I followed, and as he pulled out, I fired from directly behind a burst at 250 yards [229 metres] at the fuselage. Overtaking him, I fired a long burst at 100 to 20 yards [91 to 18 metres] at the starboard engine from underneath. The engine stopped and burst into flames. I broke off. As another Hurricane 'UC.J' went in to attack, I saw a parachute leave enemy aircraft. Enemy dived. I followed down and gave enemy aircraft a short burst, though I realised immediately that it was not necessary. Enemy aircraft crashed and exploded. I regained height, and being unable to see my flight, I returned to Northolt.[4]

On landing, the Poles were severely reprimanded – and then warmly congratulated! This encounter would later become known to millions as the 'Repeat Please' scene in the film, *The Battle of Britain*. 303 (Polish) Squadron were made operational, entering the Battle which had now been raging for over two months.

On 6 September, Urbanowicz destroyed a Messerschmitt Me 109, but during the same engagement his Commanding Officer was shot down, suffering severe burns. As the next most senior pilot, he became 303 (Polish) Squadron's acting Commanding Officer. The following day, a Dornier Do 215 and another Me 109 fell to Urbanowicz's guns, albeit the latter could not be confirmed and so was awarded only as a probable. On the 15th, Battle of Britain Day, he added a further two Dornier Do 215s to his tally, bringing the number of confirmed kills during the battle now to six. On the 26th, he sent a Heinkel He 111 into the sea, his first kill while flying P3901. The next day Urbanowicz, flying P3901, led his squadron on two occasions. During the morning engagement, he destroyed a Messerschmitt Me 109, followed by a Messerschmitt Me 110. In the afternoon, he shot down two Junker 88s over the sea. This brought his climbing tally during the battle to eleven enemy aircraft confirmed as destroyed.

On 30 September, Urbanowicz carried out a further five patrols in P3901. During one patrol, he chased a Dornier Do 215 across the English Channel as it headed back towards France. He mistakenly took two fighters also approaching the bomber to be British. After realising that they were in fact Messerschmitt Me109s, he shot both down, and then despatched the lone bomber. Three hours later, while intercepting a raid heading towards London, the squadron was bounced by Messerschmitt Me 109s. Urbanowicz engaged and shot down one of the attackers. It was to be his last kill during the Battle of Britain, bringing his tally to fifteen, nine of which were achieved while flying P3901. On 20 October 1940 he was posted to Uxbridge as the first Polish Liaison Officer, to assist in the management and coordination of an expanding Polish contingent within 11 Group. Urbanowicz epitomised the grittiness so common among Poles who had come to England to carry on the fight, evincing, 'We do not beg for freedom. We fight for it.' 303 (Polish) Squadron was accredited with downing 126 enemy aircraft over a period of forty-two days during the Battle of Britain, making it the most successful squadron in Fighter Command. In common with the scores of most Squadrons, this figure was later revised downwards, the most recent estimate being that seventy-nine enemy aircraft were destroyed, which averages to more than thirteen victories per week.[5]

This achievement speaks not only to the flying prowess of the Polish pilots, but also to their hatred for the Germans and what they had done to their Homeland. Dowding acknowledged the contribution they made to the aerial defence of Britain, while also recognising some of the inherent challenges to their integration within his Command:

> I must confess that I had been a little doubtful of the effect which their experience in their own countries and in France might have had upon the Polish and Czech pilots, but my doubts were soon laid to rest, because all three squadrons swung in the fight with a dash and enthusiasm which is beyond praise. They were inspired by a burning hatred for the Germans which made them very deadly opponents. The first Polish squadron (No.303) in No. 11 Group, during the course of a month, shot down more Germans than any British unit in the same period. Other Poles and Czechs were used in small numbers in British squadrons, and fought very gallantly, but the language was a difficulty, and they were probably most efficiently employed in their own national units.[6]

In its wartime publication on the Battle of Britain, the Air Ministry said of these highly effective additions: 'Polish and Czech pilots took their full share in the Battle. They possess great qualities of courage and dash. They are truly formidable fighters.'[7]

Immediately to the left on leaving the Bunker is a small well-manicured memorial garden. A short central path of crazy paving leads to a large

ENEMY SIGHTED

Cornish granite boulder, which is flanked by three flags. The emblems are those of the Royal Air Force, London Borough of Hillingdon, and the Union Flag of the United Kingdom. The pillar is a monument to the people who served as part of 11 Group's Operations Room between 1939 and 1946. The declaration reads:

> Beneath this stone is the site of the underground operations room from which the greater part of the Hurricane and Spitfire squadrons were controlled during the Battle of Britain. During this epic Battle these squadrons shot down over 1,300 of the 1,733 enemy aircraft destroyed. This great achievement contributed largely to our ultimate success and survival and inspired Sir Winston Churchill's now famous words, Never in the field of human conflict was so much owed by so many to so few.

Each alphanumeric character within the declaration, stands proud of the boulder, carved out of the granite itself, to ensure their story, one of courage, coordination, energy, and determination, will endure.

Churchill's famous words, 'Never in the field of human conflict was so much owed by so many to so few', were first uttered by him on 16 August 1940, when the Battle was at its height. On this day he had visited the 11 Group Operations Room with his Chief Staff Officer and military advisor, Major General Hastings Ismay. Ismay recalled:

> At one moment every single squadron in the Group was engaged; there was nothing in reserve, and the map table showed new waves of attackers crossing the coast ... As the evening closed in, the fighting died down, and we left by car for Chequers. Churchill's first words were: 'Don't speak to me; I have never been so moved.' After about five minutes he leaned forward and said, 'Never in the field of human conflict has so much been owed by so many to so few.' The words burned into my brain, and I repeated them to my wife when I got home.[8]

Four days later these words were reprised and immortalised by Churchill when he incorporated them in a speech before the House of Commons,[9] and therefore the world. The Churchillian usage of captivating language, full of imagery and awash with powerful messages, expressed in perspicacious language, destined Fighter Command's warriors to forever be known as 'the few'.

The 'erection of a suitable plaque' was first proposed in February 1955 after Fighter Command had decided that it no longer had any use for the Operations Room. The 11 Group Headquarters was to move to RAF Northolt, and the site was to be made available for use as a telephone switching centre. Acknowledging the historical significance of the underground complex, the report outlining the decision concluded that:

> This building was the first of the underground air defence operations blocks to be activated and it was from here that decisions were made during the Battle of Britain which rank with the greatest decisions ever made on the battlefields of old. These incidents were of vital importance to the survival of this country and, indeed, have been regarded by many as the vital battle of the last war, equal in importance to Trafalgar or Waterloo. It is felt that the historical importance of the building should be perpetuated by the erection of a suitable plaque in the gallery of the block.[10]

The following year, it was decided that two plaques would be erected, one inside and one outside the block. The latter, it was suggested, should be a metal plaque mounted in stone or concrete, and erected in a suitable position outside the building. Advice was sought from Sir John Heaton-Armstrong of the College of Arms, as to 'the actual design of the plaques'. Heaton-Armstrong was pleased to assist, especially as he had been stationed at 11 Group as an Administrative and Special Duties Branch Officer during the war. Subsequently, Henry Wilson, Monumental Masons and Sculptors of Uxbridge, were commissioned to complete the Cornish granite boulder,[11] referred to above.

The boulder was sited on 12 April 1958 and formally unveiled ten days later, on 22 April. A number of dignitaries were suggested as being suitable unveilers, notably Sir Winston Churchill, Sir Hugh Dowding, Sir Keith Park and the current Chief of the Air Staff. It was Hugh Dowding who had led Fighter Command during the Battle of Britain, and so it was he who was invited to carry out the unveiling ceremony. Also in attendance were Fighter Command's then Commanding Officer, Air Chief Marshal Sir Thomas Pike and 11 Group's Commanding Officer, Air Vice-Marshal

ENEMY SIGHTED

Victor Bowling. After the unveiling, a Hurricane and a Spitfire from the Battle of Britain Memorial Flight carried out a flypast over Hillingdon House, at 1,000 ft (305 metres). The aircraft were flown in loose line astern, led by the Hurricane, which was piloted by the Officer Commanding RAF North Weald, one of 11 Group's Sector stations. Both Hurricane and Spitfire had travelled from RAF North Weald, following the north-east corridor to join the RAF Northolt circuit and then on to Uxbridge.

After the flypast, Dowding and the other dignitaries made their way into the underground Operations Room to observe a reconstruction, complete with staff, of the scene as far as possible, of events when the Battle was at its height some eighteen years earlier.[12] Two pictures can be seen on display in the Bunker today; one shows Dowding unveiling the memorial dedicated to the people who served in 11 Group's Operations Room and the other shows the procession of dignitaries as they begin to negotiate the initial steps leading down to the Bunker.[13]

A futuristic building housing the Battle of Britain Visitor and Exhibition Centre is located next to the memorial garden. It occupies the site of the old above-ground Operations Room and was opened on 30 March 2018 to coincide with the 100th anniversary of the founding of the Royal Air Force. Its external design embraces the theme of stealth, reflecting the motion and dynamics of flight – a nod to today's modern aircraft, performing the role once carried out by Fighter Command's Hurricanes and Spitfires. The Centre's construction time of fifty-two weeks was within schedule and considered to have been completed in good time for today's standards. However, it is interesting to note that this is still nearly twice the time it took to complete the underground Operations Room.

The exhibition provides information surrounding the development of Britain's integrated air defence, from the response to the Zeppelin raids during the First World War, to the development and application of the Dowding System in the Second World War. Individual exhibits explore the various essential elements within the integrated air defence system and offer an excellent explanation of the underground Operations Room and its history.

There are a further two replica aircraft, a Spitfire and a Hurricane, displayed inside the Visitor Centre. Suspended from the ceiling in the centre's cavernous central hall, they portray Fighter Command's indefatigable struggle against relentless Luftwaffe attacks during the Battle of Britain. You can almost imagine the deafening roar of Merlin engines, throttles pushed hard past gate stops, set to maximum boost, both rising frantically into the air, straining to gain altitude, as they hurtle head on towards the formation of enemy bombers and fighters, depicted on the large glass windows at twelve o' clock ahead.

The Hurricane replicates a Mk I variant flown in 1940 during the Battle of Britain. It has the serial number P3873 and squadron code letters YO-H. Interestingly, another replica of this same aircraft is displayed at the Yorkshire Air Museum, site of the former RAF Elvington Station, near York. The markings are that of a fighter flown by 1 (Canadian) Squadron based at RAF Northolt in 11 Group. This Hurricane was flown by Flight Lieutenant Gordon McGregor on the afternoon of 26 August 1940, when the Squadron was one of eleven scrambled to meet a large-scale attack developing over North Foreland and the Thames Estuary. McGregor shot down one of the raiding aircraft, a Dornier Do 17, and so opened the Squadron's account for destroying enemy aircraft. The squadron also suffered its first fatality during the same engagement.[14] Flying Officer Robert Edwards, attacking another enemy bomber, managed to shear off its tail, but was himself hit by return fire from the stricken enemy aircraft's rear gunner, and both aircraft ploughed into the ground. His was the first combat death suffered by a member of the Royal Canadian Air Force while serving with a Canadian flying unit.[15]

McGregor's tally continued with a Dornier Do 17 probably destroyed and another damaged on 1 September, a Messerschmitt Me 110 damaged on the 4th, a Heinkel He 111 destroyed on the 11th, and another probably destroyed on the 15th. On the 27th he destroyed a Junker Ju 88 and damaged a Messerschmitt Me 109 and two Dornier Do 17s. His last two kills during the Battle of Britain came on 30 September and 5 October, when he destroyed a Messerschmitt Me 109 on each occasion. At 39, McGregor was both the oldest Canadian fighter pilot in the Battle of Britain and also the highest scoring one, having destroyed six Luftwaffe aircraft, probably destroying a further seven, and damaging a further eight.

Flying Officer Hartland de Montarville Molson was at the controls of P3873 on 5 October, when 1 (Canadian) Squadron intercepted enemy formations over Canterbury, as they headed towards London.[16] Molson spotted two Messerschmitt Me 109s hiding in the sun, and after knocking pieces from the wings of one, followed the other downwards. He was just about to fire, at a distance of about 100 yards (91 metres), when tracer bullets from behind reminded him that he had failed to look back; the second Me 109 was on his tail. Seconds later his control panel disintegrated and he was hit three times in the leg. The plane spun out of control.

ENEMY SIGHTED

Extricating himself from the cockpit, he fell out stomach first, waited to clear the German fighters in case they attacked his parachute, and then pulled the ripcord at about 7,000 ft (2,134 metres). In a letter to his wife afterwards, Molson described how his speed slowed and he felt as if he were on a child's swing, swinging back and forth in the breeze. He tried to use the metal ripcord as a tourniquet for his bleeding leg, but threw it away in disgust, only to look down in panic lest he had killed someone; there were, however, only sheep to be seen as he drifted to land softly 'with a plunk' in some woods at Smarden, in Kent. 'I hobbled about 30 yards to a wide path and sat down, then started to call every minute or so,' he continued. 'Soon I heard an answer, and about ten minutes from landing, half a dozen cockney soldiers were mothering me wonderfully.'[17] It was the last operational flight for both pilot and P3873. Prior to this day, Molson had damaged a Dornier Do 17 on 26 August, damaged two Messerschmitt Me 110s on 4 September, and claimed a Heinkel He 111 as destroyed on the 11th. Molson, the son of a wealthy family with large commercial interests including a famous brewery, would play no further role over Britain. After the war, he remained very active in business circles and was appointed an independent Senator in the Dominion of Canada.

The Spitfire seen beside the Hurricane replicates a Mk I variant, also flown in 1940. It has the serial number L1035 and squadron code letters SH-D. As well as seeing the aircraft 'airborne', visitors can also observe it taking off, thanks to original wartime footage, which is continuously projected onto the wall leading up to it. On closer examination, the reversed identification lettering on the Spitfire reveals that the film has in fact been flipped. This is deliberate, so the viewer can walk alongside L1035 as it takes to the sky, having been scrambled by the Bunker, and watch in awe as it approaches the enemy raid head on. The actual footage of L1035, plus more, can be seen on a British Pathé newsreel titled *Spitfires – Kenley Fighter Station* (1940).[18]

The markings are that of a fighter flown by No.64 Squadron, based at RAF Kenley in 11 Group. This Spitfire was flown by a Fleet Air Arm pilot Sub-Lieutenant Francis Dawson-Paul, who had been loaned to the beleaguered Royal Air Force. He had a flying pedigree, having learnt to fly from the age of 14. His father, Captain Joseph Dawson-Paul, was a Director at Boulton Paul Aircraft Limited, which is best known for developing the Boulton Paul Defiant, operated by Fighter Command first as a day fighter and then as a night fighter during the Battle of Britain. Perhaps less well known about that company is that in 1922 it was the first manufacturer to deliver an all metal aircraft, a prototype of their P.15 twin-engine fighter bomber, to the Royal Air Force. Specialising in the construction of high quality structures from rolled sheet metal, the company would also produce the longitudinal girders of the R101 airship, which crashed near Beauvais, in France in 1930.

Dawson-Paul was one of fifty-six naval aviators who flew in the Battle of Britain. Twenty-three, of whom he was one, served with twelve Fighter Command squadrons, and a further thirty-three served with two Fleet Air Arm squadrons, No. 804 and No. 808, who operated under the direction of Fighter Command to provide dockyard defence. Four of these naval aviators would become 'aces', that is someone who is accredited with shooting down five or more enemy aircraft during aerial combat. Dawson-Paul was the first to do so. On 1 July, the day of his arrival at RAF Kenley, he shared in the destruction of a Dornier Do 17 south of Beachy Head. Four days later, he engaged and shot down a Messerschmitt Me 109 over Rouen, France, before having to make a forced landing at RAF Hawkinge on the way back to his home airfield. Dawson-Paul claimed a Messerschmitt Me 110 destroyed on the 7th. Two more Me 110s, and probably a third, were brought down on the 10th. Dawson-Paul destroyed another Me 110 on the 13th and a Dornier Do 17 on the 24th. He recalled that engagement:

> As Blue One, I was ordered to patrol Dover at 08.50 hours, as enemy aircraft were approaching. I took off and climbed to 20,000 ft [6,096 metres], and carried out patrol with Blue Three, Blue Two having got separated from the section. After about five minutes, Blue Three broke away and disappeared. I then proceeded to patrol a convoy, which was near to the Goodwin Sands. Observed six Do 215s in two vics, very tight, approaching the convoy. Their height was approx. 11,000 ft [3,353 metres]. I dived towards them and positioned myself for a beam attack on their port side. Fired three, three second bursts at one aircraft and he broke away and fell in a spin. I fired the remainder of my ammunition into the enemy, and he broke away downwards. In doing so, I received a burst from the rear gunner of the enemy aircraft, which holed my bottom petrol tank. I proceeded to fire … The Do 215 has been confirmed as having crashed into the sea off the north-east end of the Goodwin. These enemy aircraft bombed the convoy heavily, but all their bombs fell short.[19]

ENEMY SIGHTED

His final engagement took place on 25 July when, throughout the day, numerous attacks on shipping took place in the Dover area.[20] Dawson-Paul destroyed an Me 109, before being himself shot down into the English Channel off the south coast, near Folkestone. Badly injured, he was picked up by a German E-boat and became a prisoner of war, but unfortunately he died of his wounds five days later. Interestingly, in 2010 the Falkland Islands issued a number of commemorative postage stamps to mark the seventieth anniversary of the Battle of Britain. One such stamp depicts Dawson-Paul strapped into L1035 while ground crew attend to his Spitfire.[21] It is a fitting tribute to an aviator who fought so valiantly and died so young.

A pageant of flags is permanently raised outside the Visitor Centre; they are a testament to the fact that a sizeable number of 'Churchill's few', had in fact travelled from abroad to assist Britain in her time of need. Like warriors stood in line abreast, the assemblage of fifteen flags, represent the airmen who had chosen to fight, not only for the Royal Air Force in the Battle of Britain, but also for the cause of freedom in the Battle for Democracy. Some of the flags and the countries they symbolised have now changed, but it reflects the situation as it was during the summer of 1940. The fifteen emblems correspond to the United Kingdom, which provided 2,342 airmen; Poland, 145 airmen; New Zealand, 127 airmen; Canada, 112 airmen; Czechoslovakia, now the Czech Republic and Slovakia, eighty-eight airmen; Australia, thirty-two airmen; Belgium, twenty-eight airmen; South Africa, twenty-five airmen; France, thirteen airmen; Ireland, ten airmen; the United States of America, nine airmen; Southern Rhodesia, now Zimbabwe, three airmen; Barbados, one airman; Jamaica, one airman; and Newfoundland, now a province of Canada, one airman. In fact, 595 airmen – that is just under 20 per cent of Fighter Command aircrew during the Battle of Britain – came from overseas nations and the Commonwealth. It is thought that they were responsible for downing between 25 to 30 per cent of the 1,733 enemy aircraft destroyed during the Battle.

A short distance from the flags, in the visitors' car park, is a large statue surrounded by neatly maintained shrubbery. It is a figure of Keith Park, wearing not only the uniform of an Air Vice-Marshal, but also the flying boots, flying helmet and life preserver vest donned by Fighter Command pilots during the Battle of Britain. The life preserver had been introduced in 1932 and so was known as the '1932 pattern'. Pilots referred to it as the 'Mae West' because when inflated, the wearer often appeared to be large breasted, like the American actress Mary Jane 'Mae' West. The official name, 'Waist, Lifesaving, Stole Pattern Temperate', was unsurprisingly less used. The pose adopted by the statue shows Park stood unbowed, pulling on his flying gloves, ready to climb onto his waiting Hurricane. 'Unbowed' in the sense that he is neither slouched, nor defeated.

Although bronze in colour, this sculpture is in fact constructed from glass fibre and is 16 ft 4 in (5 metres) tall. It was unveiled on the empty fourth plinth in Trafalgar Square, London, on 4 November 2009, until its removal and relocation in May 2010, to its penultimate location, the Royal Air Force Museum in Hendon. While at Trafalgar Square, Park's statue stood under that of Nelson, another great warrior-leader who had defended Britain from invasion some 135 years earlier. This view of Park as saviour is all the more indubitable when expressed by an enemy; in early 1944, Air Ministry Intelligence had obtained and translated some German appraisals of leading British and American personalities. Park, it was said, had earned the title 'Defender of London'.[22] Standing at 6 ft 5 in (1.96 metres), Park was in reality a tall man, but metaphorically, he was colossal.

For the sake of completeness, it is worth stating that an identical statue of Park, is placed permanently on display in Waterloo Place, London. This figure, cast by sculptor Les Johnson, is actually made from bronze, and is smaller than the one at Uxbridge, standing at 9 ft (2.78 metres). It was unveiled on 15 September 2010, the 70th anniversary of Battle of Britain Day, by Wing Commander Bob Foster and Park's great-great niece. Foster was well placed to unveil Park's statue, as he had flown as a Pilot Officer with 605 (County of Warwick) Squadron during the Battle of Britain. In a combat on 27 September, he damaged a Messerschmitt Me 110, as a result of which his aircraft was damaged and he had to make a forced landing at Gatwick. The following day, he damaged a Ju 88. On 7 October, he claimed the destruction of a Messerschmitt Me 109. The next day he shared in the destruction of another Ju 88. On 15 October, he claimed an Me 109 as probably destroyed. His last claim during the Battle of Britain was on the 26th, when he damaged an Me 109. The statue, fittingly, stands close to New Zealand House, and faces the direction Park's pilots would have looked while waiting for the Luftwaffe in the summer of 1940.

Chapter 14

Major Campaigns & Engagements
'Dynamo' to 'Seelöwe'

On 31 March 1939, the then British Prime Minister Neville Chamberlain told the House of Commons:

> In the event of any action which clearly threatened Polish independence, and which the Polish Government accordingly considered it vital to resist with their national forces, His Majesty's Government would feel themselves bound at once to lend the Polish Government all support in their power. They have given the Polish Government an assurance to this effect. I may add that the French Government have authorised me to make it plain that they stand in the same position in this matter as do His Majesty's Government.[1]

Poland was invaded five months later on 1 September, and on 3 September Chamberlain announced to Parliament that an ultimatum had been served:

> that unless the German Government were prepared to give His Majesty's Government in the United Kingdom satisfactory assurances that the German Government had suspended all aggressive action against Poland and were prepared promptly to withdraw their forces from Polish territory, His Majesty's Government in the United Kingdom would, without hesitation, fulfil their obligations to Poland. Although this communication was made more than twenty-four hours ago, no reply has been received, but German attacks upon Poland have been continued and intensified ... No such undertaking was received by the time stipulated, and, consequently, this country is at war with Germany.[2]

MAJOR CAMPAIGNS & ENGAGEMENTS

Following the declaration of war, a large part of Britain's professional army, the British Expeditionary Force (BEF), was immediately sent to France to check further aggression. Five squadrons within 11 Group were moved to forward airfields in Kent, to provide fighter cover on the BEF's left flank, as it advanced rapidly north through France, and into the Low Countries. The aircraft were controlled from the Bunker at Uxbridge, as they maintained offensive patrols, to the limit of their range, along the Belgium and Dutch coast.[3]

The deployment of British ground and air forces overseas, not only fulfilled an obligation to support an imperilled ally, but also met an imperative to protect Britain itself. Even though the two were geographically separated by a stretch of water, Britain's security was inextricably linked with the countries of north-western Europe. This realism was enunciated three years earlier in the House of Commons, by the then Secretary of State for War, Alfred Duff Cooper:

> It was said in the leading article of *The Times* this morning: For more centuries than need be counted, the destiny of Northern France and of the Low Countries has been held vital to the security of Britain. That situation has not been changed by modern inventions. It was Napoleon who said that Antwerp, in the possession of a hostile nation, was like a pistol held at the head of Great Britain. The result of new inventions is that that menace is greater than it was before, because today it is a double-barrelled pistol. It is not only a base for shipping and submarines but is also a taking-off ground for aeroplanes. The invention of flying, so far from rendering us more immune, has robbed us of a great part of our immunity. The sea, as Shakespeare said, 'the silver sea which serves it in the office of a wall', serves no longer in that office. More than ever, we are part of the Continent of Europe; less than ever can we rely upon any special advantage from our insular position.[4]

If France and the Low Countries were to fall, then bombing raids could be launched from Duff Cooper's 'taking-off ground', and crucially for 11 Group, the bombers would have Messerschmitt Me 109 and 110 fighter escort. Fighter Command pilots, schooled in attacking unescorted bombers, would be forced to engage in aerial combat with their more ferocious guardians.

ENEMY SIGHTED

Britain and France had expected the main German thrust to originate in the north around Belgium, as had been the case in the previous war. This belief was reinforced by their faith in the heavily fortified 'Maginot Line', which had been built to protect France from any attack along its eastern border with Germany. Even Churchill, who visited this elongated citadel of forts and tunnels just one month prior to becoming Prime Minister, considered it to be unbreachable. 'The French front cannot be surprised. It cannot be broken at any point except by an effort which would be enormously costly in life and would take so much time that the general situation would be transformed while it was in progress.'[5]

The weakness in the defence was what lay between the combined French and British Armies along the Franco-Belgium Border to the north, and the Maginot Line to the east. That weakness was an area of dense forest, known as the Ardennes, sprawled between the two. The Allies considered it to be impenetrable to columns of armoured vehicles, and so had not chosen to make any preparations to counter a mechanised incursion there. Unbeknown to them, the German High Command held a contrary view, considering a thrust through the thickly populated forestland a risk worth taking. This miscalculation on the part of the Allies would turn out to be strategically cataclysmic.

By the beginning of May 1940 much of Eastern and Northern Europe, namely Poland, Czechoslovakia, Norway and Denmark, was already under Nazi domination. Then, on the 10th of that month, the period of relative calm known as the Phoney War ended abruptly when Hitler's Heer and Luftwaffe launched Operation *Fall Gelb*, or *Case Yellow* – their 'blitzkrieg', or 'lightning war', offensive against the Low Countries and France. Elements of the German Army advanced south, entering Belgium, and the Allies moved north to confront them, as was anticipated by both sides. At the same time, as had been planned by the aggressors, other motorised elements of the German Army charged through the Ardennes Forest, to the rear of the advancing Allied Armies. With the enemy on both their northern and southern flanks, the Allied Armies were soon at risk of becoming encircled and overwhelmed. The Germans' big gamble had paid off. The only option left available to the Allies was to fight a rear guard action, and retreat to a location some six miles (ten kilometres), from the Belgium border. It was a town on the north coast of France, whose name would become synonymous with British fortitude and intrepidity. That town was Dunkirk.

As the fighting intensified, a further three squadrons of Hurricanes from 11 Group were despatched to operate from French airfields, where

MAJOR CAMPAIGNS & ENGAGEMENTS

they conducted offensive patrols under the control of the British Air Force in France (BAFF), and the Air Component of the BEF. Soon, even more fighter squadrons, operating from 11 Group airfields, were thrown into the fray to support those already in France, fighting a predominant enemy. The French airfields, vital for refuelling and maintaining British fighters, were repeatedly bombed by the Luftwaffe. This forced them to return to forward airfields in Kent between operational sorties, so adding further pressure on the Operations Room at Uxbridge.

From 20 May, the BEF and Allied Armies began to withdraw into the Dunkirk area, and 11 Group was called to provide an increasing number of offensive patrols over the surrounding coastal region and further inland. The Battle of France was lost, and the Battle of Britain was sure to follow. Those elements of the BEF that could be saved, needed to be saved. The Royal Navy, under the command of Admiral Bertram Ramsay, prepared an audacious plan, codenamed Operation *Dynamo*, to recover as much of the BEF and Allied Armies as possible. The British Cabinet hoped that as many as 30,000 troops could be rescued. The evacuation would last ten tumultuous days, beginning on 26 May and ending on 4 June. During this period, 11 Group provided almost continuous protection, facilitating the troops' evacuation and safe passage across the English Channel. An average of sixteen squadrons took part daily throughout this action, and the one Defiant, five Spitfire, and ten Hurricane squadrons were all controlled and directed from the Bunker at Uxbridge.

The remaining squadrons within 11 Group were retained to carry out Fighter Command's raison d'etre, the home defence of the British Isles. As well as providing fighter cover over France and the English Channel, Uxbridge was required 'to maintain the highest possible state of preparedness to meet the possibility of a heavy scale air attack on southern England'. All squadrons automatically reverted to being on call for home defence between offensive missions over France. On occasions, the Operations Room would despatch them from the ground, or divert them after they had left for France, to intercept raids reported to be approaching Britain. The Senior Controller at Uxbridge had to be cognisant of the state, whereabouts and function of as many as twenty-five squadrons operating from ten of 11 Group's airfields. The risk of his becoming dangerously distracted was, to a degree, mitigated by the creation of a subsidiary Operations Room, from which aircraft patrolling over France could be controlled.[6]

The majority of troops waiting to be evacuated from Dunkirk did not see and therefore did not know of the battle being fought further inland to

ENEMY SIGHTED

protect them, so it is understandable, although regrettable, that some dubbed the Royal Air Force, the 'Royal Absent Force'. The truth, however, is that the Royal Air Force was locked in a deadly struggle to repel Luftwaffe attacks targeting those same troops, as they fell back to the coast, stood in orderly lines on the beaches, and waited to be rescued by the armada of 'little ships' and larger ships that had raced from England to extricate them. Those who knew how much was being sacrificed did voice their gratitude as the evacuation progressed, such as Admiral Bertram Ramsay, who signalled Fighter Command on 29 May: 'I am most grateful for your splendid cooperation. It alone has given us a chance of success.'[7]

11 Group's losses, just on the day he sent the signal, were eighteen pilots missing and three wounded. Five would later rejoin their squadron, but sixteen were lost permanently.[8] The 'cooperation' was costing Fighter Command dearly in pilots, especially those squadrons being directed from Uxbridge.

One of those pilots, Flying Officer Peter Cazenove of 92 Squadron, was lost on 24 May, before the full evacuation from Dunkirk had even been initiated. He was one of seven pilots sent by Uxbridge that day who were either killed or taken prisoner.[9] Cazenove was flying Spitfire, serial number P9374 and squadron code letter J, on his first operational sortie. The squadron had taken off from 11 Group's satellite airfield at RAF Croydon, to head towards a patrol line between Calais and Dunkirk. When they reached the French coast, the squadron spotted a formation of twenty Dornier Do 17 at about 12,000 ft (3,658 metres) far inland, heading towards the beaches to bomb the cornered troops and the gathering evacuation fleet.[10] They could also see that the bombers were being escorted by Messerschmitt Me 110, flying 7,000 ft (2,134 metres) higher than their wards, and 4,000 ft (1,220 metres) above 92 Squadron's own Spitfires. Then miraculously, a squadron of Hurricanes appeared from out of the blue expanse, and 'bounced' the fighter umbrella, relieving the bombers of their chaperon, leaving them exposed to attack from 92 Squadron.

As Cazenove's section scythed through the enemy formation, his machine was hit by return fire, disabling his engine. Realising he could no longer fly home, he looked for a suitable place to bring his crippled aircraft down and spotted the vast expanse of sand below him. The tide was out, providing a wide, flat, unobstructed surface for him to bring his stricken machine down, without the assistance of wheels. Having ploughed into the sand, he made his way on foot along the beach towards Calais. On the way, he stumbled across the burnt wreckage of another Spitfire. Examining the

MAJOR CAMPAIGNS & ENGAGEMENTS

remains, Cazenove found 'the blackened, twisted buckle from a parachute harness'.[11] Tragically, he had discovered the mortal remains of his friend, Pilot Officer Pat Learmond, whose aircraft, serial number P9370, had been shot down the day before.

Cazenove was eventually taken prisoner, ending up in the infamous Stalag Luft III, near the town of Sagan, Lower Silesia, in what was then Eastern Germany; here, he was reacquainted with Roger Bushell, who until very recently had been his Commanding Officer at 92 Squadron. Bushell, like Learmond, had also been shot down over Dunkirk the day before Cazenove. Bushell was now known as 'Big X', the senior officer charged with planning 'the Great Escape'. Cazenove assisted him by preparing forgeries to be used during the breakout, but fortunately for him, his large build meant he could not be offered a place in the escape tunnel, and so he did not suffer the same fate that befell Bushell and many others, who were shot after being recaptured.

Another pilot lost over Dunkirk was Squadron Leader Geoffrey Stephenson, who, on the morning of 26 May, led 19 Squadron from RAF Hornchurch in 11 Group, to patrol over Calais and Dunkirk.[12] Stephenson, flying his Spitfire, serial number N3200 and squadron code letters QV, downed a Ju 87 'Stuka' dive bomber, one of five claimed destroyed and four possibly destroyed by the squadron during that engagement. They then came under attack from Messerschmitt Me 109s and Stephenson's Spitfire was hit in the radiator, forcing him to put his Spitfire down on the beach at Sangatte, to the west of Calais. His was one of two 19 Squadron aircraft shot down that morning. Stephenson was captured nearby and, after numerous escape attempts, was incarcerated in Oflag IV-C, at Colditz Castle, near the city of Leipzig in Eastern Germany. There, he busied himself by working with other detainees to build a glider, the 'Colditz Cock', which they hoped to launch from the castle loft. It was never flown, as the camp was liberated by the American Army before an escape attempt using it could be made. After the war, Stephenson resumed his flying career and went on to become the personal pilot to King George VI.

Flying Officer Peter Cazenove's and Squadron Leader Geoffrey Stephenson's actions are representative of so many 11 Group pilots, who helped make evacuation possible, their shattered Spitfires, halted by the adamantine sand and frozen in time, attestations to the violent episode that brought about their demise. Serving initially as photo opportunities, exalting the mastery of the German warrior, before becoming totally submerged, only to resurface many years later. Remarkably, and appropriately, both

131

ENEMY SIGHTED

P9374 and N3200, have been painstakingly reclaimed, rebuilt, and are now flying again.

The final number of troops extracted from the Dunkirk area was not, in fact 30,000, but 338,000 – over twelve times what was originally considered possible. In the House of Commons on 4 June, Prime Minister Winston Churchill described the evacuation of troops:

> Meanwhile, the Royal Air Force, which had already been intervening in the battle, so far as its range would allow, from home bases, now used part of its main metropolitan fighter strength, and struck at the German bombers, and at the fighters which in large numbers protected them. This struggle was protracted and fierce. Suddenly the scene has cleared, the crash and thunder has for the moment, but only for the moment, died away. A miracle of deliverance, achieved by valour, by perseverance, by perfect discipline, by faultless service, by resource, by skill, by unconquerable fidelity, is manifest to us all. The enemy was hurled back by the retreating British and French troops. He was so roughly handled that he did not harry their departure seriously. The Royal Air Force engaged the main strength of the German Air Force and inflicted upon them losses of at least four to one; and the Navy, using nearly 1,000 ships of all kinds, carried over 335,000 men, French and British, out of the jaws of death and shame, to their native land and to the tasks which lie immediately ahead. We must be very careful not to assign to this deliverance the attributes of a victory. Wars are not won by evacuations. But there was a victory inside this deliverance, which should be noted. It was gained by the Air Force. Many of our soldiers coming back have not seen the Air Force at work; they saw only the bombers which escaped its protective attack. They underrate its achievements. I have heard much talk of this; that is why I go out of my way to say this. I will tell you about it. This was a great trial of strength between the British and German Air Forces. Can you conceive a greater objective for the Germans in the air than to make evacuation from these beaches impossible, and to sink all these ships which were displayed, almost to the extent of thousands? Could there have been an objective of greater military importance and

MAJOR CAMPAIGNS & ENGAGEMENTS

significance for the whole purpose of the war than this? They tried hard, and they were beaten back; they were frustrated in their task. We got the Army away; and they have paid fourfold for any losses which they have inflicted. Very large formations of German aeroplanes, and we know that they are a very brave race, have turned on several occasions from the attack of one-quarter of their number of the Royal Air Force and have dispersed in different directions. Twelve aeroplanes have been hunted by two. One aeroplane was driven into the water and cast away, by the mere charge of a British aeroplane, which had no more ammunition. All of our types, the Hurricane, the Spitfire and the new Defiant, and all our pilots have been vindicated as superior to what they have at present to face.

When we consider how much greater would be our advantage in defending the air above this island against an overseas attack, I must say that I find in these facts a sure basis upon which practical and reassuring thoughts may rest. I will pay my tribute to these young airmen. The great French Army was very largely, for the time being, cast back and disturbed by the onrush of a few thousands of armoured vehicles. May it not also be that the cause of civilisation itself will be defended by the skill and devotion of a few thousand airmen? There never had been, I suppose, in all the world, in all the history of war, such an opportunity for youth. The Knights of the Round Table, the Crusaders, all fall back into a prosaic past: not only distant but prosaic; but these young men, going forth every morn to guard their native land and all that we stand for, holding in their hands these instruments of colossal and shattering power, of whom it may be said that when every morning brought a noble chance, and every chance brought out a noble knight, deserve our gratitude, as do all of the brave men who, in so many ways and on so many occasions, are ready, and continue ready, to give life and all for their native land.

It is clear that the air operation, so vital to the success of 'Operation Dynamo', would not have been possible without the control and direction provided by those working in the 11 Group Operations Room at Uxbridge.

ENEMY SIGHTED

The Prime Minister also announced to the country that it should brace itself for a further blow: 'We are told that Herr Hitler has a plan for invading the British Isles.' He provided a degree of optimism by stating that Britain was secretly engaged in putting her 'defences in this island into such a high state of organisation that the fewest possible numbers will be required to give effective security and that the largest possible potential of offensive effort may be realised'. Could Churchill have used this oblique language to describe Britain's integrated air defence system, hoping to offer reassurance to his compatriots without revealing secrets to his enemies?

Churchill ended his address on 4 June with words that would embolden and galvanise an embattled country:

> I have, myself, full confidence that if all do their duty, if nothing is neglected, and if the best arrangements are made, as they are being made, we shall prove ourselves once again able to defend our island home, to ride out the storm of war, and to outlive the menace of tyranny, if necessary for years, if necessary, alone. At any rate, that is what we are going to try to do. That is the resolve of His Majesty's Government, every man of them. That is the will of Parliament and the nation. The British Empire and the French Republic, linked together in their cause and in their need, will defend to the death their native soil, aiding each other like good comrades to the utmost of their strength. Even though large tracts of Europe and many old and famous States have fallen or may fall into the grip of the Gestapo and all the odious apparatus of Nazi rule, we shall not flag or fail. We shall go on to the end. We shall fight in France, we shall fight on the seas and oceans, we shall fight with growing confidence and growing strength in the air, we shall defend our island, whatever the cost may be. We shall fight on the beaches, we shall fight on the landing grounds, we shall fight in the fields and in the streets, we shall fight in the hills; we shall never surrender, and even if, which I do not for a moment believe, this island or a large part of it were subjugated and starving, then our Empire beyond the seas, armed and guarded by the British Fleet, would carry on the struggle, until, in God's good time, the new world with all its power and might, steps forth to the rescue and the liberation of the old.[13]

MAJOR CAMPAIGNS & ENGAGEMENTS

In choosing to say, 'we shall fight with growing confidence and growing strength in the air', Churchill understood that Fighter Command had to retain control of the sky above Britain, in order to make invasion a less viable military option for Hitler. He was well aware of Fighter Command's heightened state of preparedness and had great faith in both Hugh Dowding and Keith Park. He also had good reason to believe that the availability of Spitfires and Hurricanes, under the direction of his friend Lord Beaverbrook, the Minister for Aircraft Production, would continue to increase over the coming months.

On 18 June, as the situation continued to worsen, the Prime Minister again addressed the House of Commons:

> I indicated a fortnight ago as clearly as I could to the House that the worst possibilities were open, and I made it perfectly clear then that whatever happened in France would make no difference to the resolve of Britain and the British Empire to fight on, 'if necessary for years, if necessary alone'.
>
> This brings me, naturally, to the great question of invasion from the air and of the impending struggle between the British and German air forces. It seems quite clear that no invasion on a scale beyond the capacity of our land forces to crush speedily is likely to take place from the air until our Air Force has been definitely overpowered. But the great question is, can we break Hitler's air weapon? Now, of course, it is a very great pity that we have not got an Air Force at least equal to that of the most powerful enemy within striking distance of these shores. But we have a very powerful Air Force which has proved itself far superior in quality, both in men and in many types of machine, to what we have met so far in the numerous fierce air battles which have been fought. In France, where we were at a considerable disadvantage and lost many machines on the ground, we were accustomed to inflicting losses of as much as two to two and a half, to one. In the fighting over Dunkirk, which was a sort of no man's land, we undoubtedly beat the German Air Force, and this gave us the mastery locally in the air, and we inflicted losses of three or four, to one. Anyone who looks at the photographs which were published a week or so ago of the re-embarkation, showing the masses of troops assembled on the beach and forming an ideal target for hours at a time, must realise that this re-embarkation

would not have been possible unless the enemy had resigned all hope of recovering air superiority at that point.

In the defence of this island the advantages to the defenders will be very great. We hope to improve on the rate of three or four to one which was realised at Dunkirk, and in addition all our injured machines and their crews which get down safely, and, surprisingly, a very great many injured machines and men do get down safely in modern air fighting, all of these will fall, in an attack upon these islands, on friendly soil and live to fight another day, whereas all injured enemy machines and their complements will be total losses as far as the war is concerned. During the great battle in France, we gave very powerful and continuous aid to the French Army both by fighters and bombers, but in spite of every kind of pressure we never would allow the entire Metropolitan strength of the Air Force, in fighters, to be consumed. This decision was painful, but it was also right, because the fortunes of the battle in France could not have been decisively affected, even if we had thrown in our entire fighter force. The battle was lost by the unfortunate strategical opening, by the extraordinary and unforeseen power of the armoured columns, and by the great preponderance of the German Army in numbers. Our fighter Air Force might easily have been exhausted as a mere accident in that great struggle, and we should have found ourselves at the present time in a very serious plight. But, as it is, I am happy to inform the House that our fighter air strength is stronger at the present time, relatively to the Germans, who have suffered terrible losses, than it has ever been, and consequently we believe ourselves to possess the capacity to continue the war in the air under better conditions than we have ever experienced before. I look forward confidently to the exploits of our fighter pilots, who will have the glory of saving their native land, their island home, and all they love, from the most deadly of all attacks.

Within his speech that day, he gave the forthcoming onslaught a name:

What General Weygand called the 'Battle of France' is over. I expect that the battle of Britain is about to begin. Upon this battle depends the survival of Christian civilisation. Upon it

MAJOR CAMPAIGNS & ENGAGEMENTS

depends our own British life and the long continuity of our institutions and our Empire. The whole fury and might of the enemy must very soon be turned on us. Hitler knows that he will have to break us in this island or lose the war. If we can stand up to him, all Europe may be free, and the life of the world may move forward into broad, sunlit uplands; but if we fail, then the whole world, including the United States, and all that we have known and cared for, will sink into the abyss of a new dark age, made more sinister, and perhaps more prolonged, by the lights of perverted science. Let us therefore brace ourselves to our duty and so bear ourselves, that if the British Commonwealth and Empire lasts for a thousand years, men will still say, 'This was their finest hour.'[14]

Efforts to recover troops did not end following the evacuation from Dunkirk, 'the pressure on the Fighter Command became less intense, but it by no means disappeared. Hard fighting took place along the coast from Calais to Le Havre to cover the successive evacuations from that coast.'[15] Fighter cover was coordinated from Uxbridge, as part of 'Operation Cycle' and 'Operation Aerial', in which the Royal Navy rescued a further 206,000 troops. That brought the total number of British and Allied troops removed from France and brought back safely to England to around 544,000. Their heavy equipment could not be saved and most of it – planes, lorries, tanks, weapons, ammunition and communications equipment, had been destroyed, captured or abandoned. However, despite this alarming loss of accoutrements, the fact remained that more than half-a-million men had not fallen into the hands of the Germans, and therefore the war was not yet lost.

By 25 June, the Germans had attacked, conquered and occupied, Luxembourg, the Netherlands, Belgium and France. The Royal Air Force had suffered substantial losses during the campaign, during which Dowding had seen his 'resources slipping away like sand in an hour glass'.[16] In the six weeks since 10 May, the British had lost nearly 1,000 aircraft, including 463 fighters, of which 396 were Hurricanes and 67 were Spitfires. Of even greater consequence was the loss of around 330 pilots, either killed, missing or made prisoner, of which 280 were fighter pilots.[17] Many more Hurricanes were lost than Spitfires, mainly because unlike the latter, they were deployed throughout all phases of the campaign, operating over France itself. Fighter Command had wanted to preserve its Spitfires for home defence, and so they were used only during the withdrawal and evacuation phase, and then

ENEMY SIGHTED

only deployed over the English Channel and evacuation areas. Fighter Command was unable to preserve its pilots to the same extent, and those lost during the Battle of France would be sorely missed in the fighting yet to take place over Britain itself.

Britain, with her Commonwealth and her Empire, now stood alone, in anticipation of the aerial battle to come, and subsequent invasion if it were lost. The French Generals had told their Prime Minister they were convinced Germany would successfully invade Britain as it had done France, and in three weeks Britain would 'have its neck wrung like a chicken'. History would prove otherwise and in a speech to the Canadian Parliament on 30 December 1941, Winston Churchill, was able to jeer at this false prophesy. 'Some chicken! Some neck!'[18]

Operation *Seelöwe*, or *Sealion*, the plan to invade the British Isles and subjugate the British People, depended on the Luftwaffe defeating the Royal Air Force's Fighter Command, and achieving air superiority over the English Channel and invasion area. For the British people, this would, in Churchill's words, be 'their finest hour'.

Hermann Goering, Head of the German Luftwaffe, had 2,500 aircraft available to him. This vast armada contained four types of bombers, Heinkel (He) 111s, Dornier (Do) 17s,[19] Junkers (Ju) 88s, and Junkers (Ju) 87 Stukas dive bombers, and two types of fighters, single-engine Messerschmitt (Me) 109s, and twin-engine Messerschmitt (Me) 110s. Against this formidable aerial flotilla, Air Chief Marshal Sir Hugh Dowding, Head of Fighter Command, had less than 700 fighters to defend the whole of the United Kingdom, not just the south-east of England, where most of the fighting would take place. Hurricanes and Spitfires would protect Britain during the day, and Boulton Paul Defiants and Blenheims would intercept enemy raiders during the night. There were roughly twice as many operational Hurricanes as Spitfires during the Battle of Britain, and they accounted for 1,593, just over half of the 2,739 kills claimed during the fighting over Britain. They were not as fast as Spitfires but were more robust and easier to repair. When engaging the massed formations of German aircraft, Hurricanes were generally directed at the bombers; they were a steady gun platform and had a speed difference over Dornier Do 17 and Heinkel He 111 bombers, that they did not have over the Messerschmitt Me 109s. The Spitfires were directed at the German fighters. As in many cases during war, things did not always go as planned, and often the Hurricanes took on their Messerschmitt Me 109 counterparts, acquitting themselves admirably.

MAJOR CAMPAIGNS & ENGAGEMENTS

Aerial skirmishes continued after the evacuation of troops from France, into the period that became known as the Battle of Britain, 'without any appreciable opportunity to rest and re-form the units which had borne the brunt of the fighting'.[20] The Battle is officially recognised by the British as having started on 10 July and ending four months later on 31 October. Dowding had acknowledged in his Despatch the difficulty of fixing the exact date on which the Battle started, as:

> operations of various kinds merged into one another almost insensibly, and there are grounds for choosing the date of 8 August, on which was made the first attack in force against land objectives in this country, as the beginning of the Battle … on the other hand, the heavy attacks made against our Channel convoys probably constituted, in fact, the beginning of the German offensive; because the weight and scale of the attack indicates that the primary object was rather to bring our fighters to battle, than to destroy the hulls and cargoes of the small ships engaged in the coastal trade … I have therefore, somewhat arbitrarily, chosen the events of 10 July as the opening of the Battle.[21]

On the opening day, the Luftwaffe commenced the first phase of the battle it called '*Kanalkampf*' or 'Channel Fight', attacking British merchant shipping in the English Channel. The Operations Room at Uxbridge despatched thirty-nine patrols, a total of 173 Hurricanes and Spitfires, to protect 'Convoy Bread', which had come under attack from around 150 Dornier Do 17s and Messerschmitt Me 109s.[22] The Luftwaffe's intention was twofold, to entice Fighter Command into the air, into a war of attrition that it thought the Royal Air Force could not hope to win against vastly superior numbers, and deny the British use of the English Channel, in order for invasion to take place.

Whether or not Adolf Hitler would have attempted to invade Great Britain if the Royal Air Force had been defeated is still the subject of deliberation among historians today. It is true that Operation *Seelöwe* existed, but it is also true that many senior figures in the German military were against such an operation. Whether or not he could have attempted to invade Great Britain if the Luftwaffe was victorious is equally contentious. The eradication, or significant weakening of the threat to his troops from the air, could have allowed an attempt to be made. However, Britain's Royal Navy would still pose a significant threat on the ocean, and the British Army, albeit ill-equipped, could not be easily dismissed. A report on 4 July from the Joint Intelligence Sub-Committee advised the War Cabinet that, 'We consider that large-scale raids, on the British Isles involving all three arms, may take place at any moment. A full-scale invasion is unlikely to take place before the middle of July. This matter is under our daily review.'[23] What is clear, is that Britain, weakened by her defeat in France, was in a perilous state and invasion seemed to the British to be a question of when, not if.

The sense of inevitability deepened following Adolf Hitler's infamous 'Führer Directive 16' on 16 July, when he declared:

> Since England, despite its hopeless military situation, still gives no sign of any readiness to come to terms, I have decided to prepare for invasion of that country and, if necessary, to carry it through. The aim of this operation will be to eliminate England as a base for carrying on the war against Germany, and, should it be requisite, completely to occupy … The English Air Force must be beaten physically and morally to a point that they cannot put up any show of attacking force worth mentioning.[24]

It was clear that the battle being fought over Britain was an existential one.

As the battle progressed, it wasn't the lack of fighters that would concern Fighter Command. Britain, under Lord Beaverbrook, the Minister for Aircraft Production, was building more Spitfires and more Hurricanes than the Germans were Messerschmitt Me 109s and 110s.[25] Between July and October, the average number of Hurricanes built each month was 256, while the average lost each month was 151. The numbers for Spitfires produced and lost each month, were 157, and 99 respectively.[26]

It was the loss of experienced fighter pilots, that was threatening Fighter Command's very existence. While the total number of fighter pilots continued to increase, beyond the 1,341 available at the beginning of the Battle,[27] it was the attrition of seasoned pilots that risked undermining Fighter Command's ability to resist Luftwaffe raids. In the opening month of the battle, seventy-four pilots were killed, missing, or taken prisoner, and forty-nine were wounded or injured. That was, astonishingly, almost one in ten of all pilots across the Command.

As the fighting increased, so too did the losses. In August, 148 were killed, missing, or taken prisoner, and 156 were wounded or injured. September was

MAJOR CAMPAIGNS & ENGAGEMENTS

even worse, when 159 were killed, missing, or taken prisoner, and 152 were wounded or injured. The losses continued during October, albeit at a reduced level, with 100 killed, missing, or taken prisoner, and sixty-five wounded or injured.[28] Although lower than the preceding two months, it was still significantly higher than at the beginning of the Battle and was not a level of attrition that could be sustained without undermining Fighter Command's effectiveness.

The pressing need to put up sufficient pilots meant that many were required to engage Luftwaffe raids with little or no experience of flying a fighter aircraft, or flying one operationally in a front line squadron. Fresh aircrew had learnt to fly, but they had not yet learnt to fight, and so were not a 'like for like' for the seasoned pilots they replaced. This inevitably exposed new pilots to significant risk when confronting Luftwaffe raids over Britain. A case in point was 19-year-old Sergeant Pilot Tony Pickering, who towards the end of July was posted from training school to 32 Squadron, operating Hurricanes within 11 Group, at RAF Biggin Hill. On being asked by his Squadron Commander, 'Pickering. How many hours have you done on Hurricanes?' Pickering replied, 'I have never seen one before, Sir.' To which his commanding officer replied:

> Well tomorrow morning you'll be in action. There's a Hurricane out there, Pilot Officer Flinders will take you and he'll show you the controls. You'll do three circuits and bumps and then tomorrow morning at half past three you'll be awoken, have a cup of tea, then meet at dispersal at quarter past four and take off and we'll go down to Hawkinge. We'll sit there until the Hun comes over. You'll fly as number two to a Flight Lieutenant Proctor, and he'll tell you what to do.

Pickering met Proctor the following morning and was told:

> Pickering you'll fly as my number two. You'll sit directly behind me; you will not be more than about 10 or 12 ft [3 or 4 metres] from me at all times whatever I do. You won't put your gun button on fire. I don't want you to blow me out of the sky. We'll attack the Hun.[29]

Pickering's squadron was soon scrambled to intercept a German raid, and fortunately for him he survived his first operational sortie. Three pilots from other squadrons, despatched that day by Uxbridge, failed to return.[30]

ENEMY SIGHTED

On 1 August, Adolf Hitler issued 'Führer Directive 17',[31] in which he ordered an intensification of 'air warfare against the English homeland'. He ordered the Luftwaffe to 'overpower the English Air Force with all the forces at its command, in the shortest possible time.' The attacks were to be 'directed primarily against flying units, their ground installations, and their supply organisations, but also against the aircraft industry, including that manufacturing anti-aircraft equipment.' Once air superiority was achieved, then attacks were to 'be continued against ports, in particular against stores of food, and also against stores of provisions in the interior of the country.' Ports along the south coast would be spared large-scale attacks, 'in view of forthcoming operations', and so too would 'warships and merchant ships', unless they presented a 'particularly favourable target', or it was 'necessary for the training of aircrews for further operations'. Crucially, the Luftwaffe had to 'be ready to take part in full force in undertaking *Seelöwe*. It is notable that at this point of the battle, Hitler personally still reserved 'the right to decide on terror attacks as measures of reprisals'. London would, therefore, not be targeted by the Luftwaffe, yet. The focus of its attacks would continue to be on Fighter Command's airfields, and the aircraft factories at Langley, Southampton and Brooklands, all within Uxbridge's area of responsibility. The Führer had decreed that the intensification should commence, 'on or after 5 August, whenever weather conditions permitted, and necessary preparations had been completed'.

The intensification of the air war began on 12 August, with a series of attacks along the south and south-east coast of England, striking convoys in the English Channel, the harbour towns of Dover and Portsmouth, and now, 11 Group's Sector stations and Radar stations. Among a number of smaller incursions, there were several much larger raids, geographically distanced and coordinated to stretch and test the integrated air defence system. It was a pattern which the Luftwaffe would repeatedly follow as the battle progressed. The Operations Room at Uxbridge, in responding to the burgeoning assaults, was compelled to direct nearly 500 sorties on this day,[32] during which twelve of 11 Group's pilots became casualties, four wounded, seven missing and one killed.[33]

Lympne, a satellite airfield within the Biggin Hill Sector, was heavily bombed, and so too were Manston and Hawkinge, both satellite airfields within the Hornchurch Sector. Although the damage was considerable, all were operational by the following day, thanks to the determination of resolute ground staff. The Luftwaffe had hoped that by targeting Radar stations, they could nullify the defending force's ability to see them coming.

MAJOR CAMPAIGNS & ENGAGEMENTS

The sites at Pevensey, Rye, Dover and Dunkirk all sustained damage, but were operational again the same day or the day after. The damage to Ventnor, on the Isle of Wight, was far more serious, resulting in the site having to be evacuated. The bombing had started a fire which could not be brought under control as there was little or no water available. Full Radar coverage did not return until a new site became operational eleven days later, at Bembridge, also on the Isle of Wight. However, limited radar cover was provided in the meantime by positioning a mobile unit near to the defunct Ventnor station. This not only helped to plug the detection gap, but also unwittingly misled German Signals Intelligence who, having picked up the signal, wrongly assumed that Ventnor Radar station had not been destroyed and that all essential equipment must be shielded below ground. In fact, it was in plain sight, inside the wooden buildings located directly under the vast transmitting towers.

The Germans decided targeting Radar stations was no longer worthwhile. It was a major strategic error, that would undermine the enemy's ability to gain air superiority over England. If the Germans had continued with their attacks, they could well have succeeded in putting radar out of action. Britain's all-seeing eye would have been unable to alert Stanmore as to when and where the Luftwaffe were coming. Uxbridge would not have been notified in advance. Interceptions could not have taken place and the battle would have been lost, paving the way for invasion. The Royal Air Force would have been forced to maintain standing patrols in the air, requiring additional aircraft, more pilots and extra fuel, all of which it did not have.

The following day, 13 August, saw a number of larger raids, geographically dispersed across 11 Group's eastern, southern and western flanks, attacking Margate, Dover, Thames Estuary, Portsmouth and Weymouth. The Operation, named *Adler Tag*, or *Eagle Day*, involved a total of 1,485 Luftwaffe sorties. Coastal Command airfields at Eastchurch and Detling, and Fighter Command airfields at Manston and Lympne, were also targeted. Although the Operations Room at Uxbridge scrambled twelve of 11 Group's squadrons on that day, the Group's casualties were 'exceptionally small', with only three pilots being wounded.[34]

The Luftwaffe were, in effect, challenging British fighters to a duel, hoping to knock down enough Spitfires and Hurricanes, reducing Fighter Command's ability to operate effectively across the south-east of England. Disastrously for the Germans, this phase of the battle, *Adler Angriff*, or *Attack of the Eagles*, was predicated on flawed intelligence. They erroneously believed that in the lead up to *Adler Tag* Fighter Command's losses had been far higher than was the case, and that lost aircraft were not being replaced swiftly, when in fact production of new aircraft was accelerating. Also, while coming to realise that Spitfires and Hurricanes were being directed from the ground, there was a failure to understand how malleable the air defence system was. Thinking that defending fighters were limited to operating over their individual Sector stations, they mistakenly assumed that Fighter Command was incapable of putting up large formations in response to 'sizeable German raids over distant locations'.[35]

There was also an element of over-confidence on behalf of Luftwaffe leaders who, following the victories in Poland, Belgium, Holland and France, believed unquestionably that they would drive Dowding's Command out of south-east England within four days and eliminate the entire Royal Air Force within four weeks.[36] However, Britain's aerial armour was more durable than had been the case for the fallen countries of Western Europe. Preparing the ground, or air, for invading an island that was fortified by a purposefully developed and competently controlled integrated air defence system would prove to be much more challenging for the Luftwaffe.

Four weeks after *Adler Tag*, while the fighting continued above 11 Group, Dowding requested that Park send him an account of the battle so far. Park presented a report in which he chronicled the epochal events taking place and provided a historically veracious picture of what had and was still happening over the south and south-east of England.[37] The following account draws from this report. Park, the 'Defender of London', did not seek to underplay the pressure those working at Uxbridge were under, 'As the battle still continues unabated by day, and has increased greatly in intensity by night, neither I nor any of my Staff have opportunity to write a lengthy report.'

Park identified three distinct phases of the battle so far, choosing to start on 8 August, a date which Dowding would acknowledge, could also have been when the battle commenced. It is certainly closer to the Luftwaffe's thinking, who had hoped to launch *Adler Tag* on 10 August, but the weather had forced a postponement until the 13th. Park's first phase covered the period up to 18 August, and the second phase from 19 August to 5 September. The third phase began on 6 September and was still occupying 11 Group's attention night and day at the time the report was written. The phases described in Park's report were adopted as the timeline outlined by the Air Ministry in its wartime publication on the Battle of Britain.[38] The truth, as often is the case, is that it was an imprecise situation, convoluted by the 'fog of war'. Fighting had not stopped, but continued after the withdrawal

MAJOR CAMPAIGNS & ENGAGEMENTS

from France, beginning to increase after 17 July, when the Luftwaffe was ordered to be at full readiness. This, in turn, resulted in more activity over the following four weeks, which 'worked up to a crescendo', leading to the launch of the full scale offensive known as *Adler Tag*.[39]

During the first phase, bombing attacks had been directed against shipping and ports on the south-east and south coast, between North Foreland and Portland. Massed attacks were conducted against Portland and Portsmouth; Fighter Command aerodromes on the coast, and then Bomber Command and Coastal Command aerodromes on the coast were attacked; and finally, towards the end of this period, comparatively light attacks were pressed inland by day, to various objectives.

The enemy usually made an attack against coastal objectives in Kent, as a diversion in order to draw defending fighters. Then about thirty to forty minutes later, the enemy would put in his main attack against ports or aerodromes on the south coast, between Brighton and Portland. This phase introduced bombing by Messerschmitt Me 110s and 109s, the latter also carrying out machine gun attacks on forward aerodromes. When escorting bombers, the fighters were employed in unwieldy mass formations, usually flying much higher, about 5,000 to 10,000 ft (1,524 to 3,048 metres) above the bombers. The tactic was observed to be 'not very effective' in protecting the bombers.

The main problem was to know which was the diversionary attack and to hold sufficient fighter squadrons in readiness to meet the main attack, when this could be discerned from the very unreliable information received from the RDF, after they had been heavily bombed. The unreliability was in part due to the damage sustained following Luftwaffe attacks, and the fact that maintaining the 'elaborate scientific apparatus equipment presented great difficulties'.[40] To meet these attacks on coastal objectives, it was essential to keep nearly all 'Readiness' squadrons at forward aerodromes, such as Lympne, Hawkinge, Manston and Rochford. The greatest vigilance had to be observed by the Group Controller at Uxbridge, not to have these squadrons bombed or machine-gunned on the ground at forward aerodromes. On only one occasion was any squadron at a forward aerodrome attacked while on the ground refuelling, and this was because the squadron failed to maintain a protective patrol over the base during refuelling. Controllers were instructed to 'keep some units in hand within the Group during intensive engagements to ensure that quick follow up raids could be met if they developed.'[41]

A very high state of preparedness had to be maintained in order to engage the enemy before he reached his coastal objectives. The general plan in employing the fighters was to detail about half the available squadrons, including the Spitfires, to engage the enemy fighters, and the remainder to attack the enemy bombers, which normally flew at between 11,000 and 13,000 ft (3,353 and 3,962 metres), and carried out their attack frequently from 7,000 to 8,000 ft (2,134 to 2,438 metres).

During this phase, defending fighters were mainly employing the Fighter Command attacks from astern, which Park considered gave good results against enemy fighters as they were unarmoured, but were not so effective against bombers. He instructed his fighters to therefore attack Heinkel He 111s and Dornier Do 17s and 215s from quarter astern, from above or from below, and use deflection shots, which is the same principle used by shooters firing at clay pigeons or game birds in flight.

At this point, pilots were suffering increasingly from physical and mental exhaustion, being scrambled on average four times a day. The fitting of armour to enemy bombers, and the absence of trained section and squadron leaders to show inexperienced pilots how to kill without being killed, meant that casualties were higher than they had been in May and June, when fighting over France and Belgium. They were also higher now, due to the fact that much of the fighting was taking place over the Channel rather than over land, and so Controllers were instructed to not allow their fighters 'to pursue enemy raids unnecessarily far out to sea where we are liable to lose pilots through their being shot down into the sea'.[42]

Park considered his fighter defences were proving too good for the enemy. He was pleased that escorting enemy fighters were frequently too high to protect their bombers, allowing his Spitfires and Hurricanes to get in among the bomber formations. British fighters had also decimated the formations of Ju 87 Stuka dive bombers sent to attack targets across 11 Group's coastline. Their bloodcurdling banshee wail had terrorised British and Allied troops desperately seeking cover on the beaches at Dunkirk, but they were no match for Spitfires and Hurricanes, inspiring the 'like shooting rats in a barrel' scene in *The Battle of Britain*. However, while it appeared that Stukas had become the imperilled 'fly' to the Spitfires' and Hurricanes' predacious 'spider', they could still prove lethal to attacking fighters.

A case in point is that of Pilot Officer William 'Billy' Fiske, who flew with 601 (County of London) Squadron at 11 Group's Tangmere Sector station. The Neutrality Acts of the time officially forbade him as an American citizen from fighting in a foreign war, and so he enlisted in the Royal Air Force by pretending to be Canadian. Fiske was the first of nine

MAJOR CAMPAIGNS & ENGAGEMENTS

American pilots who would go on to fly in the Royal Air Force during the battle. 601 (County of London) was an Auxiliary outfit, dubbed the 'Millionaires' Squadron' because many of its pilots were wealthy and well connected. Fiske himself came from a wealthy American banking family, was a Cambridge Economics and History graduate, and had successfully led the American bobsled team in two Winter Olympics.

On 16 August, four squadrons, including 601, were scrambled by Uxbridge in response to a large raid approaching the Portsmouth area.[43] The squadrons that had been scrambled engaged a number of Ju 87 Stukas, about to dive bomb Tangmere itself. Fiske's Hurricane was hit by return fire from the rear gunner of one of the Stukas he was attacking. His Hurricane began to stream glycol, causing the engine to seize. He chose to remain with his stricken aircraft in order to preserve it, gliding over the airfield boundary and making a wheels up landing. His aircraft immediately burst into flames, severely burning Fiske from the waist down. Two nursing orderlies rushed to the machine, and despite bombs still falling all around them, they managed to extract him. Fiske was rushed to hospital and his injuries were initially thought not to be life threatening. The Hurricane he saved was repaired and returned to operational duties, but tragically the brave Fiske died of shock the following day, as a result of the injuries he had sustained. On 18 August, the Germans withdrew their much vaunted dive bombers, heralding a break of five days in intensive operations.

As for Fiske, he was buried in nearby Boxgrove Cemetery on 20 August, the coffin draped in both the Stars and Stripes and Union Flags. The funeral was conducted with full military honours and filmed.[44] As well as being the first American airman to fly with Fighter Command, Fiske was also the first American airman to die fighting for Britain. The United States had not yet entered the war and Fiske's sacrifice was a powerful exemplar to advocate joining the fight against fascism. In an uncustomary act, a memorial to Fiske was placed at St Paul's Cathedral in London and unveiled on 4 July 1941. At the presentation, Sir Archibald Sinclair, Secretary of State for Air, said: 'Here was a young man for whom life held much. Under no compulsion he came to fight for Britain. He came and he fought, and he died.' The plaque reads: 'An American citizen who died that England might live.'[45] It is poignant that the unveiling took place on American Independence Day, for a man who had fought so valiantly to preserve and was willing to give his life for Britain's independence.

Another pilot seeing action over southern England on 16 August was Flight Lieutenant James Brindley Nicolson of 249 Squadron flying a

ENEMY SIGHTED

Hurricane from RAF Boscombe Down, in the neighbouring 10 Group. Although the squadron had not been scrambled by 11 Group, it would engage the enemy over Southampton, an area covered by Uxbridge. Nicolson, who had never fired at the enemy before, would on this day become the only pilot fighting in the Battle of Britain, and the only member of Fighter Command throughout the course of the Second World War, to be awarded Britain's highest military decoration – the Victoria Cross, awarded for valour 'in the face of the enemy'.

His citation in the *London Gazette* read:

> During an engagement with the enemy near Southampton on 16 August 1940, Flight Lieutenant Nicolson's aircraft was hit by four cannon shells, two of which wounded him while another set fire to the gravity tank. When about to abandon his aircraft owing to flames in the cockpit, he sighted an enemy fighter. This he attacked and shot down, although as a result of staying in his burning aircraft he sustained serious burns to his hands, face, neck and legs. Flight Lieutenant Nicolson has always displayed great enthusiasm for air fighting and this incident shows that he possesses courage and determination of a high order. By continuing to engage the enemy after he had been wounded and his aircraft set on fire, he displayed exceptional gallantry and disregard for the safety of his own life.[46]

In an account provided to the BBC[47] as an anonymous Fighter Command pilot, Nicolson described the enemy aircraft as a Messerschmitt Me 110, but Luftwaffe records show no records of Me 110s operating in the area, but do show an Me 109 claiming two victories, which could have been Nicolson and another 249 Squadron aviator, Pilot Officer Martyn King, who was shot down and killed that day. In his broadcast, Nicolson also reported that he had been shot in the buttocks as he was about to fall to the ground in his parachute, and he blamed this on a member of the Home Guard who he had seen nearby. However this account is challenged by a witness who believes Nicolson may have been shot at by soldiers who were also on the ground.[48] To add further mystery, there is a view that the injury to his buttocks may be the result of splinters from the German cannon shells that had entered his cockpit and exploded around him. This is likely to have been the case as injury from rifle fire would have resulted in far larger wounds in that area of his body and is supported by the damage to his tunic, trousers, and Mae West life preserver, which are now displayed at the Tangmere Aviation Museum.

Regardless of whether Nicolson had been duelling with an Me 109 or Me 110, and regardless of how he had sustained the injuries to his buttock, it is clear that he had remained in his burning Hurricane to continue dogfighting, and in doing so had shown the bravery so typical of many other pilots across Fighter Command.

In the second phase of Park's report, the Luftwaffe turned its attacks to inland aerodromes and aircraft factories, industrial targets and residential areas. The daylight raids diminished markedly to the west of Sussex, and greatly increased over Kent, Thames Estuary and Essex. Night time raids continued, greatly increasing in strength. Either because the tactic had not proved profitable, or because the number of necessary aircraft were unavailable, diversionary attacks against different parts of the country were not made, and instead attacks were carried out across a wider front, using smaller bomber formations, escorted by a greater number of very high fighter screens.

The greater number of fighters meant that some bomber formations were boxed in by close fighter escorts, some of which flew slightly above to a flank or to the rear, others slightly above and ahead, with a third lot of fighters weaving between the sub-formations of bombers. 'One Squadron Leader described the appearance of one of these raids as like looking up the escalator at Piccadilly Circus.'[49]

On several occasions, raids of this type barged through Park's first and second screen and reached their objectives by sheer weight of numbers, even after having suffered numerous casualties to stragglers and flank sub-formations. On others, smallish formations of long range bombers deliberately left their fighter escort immediately on being engaged by defending fighters, and on losing height, they proceeded towards targets in the south or south-west of London, without any close fighter escort. Most of these raids were engaged by Park's rear rank of fighters, either when about to bomb or when retreating, and consequently suffered heavy casualties.

As the Luftwaffe penetrated further inland, 11 Group adopted the tactics of meeting the enemy formations in pairs of squadrons, while calling on 10 and 12 Groups to provide close cover for Park's aerodromes near London and for the suburban aircraft factories to the west of London. This allowed the Senior Controller at Uxbridge to meet the enemy further forward, in greater numbers, while giving a measure of close protection against enemy raids which might otherwise elude him at various heights. It was therefore possible, on some occasions, for him to direct a wing of two Spitfire squadrons to take on the fighter escort, while a further wing of two Hurricanes would attack the bomber formation. Although the intention was to meet raids nearer to the coast, the use of forward airfields at Hawkinge and Manston became rarer at this point, owing to the heavy scale of attack to which they were subjected, and the fact that squadrons were required to go into action in pairs and were consequently based together in inland aerodromes. German Intelligence misread the decision as relating to the forward aerodromes and wrongly assumed that 'the main forces of Fighter Command had been withdrawn to the area surrounding London, and the main strength of the German attack was shifted accordingly'.[50]

The heavy fighting was taking its toll on squadrons operating across 11 Group, but the stark truth was that they could not easily be extricated and replaced with fresh units. Fighter Command simply did not have sufficient squadrons or pilots, especially experienced ones. Dowding had introduced a policy of rotating units as they became numerically and physically exhausted, replacing them with those from his Northern Groups, but this did not fully address the situation. Newly arrived squadrons, with their inexperienced pilots, were suffering the worst attrition level, even though they were the strongest in numbers. As a result, resting squadrons were often returned to the south-east of England before they had adequately revitalised and regrouped.

Park considered the results following combats during this phase, to be numerically satisfactory. However, he wanted far more bombers to be destroyed than fighters, but a number of factors had conspired against this. Goering's instruction for fighters to fly closer to the bombers they were chaperoning meant they were engaging more closely, and so reduced the number of bombers turned back or shot down.[51] It seemed to Park that the Luftwaffe's bombers were more heavily armoured than previously, were operating in greater numbers, so providing mutual protection, and were generally being flown more proficiently as their crews became more experienced. However, a contrary view is expressed by Tantum and Hoffschmidt in *The Rise and Fall of the German Air Force*, who considered that bombers at this stage of the battle were beginning 'to suffer more heavily, both in losses and in damaged aircraft. Their own armament was not sufficient even to discourage fighter attack.'[52] Regardless of the situation in relation to bombers, it is evident that in engaging them, Fighter

Hawker Hurricanes scrambling
A pair of 501 Squadron Hurricanes taking off from Hawkinge in 11 Group on 16 August 1940. This was the day Churchill had visited the Bunker at Uxbridge and was moved to utter his famous 'Never in the field of history' statement, later to be incorporated into his speech before parliament. Bomb damage can be seen to number five hanger in the background, which had been caused during a raid four days earlier by the Me 110s of Erprobungsgruppe 210. (Public Domain)

Supermarine Spitfires scrambling
Three Spitfires of 65 Squadron taking off from Hornchurch in 11 Group in August 1940. After leaving the ground, Spitfires would take around fourteen minutes to reach an operating altitude of 20,000 feet. Hurricanes, being somewhat slower, would take around sixteen minutes. Height was vital when engaging the enemy, so Fighter Command's aircraft had to be airborne within five minutes when scrambled from 'Readiness' state. (Public Domain)

View from Heinkel He 111
The view as seen by the pilot and nose gunner of a Heinkel He 111, flying in formation over the English countryside during a bombing raid. (National Museum of Denmark)

Sector airfield being bombed
A view of 64 Squadron's Spitfires and their shelters at Kenley in 11 Group, under attack by a Do 17 bomber of KG76 on 18 August 1940. The picture was taken from the aircraft flown by Rolf von Pebal as it passed over the northern part of the airfield. This is a heavily retouched version that was published in *Der Adler*; it was used as German propaganda to present a more dramatic scene. The two large clouds of smoke nearest the camera were not on the original. The smaller clouds beyond are probably the rest of gunfire from the Do 17 flown by Gunther Unger as it engaged a machine-gun post on the ground. (Historic Military Press)

Hawker Hurricanes returning after combat
During periods of intensive enemy action, fighter pilots were expected to fly up to six sorties in a day. Seen here are a pair of 32 Squadron Hurricanes landing at Biggin Hill in 11 Group in August 1940, during the Battle of Britain, to rearm and refuel and, very likely, to re-engage the enemy. (Public Domain)

Hawker Hurricane refuelling after combat
As a general rule of thumb, defending fighters had to return in around sixty minutes to refuel. Seen here, a Hurricane of 32 Squadron has returned and is being refuelled at Biggin Hill in August 1940. The pilot is sat waiting in his cockpit, indicating that he will most likely have to take to the sky imminently. (Public Domain)

Supermarine Spitfire refuelling after combat
Ground crew at work refuelling a 19 Squadron Spitfire at Fowlmere in 12 Group in September 1940. Note the Albion fuel bowser with its three overhead booms, which would allow simultaneous fuelling of three aircraft. (Public Domain)

Supermarine Spitfire rearming after combat
Fighter Command's day fighters had enough ammunition to provide around eighteen to twenty seconds of fire, normally in several shorter bursts. Seen here is a Spitfire flown by Pilot Officer David Moore Crook of 609 (West Riding) Squadron being tended to by ground crew. The image has the following handwritten caption: 'Rearming my Spitfire after the fight above Portland, 13 August 1940'. (Public Domain)

Hawker Hurricanes taxiing to take off
Hurricanes of 32 Squadron pictured taxiing for take-off at Hawkinge in 11 Group on 29 July 1940. The centre aircraft, serial number N2459 and squadron code letters GZ-C, was normally flown by Pilot Officer 'Grubby' Grice. It was shot down in flames on 15 August over the English Channel, with Grice at the controls, during an engagement with enemy fighters. Grice suffered severe burns and subsequently became a Sector Controller at Biggin Hill, Northolt, North Weald, Tangmere, and then Group Controller at Uxbridge. (Public Domain)

Gun-camera showing Messerschmitt Me 109 being shot down
A still taken from the camera gun footage of the Spitfire flown by Pilot Officer David Moore Crook of 609 (West Riding) Squadron on 30 September 1940. In his memoir, he wrote: 'The Me 109 on fire and turning on his back just before diving into the sea.' (Public Domain)

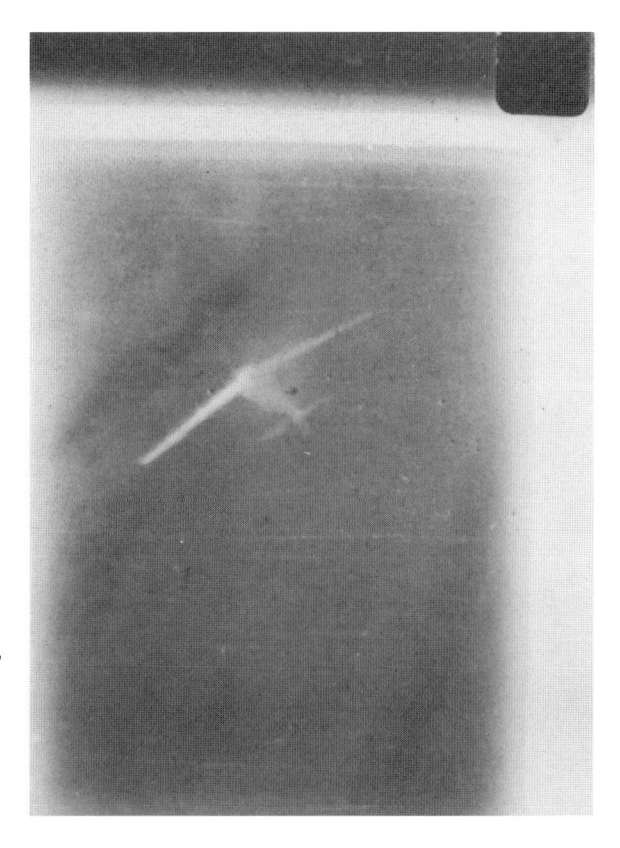

Wreckage of Dornier Do 17 shot down over London
The wreckage of a Dornier Do 17Z at Victoria Station. This aircraft, F1+FH from 1/KG 76, which had taken off earlier from its base at Nivelles, Belgium, with 27-year-old Oberleutnant Robert Zehbe at the controls, was brought down by Sergeant Ray Holmes of 504 Squadron, flying from Hendon in 11 Group. (Historic Military Press)

Wreckage of Heinkel He 111 shot down over Kent
The wreckage of Heinkel He 111 Werke 5680 on fire at Burmarsh, Kent, on 11 September 1940, during the Battle of Britain. The aircraft had been shot down by anti-aircraft fire over London and force-landed at 16.00 hours. The crew of Unteroffizier Hofmann, Feldwebel Heinz Friedrich (pilot), Feldwebel George, Unteroffizier Dreyer and Unteroffizier Stirnemann were all captured. One of the crew can be seen being carried away on a stretcher. Note the triumphantly circling Spitfire in the air and anti-invasion poles in the ground. (Historic Military Press)

Wreckage of Messerschmitt Me 109 shot down over Sussex
Downed German aircraft appeared to litter the English countryside across Essex, Kent, Sussex, Hampshire, and Surrey. Messerschmitt Me 109 E-1, Werke 5068, crashed at New Salts Farm, Shoreham, Sussex, at 07.10 hours on 13 August 1940. This was the aircraft of Oberleutnant Paul Temme, Gruppe Adjutant of I/JG 2. (Public Domain)

Aerial battle over London
For the first time in modern history, the British public were witness to a major battle taking place around them. Here the photograph captures combat over London. Vapour trails fill an otherwise clear sky over Saint Pauls Cathedral, in the middle of, or immediately after, a significant skirmish during the Battle of Britain. (Air Force Museum of New Zealand)

Blitz on London
A Heinkel He 111 bomber seen here over the River Thames on 7 September 1940, during the first large scale raid on London. The bombing on this day signalled the beginning of the Blitz. Redirecting attacks away from 11 Group's Sector airfields would prove to be a strategic blunder for the Luftwaffe. (Shutterstock)

London ablaze from the air
The first day of the Blitz on the Capital. The original caption dated 23 September 1940 states: 'German bombs fire London dock area. German sources say that this aerial picture shows the effects "of the first big, concerted attack of the German air force on London Dock and industry districts, September 7." The fire on the lower left of the picture is described as burning in the mills at the Victoria Docks.' (Historic Military Press)

Right: **London ablaze from the ground**
Firefighters of the National Fire Service at work on a fire in Britannia Row, off Essex Road, London, following a Luftwaffe bombing raid. (Historic Military Press)

Below: **Fighter Command on the offensive**
Ground crew rearming a Spitfire of 485 (New Zealand) Squadron, believed to be at Redhill in 11 Group. It is being prepared for an offensive sortie over France on 22 July 1941. (Air Force Museum of New Zealand)

Supporting the raid on Dieppe
With his head bandaged, Flight Sergeant Robert Mehew 'Zip' Zobell of 401 Squadron (Royal Canadian Air Force), is pictured by his damaged Spitfire on his return from a sortie over Dieppe during Operation *Jubilee*. The original caption states that: 'his only complaint was that the medical officer would not allow him to fly during the rest of the day'. (Library and Archives Canada)

Supporting the D-Day landings, Operation *Overlord*
D-Day operations at Ford in Sussex. Spitfires of 453 Squadron, (Royal Australian Air Force), are started up for a sortie over Normandy. Both aircraft are carrying 44-gallon long-range fuel tanks under the fuselage to extend their range over the continent, and both are displaying white and black D-Day or invasion stripes, painted to avoid friendly fire incidents. (Public Domain)

Above: **V1 launched against London**
Released to the press on 3 August 1944, this image shows a V1 'Doodlebug' flying bomb, diving onto London. The buildings in the foreground are the Royal Courts of Justice (Law Courts) on the north side of the Strand. It is stated in the Blitz: Then and Now, that this V1 fell on Wild Street on 28 June 1944, this being when the Peabody Buildings were struck. (NARA)

Right: **Engaging a V1**
A grainy image taken on 22 September 1944, capturing the moment a Spitfire deliberately flies alongside a V1, to tip its wing to destabilise it and cause it to crash. (Everett Collection/Shutterstock)

Left: **The more lethal V2**
The moment that a German V2 rocket is fired. Fuelled by a propellent feed system, it was the world's first ballistic missile. It was too fast to be intercepted once in flight and had to be destroyed whilst still on the ground. (NARA)

Below: **Gloster Meteor – Britain's first operational jet fighter**
A Gloster Meteor pictured at the very end of the war. These modern fighter jets did not see action against German jet aircraft, but were used effectively against the V1 Doodlebug. (National Museum of Denmark)

External view of Bunker
A view of the main entrance to the underground Operations Room at Uxbridge. Its nondescript appearance camouflaging the world-leading technology that lay beneath. Note the metal blast-proof door, designed to protect against assault by enemy ground forces and bomb blast. (Dilip Amin)

First half of main staircase leading into the Bunker
A view from the 'L' shaped half landing, looking up towards the guard room, which visitors would have had to pass before descending the Bunker's steep staircase. Note the original black conduits, which conveyed electricity, water, sewage, telephone, and teleprinter lines to and from the Bunker. (Dilip Amin)

Left: **Second half of main staircase leading into the Bunker**
A view from the ring corridor at the bottom of the staircase, looking up towards the 'L' shaped half landing. Note the cream-coloured metal ducting, which forms part of the Bunker's air ventilation unit. (Dilip Amin)

Below: **Operations room looking at tote board from controller cabin**
A view through the curved glass of the Senior Controller's cabin, looking down across the floor of the Operations Room. Note the plotting table with its original map of Southern England, and the illuminated panel wall showing the states of 11 Group's fighter squadrons, as they were at 11.30 hours on 15 September 1940, Battle of Britain Day. (Dilip Amin)

Blocks and arrows
The angular wooden blocks placed on the general situation map depict both enemy and friendly aircraft. They were arranged so that the tilted side faced the gallery, making it more visible to the Senior Controller. Those shown reflect the situation as it was at 11.30 hours on 15 September 1940. Raids 'Hostile Zero Four', 'Zero Six', and 'One Zero', are Luftwaffe bombers and fighters crossing the English coastline over Kent. The blocks with rectangular yellow counters marked '72', '92', and '603', are the Spitfire squadrons sent to engage with the Messerschmitt fighter escort, whilst those marked '253' and '501', are the first pair of Hurricane squadrons that will carry out head-on attacks on the temporarily unescorted bombers. (Dilip Amin)

Tote board showing multi-colour and all-red lights
Each light spot on the squadron indicator panel represents a 'section' of three aircraft, identified as 'red section', 'yellow section', 'blue section', and 'green section'. Two 'sections' formed a 'flight' of six aircraft, 'A flight' and 'B flight', and when both 'flights' operated together, they formed a squadron. The number of lights illuminated, indicated to the Senior Controller how many fighters he had available to him. When the enemy were sighted, the different coloured light spots would all change to red, informing him that engagements were now taking place. (Dilip Amin)

Sector clock
A Sector clock was used not only to indicate the time, but also to determine the 'age' of enemy plots on the plotting table. This was achieved by correlating the colour of the triangular segment on the clock that the minute hand was on, with the colour of the arrows nearest to the raid block. The colour of the segments on the clock face changes every five minutes, alternating between 'Blue', 'Red', and 'Yellow'. This Sector clock is mounted in the centre of the illuminated panel wall in the Battle of Britain Bunker and the minute hand is shown as still being inside the 'Blue' segment. The colour of the arrows nearest to the raid blocks on the table is also 'Blue', so the position of the enemy raid as shown is no more than five minutes old. (Dilip Amin)

Keith Park statue
A towering statue of Air Vice-Marshal Keith Park, in his flying boots, helmet, and life preserver, stands prominently outside the Battle of Britain Bunker Museum and Visitor Centre. Park, described as the 'Defender of London' by German Intelligence, had led 11 Group magnificently during the Battle of Britain, a period in history which Winston Churchill had reasoned was Britain's 'finest hour'. (Dilip Amin)

MAJOR CAMPAIGNS & ENGAGEMENTS

Command was incurring a high and unsustainable casualty rate among pilots and machines.

On 20 August, having visited the underground Bunker at Uxbridge four days earlier, Churchill paid tribute to those aircrew, fighting so valiantly to prevent an invasion of the British Isles:

> We hope, we believe that we shall be able to continue the air struggle indefinitely and as long as the enemy pleases, and the longer it continues the more rapid will be our approach, first towards that parity, and then into that superiority in the air, upon which in a large measure the decision of the war depends ... The gratitude of every home in our Island, in our Empire, and indeed throughout the world, except in the abodes of the guilty, goes out to the British airmen who, undaunted by odds, unwearied in their constant challenge and mortal danger, are turning the tide of world war by their prowess and by their devotion. Never in the field of human conflict was so much owed by so many to so few. All hearts go out to the fighter pilots, whose brilliant actions we see with our own eyes day after day.[53]

Many people hearing Churchill's extolment to 'the few', believe that he was directing it towards those aircrew flying in Fighter Command, defending Britain from invasion. This is only partially correct, what is less widely known is that, within his speech on 20 August, he was also paying tribute to those aircrew flying in Bomber Command, taking the fight to the enemy:

> but we must never forget that all the time, night after night, month after month, our bomber squadrons travel far into Germany, find their targets in the darkness by the highest navigational skill, aim their attacks, often under the heaviest fire, often with serious loss, with deliberate, careful discrimination, and inflict shattering blows upon the whole of the technical and war-making structure of the Nazi power. On no part of the Royal Air Force does the weight of the war fall more heavily than on the daylight bombers who will play an invaluable part in the case of invasion and whose unflinching zeal it has been necessary in the meanwhile on numerous occasions to restrain.

ENEMY SIGHTED

So far during the battle, Bomber Command had been attacking industrial and military targets, vital to Hitler's war effort. In the view of Air Chief Marshal Sir Charles Portal, the Commander in Chief of Bomber Command, bombers remained 'the one directly offensive weapon in the whole of Britain's armoury'.[54]

Churchill had already enquired, towards the end of July, that if London was attacked, could the Royal Air Force respond with a raid on Berlin? Events the following month would soon put Bomber Command to the test and, as a result, change the course of the battle. On the night of 24 August, 'bombs were dropped over the City of London and the West India Docks'.[55] Hitler, at this point, had not authorised the bombing of London itself, and it is uncertain whether this incident was accidental or not. Regardless, it set in motion events that would have far reaching effect. Churchill seized the opportunity afforded by the Luftwaffe raid, ordering an immediate reprisal against Berlin. Bomber Command carried out its first raid on the German capital on the night of 25 August, attacking targets in and around Berlin.

There was a critical period between 28 August and 5 September when the damage to Sector stations and the ground organisation was having a serious effect on the fighting efficiency of 11 Group's fighter squadrons, who could not be given the same good technical and administrative service as previously.

Park's report reveals that contrary to general belief and official reports, the enemy's bombing attacks by day had caused extensive damage to five of 11 Group's forward aerodromes, and also to six of its seven Sector stations. The damage to forward aerodromes was so severe that Manston and Lympne were on several occasions quite unfit for operating fighters for days on end. Biggin Hill was so severely damaged that only one squadron could operate from there, and the remaining two squadrons had to be placed under the control of adjacent Sectors for over a week. Had the enemy continued its heavy attacks against the adjacent Sectors and knocked out their Operations Rooms or telephone communications, the fighter defences of London would have been in a parlous state during the last critical phase, when heavy attacks were being directed against the capital.

Sector Operations Rooms were put out of action on three occasions, either by direct hits or by damage to telephone cables, and all Sectors took into use their Emergency Operations Rooms, which were not only too small to house the essential personnel but had never been provided with the proper scale of telephone landlines to enable normal operation of three squadrons per Sector.

MAJOR CAMPAIGNS & ENGAGEMENTS

This period of the battle is described in an 11 Group report prepared after the war, as having seen 'much greater intensity and almost exclusively against 11 Group air fields'.[56] One of the worst effected Sector stations was RAF Biggin Hill, guarding the southern approaches to the capital. The 'Bump', as it was affectionately known, was attacked on no less than twelve occasions over a five-month period between August and January, underscoring its importance to London's defence. On 30 August, the Germans bombed it twice. The morning raid caused damage to the airfield, hindering the ability of its squadrons to take off and land, but it was the second visit that proved to be especially devastating. A relatively small number of Ju 88 bombers inflicted widespread damage across the Sector station, many buildings were destroyed and the supply of gas, electricity and water was cut off. Crucially, the vital telephone lines necessary for essential services across the station to speak with each other, and those required for the Operations Rooms at Biggin Hill and Uxbridge to communicate with each other, were severed.

Section Officer Felicity Hanbury, who had taken cover during the raid, now re-emerged to a scene of absolute devastation. She made her way towards what had moments ago been another WAAF shelter trench to offer support and, as the officer responsible for the 250 WAAFs on the station, coordinate a response in the aftermath of the attack. She could smell gas but, unthinkingly, lit a cigarette to calm her frayed nerves. Jolted by someone shouting, 'Put that cigarette out before you blow the place to bits!', Hanbury extinguished her cigarette and continued on her way, passing by the body of a young girl on the ground.[57] The death toll at Biggin Hill on that day would be a staggering thirty-nine people killed.

It is likely that the famous, 'Put that cigarette out! The mains have gone, can't you smell gas?', scene in *The Battle of Britain* was re-enacted by Susannah York's character, Section Officer Maggie Harvey, as a tribute to Felicity Hanbury's actions on this day.

The aerial intruders returned twice on the following day. One of the bombs dropped during the second raid fell just outside the Sector Operations Room, cutting through temporary cables and telephone lines that had been rigged up following the previous day's raids. All contact across Biggin Hill was lost, but the direct line with 11 Group's Operations Room was still functioning. The threads forming the spider's web were still holding, but they were now being severely strained.

WAAF Sergeant Helen Turner, who had remained at the switchboard despite the obvious risk to her safety, was forced to the ground by a colleague just in the nick of time as a 500 lb bomb entered through the roof and exploded, sending deadly shards across the Operations Room. Another WAAF, Corporal Elspeth Henderson, responsible for holding the direct line with Uxbridge open, had also remained at her post. Knocked down by the blast, she was helped to her feet by the Station Commander who had just walked in and was himself cut by flying debris. Picking up, refilling and lighting his pipe, which had been forced from his mouth by the explosion, he congratulated Henderson on her composure. She replied stoically, 'There wasn't much else I could do anyway, was there, sir? After all, I joined the WAAFs 'cause I wanted to see a bit of life.'[58]

A third WAAF telephonist, Sergeant Joan Mortimer, was on duty in the Station Armoury at the time of the raid. She remained at her switchboard, relaying messages to the defence posts around the airfield, even though she was surrounded by several tons of high explosives. The airfield itself was still being bombed when Mortimer ran out with a bundle of red flags to warn returning pilots, by marking where bombs had landed but not exploded. Even when one exploded nearby, knocking her off her feet, she got up and carried on.

The actions of Hanbury, Turner, Henderson and Mortimer showed beyond doubt that those who had warned against employing women in such highly pressurised environments had been utterly wrong. Hanbury was awarded the first Military MBE for 'setting a magnificent example of courage and devotion to duty during heavy bombing'. Turner, Henderson and Mortimer were each awarded the Military Medal, for their courage, their cool, calm, collected conduct, and the example they set to others that day.

The Luftwaffe was putting Fighter Command under severe pressure and while it can be said that the defending forces were fighting for their survival, it is also clear that the aggressors had so far failed to achieve their objective, the destruction of Fighter Command in the south of England within four days and were failing in their objective of eliminating the Royal Air Force within four weeks.

At the beginning of September, Hermann Goering met the Luftwaffe High Command in The Hague to discuss how the objective of defeating the British was progressing, or not progressing. There was no collective view to be found as to how many Hurricanes and Spitfires remained available to Fighter Command. The disparity between Kesselring and Sperrle, his two main Luftflotten Commanders, appeared to be as wide as the English Channel their bombers and fighters had to traverse each day. Kesselring

MAJOR CAMPAIGNS & ENGAGEMENTS

thought Fighter Command was finished, whereas Sperrle claimed it had a thousand aeroplanes still remaining. Luftwaffe Intelligence agreed with neither, reporting that the figure had gone as low as 100 at the end of August, but now risen to around 350. The truth is that at the end of August, when Fighter Command was supposed to be at its lowest ebb, it had in fact an operational strength of 670 fighters. The real threat to Fighter Command, the loss of experienced pilots, was not considered.[59] Without having the measure of their enemy, the Germans were unable to form an accurate shared understanding of its potency, and therefore they persevered with their plan, which they felt sure would deliver them victory over the British.

Adolf Hitler, incensed by the previous week's attack on Berlin, directed his Luftwaffe on 2 September to stop bombing Fighter Command's airfields, and instead ordered that 'attacks should be made on the populations and defences of the large cities, particularly London, by day and night.'[60] Targeting the civilian population in prominent cities, or the mere threat of doing so, had worked well for the Germans in Poland, Holland and Denmark. It was hoped that the British would follow suit and sue for peace, but this was not to be the case. In reality, the Germans had made a catastrophic blunder. Fighter Command had not yet been destroyed, although the constant attacks on its airfields and attrition of experienced pilots was slowly crushing it. By redirecting their attacks away from the airfields, the Germans had given Fighter Command breathing space; space which would be used to recover and regather, in time for the final phase of the battle. It is as if the Luftwaffe had had its foot pressed on Fighter Command's throat, and just as it was beginning to suffocate, the attacker lifted his foot and allowed the defender to breathe again.

The third phase commenced on 6 September, with three major daytime Luftwaffe raids over the Thames Estuary and Kent, resulting in six of 11 Group's pilots being killed or reported missing and one wounded. It was also on this day that the Bunker at Uxbridge was visited by their Majesties, King George VI and Queen Elizabeth, who witnessed first-hand the intense fighting taking place over southern England.[61] Enemy activity continued into the night, resulting in a considerable number of bombs being dropped across the Lower Thames and south-west, south and south-east London.

On 7 September, the Luftwaffe carried out their first heavy daylight raid on London, with a large mass attack on the Thames Estuary and the London Docks. Sixteen squadrons were scrambled by Uxbridge to engage around 380 enemy aircraft, resulting in nine of 11 Group's pilots being lost on that day. This raid was followed throughout the night by further waves of bombers, attacking the London Docks and parts of southern England.[62] This heralded the beginning of the 'Blitz', a protracted period of bombing towns and cities that would continue for nine months, and cost 43,500 civilians their lives.

Park speculated that the change in target, from airfields to areas of large population, was perhaps because the enemy's timetable called for it, or because intelligence staff were persuaded, as had happened in Poland, that Britain's fighter defence was sufficiently weakened by the previous month's attacks. What he could be certain of was that the change had saved his Sector stations from becoming inoperative and enabled them to carry on operations, although at a much lower standard of efficiency.

The Luftwaffe's strategy here was to overwhelm and confuse the British defences, and they employed a number of different tactics to achieve this. The Stuka dive bombers, previously withdrawn after having been mauled by Fighter Command's Hurricanes and Spitfires, now reappeared to attack coastal objectives and shipping off Essex and Kent. These attacks were made under cover of the massed raids carried out by long-range bombers against inland objectives. Other diversionary raids were carried out by formations of fighters in advance of the massed bombers and their close fighter escort making their way to London. Those larger raids were sent over in two or three distinct waves, following one another at about twenty minute intervals, with the whole attack lasting up to one hour. Each inland wave consisted of a number of raids of twenty to forty bombers with an equal number of fighters in close escort, and covered at a much higher altitude by larger formations of more fighters. The majority of the raids were at a higher altitude, above 15,000 ft (4,572 metres), in bright sunlit skies that made it practically impossible for the Observer Corps to give accurate information, as to the strength or type of the enemy formations flying overhead.

The Germans must have hoped that by using large successive waves of aircraft they could bludgeon their way past Fighter Command, or that employing diversionary attacks would stretch the defender's finite resources, allowing them to exploit any unprotected airspace to get through and press home attacks on London. The deployment of fighter aircraft, although assisted by technology and calculus, was still an 'art', and therefore interception could not always be guaranteed. Interceptions were also not being made for reasons other than the volume and spread of attacks. Height was one, as radar became less reliable when surveilling high-flying aircraft, and information passed by the Observer Corps on

MAJOR CAMPAIGNS & ENGAGEMENTS

high-flying raiders was often imprecise and incomplete. Another was the disruption to the communication network, caused by telephone lines being damaged during air raids, or being temporarily dislocated during the move to emergency Sector Operations Rooms. Mention should also be made here of the disruption caused to operations, following the dispersal and relocation of non-essential personnel from Sector stations, necessary to safeguard them against future Luftwaffe attacks.

To counter this threat, Senior Controllers at Uxbridge developed an arrangement of engaging the first wave of a large raid with six 'Readiness' squadrons operating in pairs, with Spitfires flying higher and Hurricanes flying lower to engage bombers. A further eight squadrons would be held to meet the second wave, half way to the coast. The remaining squadrons would be used to cover aircraft factories and aerodromes, or if necessary be thrown in to meet a third wave. In the event of this being the case, then reinforcements from 10 Group and 12 Group would be called upon to protect the aerodromes and vital aircraft factories in the north and west of 11 Group's area. Crucially for 11 Group, there was a willingness among its leadership to constantly monitor and refine the new dispositions, as on 7 September when Park informed his Controllers:

> it is evident that during the past week some enemy bomber formations have proceeded uninterrupted to their inland objectives. This has happened on numerous occasions when we had from twelve to twenty squadrons despatched to intercept and to cover aerodromes. The reason is mainly that our fighters are patrolling so high that they are normally becoming heavily engaged with the enemy fighter screen, flying above 20,000 ft [6,096 metres]. On one occasion yesterday, only seven out of eighteen squadrons despatched, engaged the enemy. On another occasion on the same day, seven out of seventeen squadrons engaged the enemy. It is obvious that some of our Controllers are ordering squadrons intended to engage enemy bombers, to patrol too high. When Group order a squadron to 16,000 ft [4,877 metres], Sector Controller in his superior knowledge, adds on 1,000 or 2,000, and the squadron adds on another 2,000 in the vain hope that they will not have any enemy fighters above them. The nett result has been that daily some of the enemy bomber formations slip in under 15,000 ft [4,572 metres], frequently without any fighter escort, and

ENEMY SIGHTED

bomb their objectives, doing serious damage as at Brooklands. In fact the majority of enemy bomber formations have only been intercepted after they have dropped their bombs and are on the way out.[63]

Here was the challenge of defending within a three dimensional plane. Should Fighter Command's pilots fly higher to gain a tactical advantage when engaging enemy fighters, or should they fly lower so as to prevent enemy bombers sneaking through? It was work in progress and lessons were being learnt as the fighting continued. Apart from the difficulty of determining which formations meant business, and which were feints, Fighter Command had to discover which formations carried bombs and which did not. To increase the proportion of interceptions, 11 Group decided to employ high-flying scouts, single Spitfires flying at maximum height, to shadow enemy raids and report their observations immediately by VHF radio. A special Flight was organised for this purpose and it was later recommended that the Spitfires should be employed in pairs, for reasons of security, and that the flight should become a squadron. A special receiving set was erected at Uxbridge so that reports might be obtained without any delay in transmission from the Sector Receiving station.[64]

Heavy concentrations of attacks by large numbers of single aircraft followed the day attacks. These methods of attack were followed on 9 and 11 September, when the sky was sufficiently clear of clouds. These attacks did not penetrate so well or do as much damage as on the 7th and enemy losses were consistently heavy. Of the twenty-one squadrons scrambled from Uxbridge on 9 and 11 September, nineteen successfully intercepted the enemy's raids, although one heavy raid of about forty to fifty bombers broke through and reached East London before being attacked by fighters. The more highly developed tactics of concentration and interception, and the adoption of head-on beam attacks against bombers, were inflicting a heavier proportion of German losses during this period than the previous. 11 Group was, however, still haemorrhaging pilots, though it was decided not to replace squadrons which had been hammered for the time being, but to keep them filled up to a minimum of sixteen operationally trained pilots by transfers from Northern Groups which, being less heavily engaged and more remote from the area of combat, were able to train new pilots from the training units to operational standard.

Park concluded his update to Dowding, dated 12 September, by summarising that:

MAJOR CAMPAIGNS & ENGAGEMENTS

at the time of writing, confidence is felt in our ability to hold the enemy by day and to prevent his obtaining superiority in the air over our territory, unless he greatly increases the scale or intensity of his attacks. Every endeavour is now being made to improve our fighter defences by night. To achieve this aim will require not only better equipment, but greater specialisation of pilots on night flying and fighting.

Although it was being stretched far beyond what was expected, the 'spider's web' was holding.

On 13 September, enemy aircraft dropped bombs across London and the south-east of England during the night, following up in the daytime with around seventy-five raids across 11 Group, mostly by single aircraft. London was still the main focus of their attacks and bombs were dropped on Trafalgar Square, Downing Street and Buckingham Palace. Cloud made it more difficult to intercept the enemy, resulting in only four bombers being damaged over the area covered from Uxbridge, but with no British losses.[65]

Uxbridge was a twenty-four hour Operations Room and staff working there continued to be tested throughout the night and day. London was again attacked by the Luftwaffe during the early hours of 14 September. On this occasion, a Blenheim night fighter of 25 Squadron, operating out of 11 Group's North Weald Sector Station, was tasked by Uxbridge to intercept a lone raider. The searchlights were able to hold the enemy aircraft, a Heinkel He 111, for twenty minutes and it was successfully brought down by the Blenheim crew.[66] The pressure continued into the day light hours. A number of attacks were carried out by single aircraft against seaside resorts, to test, confuse and exhaust the defences. Cloud hampered the Hurricanes and Spitfires as they hunted their prey, resulting in only three interceptions being achieved out of thirty-two ordered by Uxbridge. Then, later in the day, came the two large raids. The first, with around 200 bombers and fighters crossing the south-east coast and making for the outskirts of West London. Again cloud played a determining factor, with only five of 11 Group's squadrons out of the seventeen detailed, intercepting the enemy. The second main raid, with around 200 aircraft, appeared to have many features in common with the previous one. Around sixty managed to reach London and some ninety loitered over Kent. Of the nineteen squadrons ordered up by Uxbridge, eight successfully intercepted their designated target. The final tally was fourteen enemy aircraft claimed

ENEMY SIGHTED

destroyed, one probably destroyed and ten damaged, for the loss of three 11 Group pilots killed or missing.[67]

This, then, had been the penultimate day before the Luftwaffe launched its final all-out attack against Britain, hoping to lure Fighter Command's few remaining Hurricanes and Spitfires into the air, in a climactic, but futile, gesture of defiance before the master race. The final attack was, however, premised on flawed intelligence. Flawed because a number of inaccurate assumptions had led to a gross underestimation of the number of Hurricanes and Spitfires that would in fact rise into the sky.

First, the number of 'kills' claimed by Luftwaffe pilots was far in excess of the actual number of British fighters downed. This confusion, which occurred on both sides, is understandable when, in the midst of chaotic dogfights, pilots share only but a fleeting glance of their adversary. Second, British Spitfires and Hurricanes were failing to engage the large 'fighter only' formations sent over Britain to entice Fighter Command into the air. The Germans did not realise that Fighter Controllers, in order to conserve their precious resource, were under instructions to ignore enemy fighters and concentrate instead on the bombers. This disposition was portrayed in the 'Leave the flaming fighters! It's the bloody bombers we want!' scene in *The Battle of Britain*. Third, they did not realise that Spitfires and Hurricanes lost during the battle were being replaced faster by the British than the Germans themselves were able to replace the downed Messerschmitts, now scattered across southern England, or laying at the bottom of the English Channel. Finally, it was also flawed because Luftwaffe Intelligence Officers felt it safer to tell the acrimonious and delusional Goering what he wanted to hear, rather than what he needed to hear.

The combined effect of these erroneous assumptions was that those in the higher echelons of the Luftwaffe mistakenly believed the next day's raid over London would force Fighter Command to commit its last remaining fighters, in defence of the capital. For the Luftwaffe to win the battle, it needed to destroy Fighter Command. For Fighter Command to win the battle, it simply needed to continue to exist.

Chapter 15

Battle of Britain Day

'The Prelude'

Sunday 15 September 1940 will be a day of great significance. The orders sent to 11 Group's Sector stations from the underground Operations Room at Uxbridge, and the consequential engagements over London and south-east England, will be monumental. The date, now immortalised as 'Battle of Britain Day', will not only alter the outcome of the battle, but also the course of the war itself. The Luftwaffe, believing Fighter Command is down to its last few fighters, plans to deliver a decisive blow, leaving the Royal Air Force too weak to ward off invasion. By the end of this day, they will realise that their belief is misplaced.

As the morning progresses, the clear blue sky, which had earlier covered much of southern England, is now replete with layers of cloud. Weather will play a major part in the day's aerial battle. It has already been said that enemy aircraft could be over London within twenty minutes of their first being picked up by British Radar stations, and on some occasions, they had dropped bombs on south-east London seventeen minutes after the first radar plots were given. Today, the wind speed at 18,000 ft (5,486 metres) above England, is travelling at 96 mph (154 kph). Crucially, it is coming from the north-west,[1] meaning that any German aircraft approaching London from the Pas De Calais will be flying directly into wind, causing their ground speed to decrease, and so giving the Senior Controller at Uxbridge more time to position his squadrons.

Above ground, worshippers have congregated in churches to pray, much as they had done during peace time some twelve months before. Below ground, at Uxbridge to the west of London, another group of people have assembled – not to worship, but to keep vigil against attacks from the air. These sentinels, secreted within 11 Group's underground Bunker, are working assiduously to keep the Germans at bay, denying them the air superiority they need before an invasion can be launched. They have performed this exacting role, continuously and with distinction, throughout

ENEMY SIGHTED

the greatest aerial battle in history, which has now entered its fourth gruelling month.

Plotters and Tellers, essential artisans within Britain's integrated air defence system, stand poised and huddled around the large plotting table, overseeing the general situation map of southern England and north-west France. The women are primed, ready to receive reports filtered by others in Fighter Command's Headquarters at Bentley Priory. These despatches, emanating from a combination of Radar stations looking out to sea, and Observer Corps Posts looking inland, will come thick and fast. They will betray the presence of Luftwaffe aircraft, as they encroach British airspace and prompt a coordinated, lethal response from Britain's defensive aerial network.

A raised dais accommodates more operatives, who watch the plots being placed and moved around the table and then communicate information onwards. The Senior Controller, whose role it is to engage with and destroy the enemy, is sat in a glass-fronted gallery above them, which affords him a commanding view of the map below and an array of coloured lights on the wall opposite. As they dance around and glow, they reveal the status and availability of 11 Group's fighter squadrons on this Sunday morning. The Senior Controller has available to him a total of 375 pilots and 254 day fighters, of which eighty-four are Spitfires and 170 are Hurricanes.

Understanding the magnitude of the decisions being made here, Prime Minister Winston Churchill and his wife, Clementine, have decided to visit the Bunker, travelling from their country residence at Chequers. It is her birthday and she tells Winston that 'A good bag of German aircraft would be an excellent present.' The couple arrive around 10.30 hours and are met by Air Vice-Marshal Keith Park. Churchill, who has a great sense of history and destiny, feels that today will be a historic day; unpretentiously, he tells Park he has no wish to disturb anyone, but as he happened to be passing, he thought he would call in to see if anything was up. If not, 'I'll just sit in the car and do my homework'.[2] Park takes them to their seats behind the glass gallery where, like the Gods on Mount Olympus, they will soon look down and watch the burgeoning threat unfold and the counteroffensive rise up into the sky. Park reminds the Premier that the Bunker's air ventilation system cannot deal with cigarette or cigar smoke, and so Churchill sits acquiescently, clenching an unlit cigar between his teeth.

At 10.40 hours, Radar stations in 11 Group detect enemy aircraft taking to the air near Boulogne. By 11.00 hours, further reports signal a large formation massing over the Pas de Calais, rousing the women stood around the large plotting table into action. Like regimented croupiers, wooden blocks and coloured arrows are hurriedly prepared, ready to be placed on the map and moved around with croupier-style sticks. Vera Saies is one of those around the plotting table and her daughter will later recall being told that they were:

> reading, knitting, or doing other similar things to occupy themselves while they waited to start work ... but there was a commotion, and she dropped her book on the floor and ran over to the teleprinter. It contained a message about waves of bombers heading for the heart of London. At first, the sergeant in charge did not believe what she was reading and asked her to read the message twice. But what she was reading was true. German bombers were heading to London, in huge numbers. My mother was one of the first to find out just how many were on the way. She told me she started work straight away, plotting with other girls, not even thinking of stopping at midday when her shift should have ended.[3]

This, then, is the process by which the Gods looking down will be able to watch the large aerial battle being fought in the skies above southern England, as the Royal Air Force's young men duel with the Luftwaffe's young men, in order to repel their fusillade on London.

Churchill, observing the incoming raids being pushed along the plotting table, comments: 'There appear to be many aircraft coming in.' Park calmly reassures the Prime Minister, 'There'll be someone there to meet them.'[4] The Duty Senior Controller, Willoughby De Broke, will have to think and act fast, not only because his actions are being observed by the Prime Minister sat next to him, but because he understands that 'each minute of unnecessary delay waiting to make absolutely sure that the raid was coming in meant about 2,000 ft, or 610 metres, of vital altitude our fighters would not have when they met the enemy'. Height is a vital asset in a dogfight. The pilot who has the height advantage can see his adversary first and is able to convert that advantage into speed as he dives to attack from above. The Senior Controller, however, has to finely balance the decisions he takes and when he takes them. If he scrambles his fighters too early, then they will use up precious fuel before engaging the enemy. If too many squadrons are committed, then they will be vulnerable to attack when they land to refuel and rearm, as there may not be enough reserves to meet the next

ENEMY SIGHTED

attack. If too few are sent up, then they would be severely disadvantaged when confronting much larger enemy formations. These are life and death decisions, not only for the individual pilots, but also for the nation.

The decision is taken to immediately deploy two squadrons of Spitfires and at 11.05 hours a call is made to the Biggin Hill Sector Controller, call sign 'Carfax'. 'Biggin Hill. Serial One Three. Squadrons Seven Two and Nine Two. Patrol Canterbury. Angels Two Five.' Carfax, in turn gives the order for 72 Squadron, call sign 'Tennis' and 92 Squadron, call sign 'Gannic' to 'Scramble', instructing their combined twenty Spitfires to take off immediately. The Sector Controller's voice crackles over the radio, providing clipped instructions:

'Hello Gannic Leader. Gannic Leader. Carfax calling. Two Hundred Plus coming in over Red Queen. Vector One Two Zero. Angels Two Five.'

Flight Lieutenant Brian Kingcombe, 92 Squadron's temporary Commanding Officer replies, 'Hello Carfax. Gannic Leader. Message received. Over.'

'Hello Gannic. Gannic Leader. Carfax calling. Watch out for Snappers above! Many Snappers above. Hear me?'

'Loud and clear Carfax. Over and out.'[5]

'Red Queen' is the code for Canterbury, used by Fighter Command to confuse German eavesdroppers. 'Vector' is the compass heading which needs to be followed to reach their destination. 'Angels' is height, given in thousands of feet. 'Snappers' are the enemy fighters who are chaperoning their bombers. The Spitfires are to patrol over Canterbury at 25,000 ft (6,706 metres), and engage with the 'umbrella' escort of Messerschmitt Me 109 fighters flying above the bombers.

The deadly game of aerial chess now continues at a frantic pace. At 11.15 hours, the Senior Controller at Uxbridge orders a further six of his squadrons, totalling seventy-four Hurricanes, into the air. They too are operating in pairs. 'Northolt. Serial One Four. Squadrons Two Two Nine and Three Zero Three. Patrol Biggin Hill. Angels One Five.' 229 and 303 (Polish) Squadrons from Northolt are to patrol Biggin Hill at 15,000 ft (4,572 metres). 'Kenley. Serial One Five. Squadrons Two Five Three and Five Zero One. Patrol Maidstone. Angels One Five.' 253 and 501 (City of Bristol) Squadrons from Kenley are to patrol Maidstone at 15,000 ft. 'Debden. Serial One Six. Squadrons One Seven and Seven Three. Patrol Chelmsford. Angels One Five.' 17 and 73 Squadrons from Debden are to patrol Chelmsford at 15,000 ft. Ideally, they are to engage with the lower, slower bomber formations now approaching British airspace, while the

BATTLE OF BRITAIN DAY

Spitfires of 72 and 92 Squadrons lock horns with the Messerschmitt Me 109 fighters.

At 11.20 hours, three more of 11 Group's squadrons are committed. 'Northolt. Serial One Seven. Squadron Five Zero Four. Proceed to and patrol Maidstone.' 'Debden. Serial One Eight. Squadron Two Five Seven. Rendezvous with Squadron Five Zero Four over North Weald. Angels One Five. Proceed to and patrol Maidstone.' Thirteen Hurricanes from 504 (County of Nottingham) Squadron at Northolt and twelve Hurricanes from 257 Squadron at Martlesham are vectored to fly over Maidstone at 15,000 ft. 'Hornchurch. Serial One Nine. Squadron Six Zero Three. Patrol Dover. Angels Two Five.' 603 (City of Edinburgh) Squadron's twelve Spitfires are scrambled from Hornchurch and ordered to patrol over Dover at 25,000 ft (7,620 metres). The Luftwaffe's likely targets are London and the Hawker Hurricane factories at Langley and Brooklands, and so the Senior Controller at Uxbridge calls for reinforcements from the adjoining 10 and 12 Groups to protect his northern and western flanks. 'Ten Group. One squadron required to patrol to the west of the North South line. Brooklands-Windsor. Angels One Five. Immediately.' His request is promptly answered by the Spitfires of 609 (West Riding) Squadron from Middle Wallop in 10 Group, who are instructed to fly along the Brooklands-Windsor patrol line at a height of 15,000 ft, to guard against attacks on the Hurricane factories. 'Command. Duxford squadrons required to patrol North Weald-Hornchurch. Angels Two Five. Immediately. Protect London and the aerodromes in the absence of our own squadrons on forward patrol.' A 'Big Wing' led by Douglas Bader from Duxford in 12 Group, is directed to fly at 25,000 ft over Hornchurch and act as a final line of defence over London. He is bringing with him three Hurricane squadrons: 242 (Canadian), 302 (Polish) and 310 (Czechoslovak), and two Spitfire squadrons: 19, and 611 (West Lancashire), a total of fifty-five aircraft.

Between 11.30 and 11.40 hours, the Luftwaffe raid makes land over a wide area from Dover to Ramsgate. This is thirty minutes after the first defending fighters are scrambled. There are now seventeen Fighter Command squadrons in the air, 196 Hurricanes and Spitfires, ready and waiting to meet, attack and harry the enemy as they head inland. Leading the raid are sixty Me 109s on a 'free hunting' patrol, they are bait to lure the waiting Hurricanes and Spitfires into combat and divert them away from the bombers, which are next to cross the coast. This second formation is made up of twenty-five Do 17s, escorted by another sixty Me 109s, thirty of which are providing close protection, and a further thirty which are flying

ENEMY SIGHTED

higher to provide the bombers with an umbrella cover. The third and final formation in the raid consists of twenty-one Me 109 fighter bombers, who are escorted by a similar number of Me 109 fighters.

As they cross, a further six of 11 Group's squadrons are scrambled. 'Kenley. Serial Two Six. Squadrons Two Five Three and Five Zero One. Intercept enemy raid One Zero. Angels Two Zero. Approaching from Dover.' Twenty-two Hurricanes from 253 and 501 (City of Bristol) Squadrons at Kenley are vectored to fly towards Dover at 15,000 ft. 'North Weald. Serial Two Seven. Squadrons Two Four Nine and Four Six. Patrol south London. Angels Two Zero.' Twenty-four Hurricanes of 249 and 46 Squadrons from North Weald are sent over London's southern approaches at 20,000 ft (6,096 metres). 'Northolt. Serial Two Eight. Squadron One. Rendezvous with Six Zero Five over Kenley. Patrol base. Angels One Five.' 'Kenley. Serial Two Nine. Squadron Six Zero Five. Rendezvous with One over Kenley. Patrol base. Angels One Five.' Thirteen Hurricanes of 1 (Canadian) Squadron from Northolt and twelve Hurricanes of 605 (County of Warwick) Squadron from Croydon are to cover Kenley aerodrome at 15,000 ft. 'Hornchurch. Serial Three Zero. Squadron Four One. Patrol base. Angels Two Zero.' Seventeen Spitfires of 41 Squadron from Hornchurch are sent up to fly over their airfield at 20,000 ft. 'Biggin Hill. Serial Three One. Squadron Six Six. Intercept enemy Raid One Zero. Angels Two Zero. Approaching south London.' Eleven Spitfires of 66 Squadron from Gravesend are scrambled to fly to the south of the capital at 20,000 ft and engage the approaching enemy raid. De Broke and Park have committed twenty-three squadrons, 273 Hurricanes and Spitfires to defend the capital.

Very soon, the second formation of Dornier Do 17 bombers and their Messerschmitt Me 109 escorts are sighted over Dungeness. The uncustomary delay in waiting to cross the Channel after having taken off, combined with the wind disposition, favourable to the defenders, have provided the Senior Controller at Uxbridge with additional time to get his fighters in position. The Spitfires of 72 and 92 Squadrons are above the enemy, they have the tactical advantage as they engage them. Flight Lieutenant John 'Pancho' Villa leading 72 Squadron calls out, 'Tennis Squadron. Tally Ho!' The Sector Controller, listening on the radio at Biggin Hill, now knows that the enemy have been sighted and are being engaged. The message is relayed to the Ops 'B' team at Uxbridge, who illuminate the red 'Enemy Sighted' lights under 72 and 92 Squadrons, informing the Senior Controller that the first engagements are taking place.

BATTLE OF BRITAIN DAY

The Messerschmitt pilot providing top cover for the bombers sees the approaching Spitfires and shouts out a warning 'Achtung! Spitfires!' but his comrades have little time to react as the Spitfires swoop past.

Villa recalls:

> The main bomber force with fighter escort was about 4,000 ft [1,219 metres] below, with fighters about 3,000 ft [914 metres] below. I ordered the squadron into line astern and dived down on the fighters from out of the sun, as we dived down, I ordered the squadron into starboard echelon, thus attacking as many enemy fighters (Me 109s) as possible. The Me 109 which I attacked half rolled as I opened fire and before he could dive away, he caught fire and exploded. I was then attacked by five other Me 109s. I did a steep turn to starboard and continued to turn until I out turned one Me 109 which was on my tail. I gave him two short bursts and he burst into flames. I then spun down to get away from more Me 109s which dived down on me.[6]

The skirmishing between Spitfires and Messerschmitts is fast, furious and chaotic, as they attack each other, or are themselves attacked. Sometimes the results are clear, but often they are inconclusive. Pilot Officer Robert Holland of 92 Squadron writes:

> I was Blue One leading my section. At 23,000 ft [7,010 metres] inland of Dungeness, we sighted about fifteen Do 17s below us and various formations of Me 109s. I led my section into a group of 109s and a dogfight ensued. After spinning out down to 10,000 ft [3,048 metres], I climbed again to 15,000 ft [4,572 metres]. Later at approximately 12.00 hours, I observed a Me 109 flying over Canterbury, south to the sea. I dived from behind and gave approximately two second burst within range. Bits flew off the wing and thin black smoke emitted from the engine. I then observed two other 109s diving on me. So I broke off and dived to 8,000 ft [2,438 metres].[7]

Soon the Biggin Hill squadrons are joined by 603 (City of Edinburgh) Squadron's Spitfires from Hornchurch. Entering the fray, Squadron Leader George Denholm of 603 (City of Edinburgh) Squadron notes:

ENEMY SIGHTED

> When between Dungeness and Dover I saw an Me 109 and gave it a short burst from astern. It emitted glycol steam and dived into a cloud. I followed it but lost it in the cloud. On coming out I saw an Me 109 in difficulties, which I took to be the enemy aircraft at which I had previously fired, and I fired a short burst, and the enemy aircraft did a gentle dive landing on the sea fifty yards off Dover outer harbour.[8]

Pilot Officer James MacPhail records:

> I was on patrol with 603 Squadron and had dived to evade an Me 109. On climbing through cloud, I saw an Me 109 flying south along the top of the clouds. I turned and chased the enemy and got in a burst from astern. He turned to the left and I got in another burst. The enemy rolled on his back with pieces flying off his machine and dived into the corner of a small wood a few miles south of Detling aerodrome and burst into flames. I did not see the pilot bail [*sic*] out owing to the clouds.[9]

Some of the Spitfires were able to get to the German bombers. Pilot Officer Read of 603 (City of Edinburgh) Squadron reports:

> I became separated from the rest of the squadron after the initial attack. I saw a formation of Do 215s proceeding east down the Thames Estuary. They were below me and fairly close to cloud layer. I delivered a diving beam attack, developing into a quarter attack from starboard on a bomber that was a little behind the others. Its port engine started to smoke, and it left the formation and slid down into the cloud. Owing to my excess speed I overshot it and went through the clouds in a dive. It did not emerge below the cloud cover, at least, in my vicinity.[10]

Next to engage the raiders are the two Kenley squadrons, 501 (City of Bristol) and 253, with the former leading. They are vectored to Margate and begin to climb rapidly. Soon the rising Hurricanes spot an enemy formation of some twenty Do 17s over Maidstone, flying in a wide 'vic' formation. They are coming straight towards them, and they are not alone. There are

BATTLE OF BRITAIN DAY

around fifty yellow nosed Me 109s positioned above them. When the enemy formation is sighted, 501 (City of Bristol) is at 15,500 ft (4,724 metres) and the order is given to manoeuvre into echelon left. The Hurricanes climb to meet the bombers, attacking from below so as to make a slow closing and facilitate break away. On sighting the Hurricanes, the bombers climb to make their approach more difficult. Twelve of the thirteen Hurricanes are able to fire from a quarter below and dead ahead.[11]

A navigator in one of the bombers, Feldwebel Theodor Rehm, later recalls:

> Their thrusting attack took them right through our formation. Manning the nose gun, I dared not open fire for fear of hitting our own aircraft but the Hurricanes flashing close by, passed us and did not do much firing either, and we came out of the attack unscathed.

A pilot in another bomber, Feldwebel Wilhelm Raab, would write:

> They came in fast, getting bigger and bigger. As usual when under attack from fighters, we closed into a tight formation to concentrate our defensive fire. Four Hurricanes scurried through the formation. Within seconds they passed us. Then more black specks emerged from the bank of cloud in front, rapidly grew larger and flashed through the formation. They were trying to split us up, but neither attack had any success. Our formation remained intact.[12]

The bombers are attacked when they are at 17,000 ft (5,182 metres), after which the Hurricanes break up and efforts to reform prove difficult, owing to the ensuing dog fights with Messerschmitts that dive straight down and then climb back again. The Hurricane being flown by a Belgian, Pilot Officer Albert Van den Hove D'Ertsenrijck, is hit and catches fire as it nears the ground while its pilot attempts a force landing. Van den Hove D'Ertsenrijck is seen to stand and jump from his stricken aircraft, but tragically strikes a tree and is killed. The Hurricane being flown by 501's Squadron Leader, Henry Hogan, is also put out of commission when a cannon round finds his radiator. Although out of the fight, he fortunately will be able to return to Kenley. The Hurricanes of 253 immediately follow with head-on attacks on the bomber formation. Sergeant Allan Dredge attacks a Do 215 and

ENEMY SIGHTED

observes large pieces falling from the enemy aircraft's starboard wing and rudder. Pilot Officer Anthony Barton shoots down a Do 215 in the sea off Herne Bay.[13]

Flight Lieutenant Raymond Duke-Woolley accounts:

> I was Red Two and followed Red One into first attack on enemy aircraft from enemy aircraft's starboard quarter and from three quarters head on. I took a bad sight and only fired short burst and broke away. I lost Red One after breaking away and not being able to contact him, carried out three other attacks three quarter head on from enemy aircrafts' port quarter. The last three attacks were carried out on different aircraft of original formation intercept. On second attack I observed pilot's cockpit enclosure of one Do 215 collapse.[14]

The two opposing forces continue to clash over many cubic miles of sky, as the raiders fight their way across Kent. More defending fighters race to confront the enemy, and the next to intercept them are those from 41 and 66 Squadrons. The Spitfires of 41 Squadron are bounced by Me 109s over Gravesend. Sergeant Edward Darling reports:

> I was patrolling south-east of base as Blue Three, when attacked by 109s from above. I evaded them and lost height, then climbed up to 20,000 ft [6,096 metres] and patrolled by myself off Dover. I was returning to base, when I saw sixteen Do 215s crossing the coast and heading south. I attacked a straggler and overshot, turned, and attacked again. The port engine began to smoke and a 109 came in from astern. I turned and returned to base, as I was nearing the coast of France.[15]

Flying Officer Anthony Lovell records:

> Flying as Blue Two, we broke up to attack Me 109s who were attacking us. I sighted my Me 109 turning east and diving. I dived after him and chased him for some fifteen miles [twenty-four kilometres] in and out of cloud. After my first burst white fumes came from his port wing rout, but he carried on. I gave him two more bursts and he caught fire and I saw him bale out and was being attended to on the ground.[16]

BATTLE OF BRITAIN DAY

The Spitfires of 66 Squadron are able to get in among the bombers. Flight Lieutenant Crelin Bodie reports:

> I had lost the squadron due to an attack by 109s and saw twenty Do 17s flying north towards London. In company with two or three more friendly fighters I attacked. I made two attacks individually (diving beam attacks) and both times dived through the formation. The other fighters had also attacked individually, and we were not bothered by fighters. The formation of bombers then turned and headed south. I made another head-on dive attack at the last section of three, and damaged the port engine of one of them, and he dropped back from the formation. I made repeated attacks on him in company of Green One and a strange Hurricane, and his port engine stopped. Two of the crew baled out successfully, the under rear gunner tried, but became stuck, half in and half out of his 'dustbin'. The pilot may have been badly wounded, for although he was still at the controls, he made no attempt at a landing when his starboard engine stopped, but crashed on the edge of a wood, and the aircraft exploded, burning fiercely.[17]

Churchill, who had been watching the battle develop, will write:

> Presently the red bulbs showed that the majority of our squadrons were engaged. A subdued hum arose from the floor, where the busy plotters pushed their discs to and fro in accordance with the swiftly changing situation. Air Vice-Marshal Park gave general directions for the disposition of his fighter force, which were translated into detailed orders to each Fighter station by a youngish officer in the centre of the Dress Circle, at whose side I sat. He now gave the orders for the individual squadrons to ascend and patrol as the result of the final information which appeared on the map table. The Air Marshal himself walked up and down behind, watching with vigilant eye every move in the game, supervising his junior executive hand, and only occasionally intervening with some decisive order, usually to reinforce a threatened area. In a little while all our squadrons were

ENEMY SIGHTED

fighting, and some had already begun to return for fuel. All were in the air. The lower line of bulbs was out. There was not one squadron left in reserve. I became conscious of the anxiety of the Commander, who now stood behind his subordinate's chair. Hitherto I had watched in silence. I now asked, 'What other reserves have we?' 'There are none,' said Air Vice-Marshal Park. In an account which he wrote about it afterwards, he said that at this, 'I looked grave'. Well I might. What losses should we not suffer if our refuelling planes were caught on the ground by further raids of 'forty plus' or 'fifty plus!' The odds were great; our margins small; the stakes infinite.[18]

Now, as the German raiders fly over the capital itself, they are set upon by even more Hurricanes and Spitfires. The Hurricanes of 249 and 504 (County of Nottingham) Squadrons intercept about twenty Do 215s about five miles (eight kilometres) south-east of the London Docks. The bombers are flying towards the Docks in a diamond shaped formation at 17,000 ft (5,182 metres). They are escorted by Me 109s, at their sides and above them, stepped up to 22,000 ft (6,706 metres). As they are attacked, five bombers break formation and dive down into the cloud, probably to look for their target, but this allows the Hurricanes to get in among the remaining raiders. Squadron Leader John Sample leading 504 (County of Nottingham) Squadron writes:

> In company with about seventy Hurricanes and Spitfires, I carried out a quarter attack on about twenty Do 215s over London, just south of river, from starboard side. Saw white smoke come out of the one which I fired at. After breaking away I helped several other Hurricanes and Spitfires to bring down another Do 215 which broke up in the air.[19]

Pilot Officer Ray Holmes' combat report reads:

> I attacked the right flank machine from quarter to astern. Pieces flew from the wings and a flame appeared in the port wing but went out again. After breaking away I climbed up to a single Do 215 and made two quarter attacks. Pieces flew off. My windscreen was now splashed with black oil.

BATTLE OF BRITAIN DAY

> I attacked a third time and members of the crew baled out. On my fourth attack from the port beam, a jar shook my starboard wing as I passed over the enemy aircraft and I went into an uncontrollable spin. I think the enemy aircraft must have exploded beneath me. I baled out and as I landed, I saw the Dornier hit the ground by Victoria Street Station half a mile away.[20]

On its final dive, the bomber had spun violently, expelling its bombs, some of which struck Buckingham Palace. This particular engagement will, in fact, come to epitomise the fighting taking place over England on this day, and the bravery of those involved. The bomber in this case had previously been attacked by Hurricanes from 310 (Czechoslovak) Squadron, demonstrating how easily and understandably the destruction of the same machine could be claimed by several pilots. The pilot of the German bomber, Feldwebel Robert Zehbe, had put his doomed aircraft on autopilot before jumping, leaving it pilotless at the time of Holmes' final attack. Tragically for Zehbe, he is set upon by an angry and frenzied crowd after landing near the Oval Cricket Ground. He will die the next day as a result of the injuries he sustains following the assault. As for Holmes, his parachute becomes snared on a house roof and he is left dangling over a garden bin, but is otherwise unharmed. His Hurricane will be the only British aircraft to crash in Central London during the Second World War, and Holmes will be present when it is excavated from its final resting place at the junction of Buckingham Palace Road and Pimlico Road, sixty-four years later.[21]

Pilot Officer John Crossman of 46 Squadron, writes:

> I saw about twenty Do 215s at about 17,000 ft [5,182 metres], with very large formation of Me 109s about 5,000 ft [1,524 metres] above in tight 'vic' formation. Two Me 109s detached themselves from the formation and dived to attack me. I turned inwards and headed for bomber formation and did a stern attack on one Do 215. Firing alone four bursts. When my ammunition was almost expended, I saw black smoke pouring out from the port engine of the Do 215 and the aircraft detached itself from the formation and began to lose height. There was no answering fire. I then dived away from the oncoming Me 109s.[22]

ENEMY SIGHTED

The five squadrons forming the Duxford 'Big Wing', 242 (Canadian), 302 (Polish), 310 (Czechoslovak), 611 (West Lancashire) and 19, have travelled down from 12 Group and are patrolling south of the Thames at 25,000 ft (7,620 metres). They are led by their indefatigable commanding officer, Squadron Leader Douglas Bader, who recounts:

> Saw two squadrons pass underneath us in formation, travelling north-west in purposeful manner, then saw anti-aircraft bursts so turned 12 Group Wing and saw enemy aircraft 3,000 ft [914 metres] below to the north-west. Managed perfect approach with 19 and 611 between our Hurricanes and sun, and enemy aircraft below and down sun. Arrived over enemy aircraft formation of twenty to forty Do 17. Noticed Me 109 dive out of sun and warned our Spitfires to look out. Me 109 broke away and climbed south-east. About to attack enemy aircraft which were turning left-handed, i.e. to west and south, when I noticed Spitfires and Hurricanes (11 Group?) engaging them. Was compelled to wait for a risk of collision. However, warned Wing to watch other friendly fighters and dived down with leading section in formation onto last section of three enemy aircraft. Pilot Officer Campbell took left-hand Do 17, I took middle one, and Sub-Lieutenant Cork the right one, which had lost ground on outside of turn. Opened fire at 100 yards [91 metres] in steep dive and saw a large flash behind starboard motor of Dornier as wing caught fire, must have hit petrol pipe or tank, overshot, and pulled up steeply. Then carried on and attacked another Do 17 but had to break away to avoid Spitfire. The sky was then full of Spitfires and Hurricanes, queuing up and pushing each other out of the way to get at Dorniers which for once were outnumbered. I squirted at odd Dorniers at close range as they came into my sights but could not hold them in my sights for fear of collision with other Spitfires and Hurricanes. Saw collision between Spitfire and Do 17 which wrecked both aeroplanes. Finally ran out of ammunition chasing crippled and smoking Do 17 into cloud. It was the finest shambles I have been in since for once we had position, height and numbers. Enemy aircraft were a dirty looking collection.[23]

BATTLE OF BRITAIN DAY

Pilot Officer Stan Turner, also flying with 242 (Canadian) Squadron, reported:

> Proceeded with Wing up to 24,000 ft [315 metres.] At approximately 12.30 sighted enemy aircraft proceeding north, below us. We turned to attack from our position. Enemy aircraft sighting us turned south. Enemy fighters also turned away. Attacked bombers which split up. Sighted struggler Do 17 below me, made three attacks on it at close range. Last burst, burst oil tanks of enemy aircraft. Three people jumped by parachute and enemy aircraft crashed into field and blew up.[24]

Flight Lieutenant William Leather, a Spitfire pilot in 611 (West Lancashire) Squadron, reported when over London:

> I carried out a head-on attack on three Do 215s. No result seen. I then turned and picked out one Do 215 behind a large formation. I fired the rest of my ammunition in it and his port engine exploded and stopped. A number of other fighters also attacked this machine and Red Two saw two crew bale out and machine crashed seven to ten miles, or eleven to sixteen kilometres, south-east of Canterbury.[25]

The Messerschmitt Me 109's 'Achilles' heel' was its inadequate operational range, which limited flying time over London to about ten minutes. This period is reduced further still on this day because extra fuel was needed on the way in, to fly against a strong headwind and to engage the Hurricanes and Spitfires sent up by the Operations Room at Uxbridge. Many Messerschmitts have to turn around and head for home and as the bombers lose their fighter escorts they jettison their loads, before they too turn around and head frantically for the French coast. But the journey home is resisted by even more fighters standing in their way, as some head west over Brooklands and then south, while others fly east and then over Kent.

Those retreating west were engaged by the Spitfires of 10 Group's 609 (West Riding) Squadron, call sign 'Sorbo'. Flying Officer Dundas reports:

> I was Yellow One on patrol over London at 17,000 ft [5,182 metres] when I sighted a large formation of bombers approaching from east and informed Sorbo Leader. Sorbo

ENEMY SIGHTED

> Leader turned towards the enemy aircraft which we then identified as Dorniers and turned across them to port. There were many Me 109s on both sides of the bomber formation and above them; so having received no orders on the R/T from Sorbo Leader and thinking it unwise to wait around under the Me's for too long before making an attack, I turned in and attacked an enemy aircraft in centre of the formation from below and the beam. As I passed, I saw one of its motors stop. On breaking away I was attacked by an Me from above and astern. After evading the Me's, I made a second attack on the Dorniers, this time from almost vertically below. No results observed. The first Dornier I attacked had yellow spinners, the second red spinners. After this I was attacked by three Me's who peeled off from 2,000 ft [610 metres] above but gave themselves away by opening fire at excessive range. They did not stay to fight. After this I lost the enemy formation and after continuing on patrol for fifteen minutes I returned to base.[26]

Pilot Officer John Curchin, also of 609 (West Riding) Squadron, recalls:

> I was Green Three. One Dornier 215 broke from the formation and I attacked it. Two Hurricanes also attacked it at the same moment. I gave it a short burst of about three seconds from astern and then broke away and attacked it from quarter ahead, after the attack I noticed that both engines had stopped. The aircraft started to glide down. I followed it and two men baled out at about 3,000 ft, or 914 metres. The machine crashed immediately and burst into flames.[27]

Those withdrawing to the south were intercepted by the Hurricanes of 605 (County of Warwick) Squadron, call sign 'Turkey', from Kenley and 1 (Canadian) Squadron from Northolt. Flight Lieutenant McKellar recounts:

> Turkey Squadron ordered to scramble and orbit Kenley 15,000 ft [4,572 metres] and join up with Canadian squadron, I to lead both squadrons. At 16,000 ft [4,877 metres], I saw a bomber formation with very large fighter escort (Me 109s). I ordered a beam attack as the Do 17s were going faster than I had anticipated, and I would not get into position for a

BATTLE OF BRITAIN DAY

> head-on attack. I carried out my attack with no obvious result and broke downwards. As I was climbing up again, to again attack, I saw two Me 109s attacking a Hurricane which went down in flames. I therefore attacked them and shot both down in flames, one by a surprise beam attack, and the other in the course of a dogfight. I continued to climb and at 17,000 ft [5,182 metres] over Croydon, I noticed nine Do17s flying south-east. I did a diving beam attack without any obvious result on the outside man of the last vic.[28]

This engagement occurs almost one year after McKellar, along with Flight Lieutenant George Pinkerton, destroyed a Heinkel He 111 on 16 October 1939, over the Firth of Forth. It has the distinction of being the first enemy aircraft shot down over Britain in the Second World War. Pinkerton would write, rather tersely, 'Dogfight during which enemy aircraft crashed into sea. Ship proceeding to pick up wreckage. All ammunition was expended.'[29]

Returning to 15 September, two more of 11 Group's squadrons from Northolt engage the raiders. Flight Lieutenant John 'Johnny' Kent, a Canadian affectionately called 'Kentowski' by his Polish pilots, leads 303 (Polish) Squadron[30] in company with 229 Squadron, which was in advance. They have been sent over London where a large formation of enemy aircraft are seen hovering over south-east of the City. The squadrons fly towards it, but the enemy turns south and escapes. Another formation is then seen approaching London from the south and the two squadrons fly side by side towards it but are too far away to effect an interception. When the enemy turn, having presumably dropped their bombs somewhere over the Estuary, they flee towards the south and the two squadrons set off in pursuit. They catch up with the rear guards of Me 109s somewhere near Folkestone and a series of individual actions take place between the Hurricanes and enemy fighters. One Do 215, which had probably been damaged as it was separated from its companions, was shot down by Flying Officer Zdzislaw Henneberg:

> After a lengthy chase of Me 109s I perceived a formation of about twenty Do 215s flying towards London, protected by a number of Me 109s. I attacked a Do 215 firing a long burst from a distance of 300 yards [274 metres]. Being attacked by three Me 109s, I was forced to break off the engagement with the bombers but looking round I noticed the right engine and petrol tank of the Do 215 was in flames.

ENEMY SIGHTED

Kent and several other pilots have momentary contacts and fire short bursts at Me 109s, seeing the ammunition hit, but unable to make any claims. The few Dorniers he sees far ahead are in loose formation, and there are swarms of Me 109s in formations of all shapes and sizes. Sergeant Josef Frantisek of 303 (Polish) Squadron, a Czech flying alongside the Poles writes:

> I was flying in the last section and patrolling when I noticed above us Me's and Do's. I attacked two Me 110s and, leaving one to [the] Hurricane following me, attacked the other. Enemy aircraft tried to evade me, but I fired a burst and saw his right engine smoke. I fired another burst, and enemy aircraft immediately dived, and fell to earth in flames.

Frantisek will become the highest scoring pilot during the battle, with seventeen confirmed kills.

303 (Polish) Squadron's Pilot Officer Marian Pisarek writes:

> Flying in a Southerly direction I noticed several Me 109s and to the right Do 215. As I approached the Me 109s first, I engaged them and following on the tail on one I fired several short bursts, but only after falling to about 400 ft [122 metres] did I see enemy aircraft burst into flames and fall into the sea. I began to climb but met nothing more.

Another 303 (Polish) Squadron Pilot, Pilot Officer Witold Lokuciewski reports:

> At a height of about 18,000 ft [5,486 metres] we noticed enemy aircraft flying towards London. We approached, but enemy aircraft turned, and we attacked them from a deflected angle from the rear and above, but at that moment we ourselves were attacked from the rear by the Me 109s, at the same time I noticed another formation of enemy aircraft flying towards London, protected by Me 109s and Me 110s. I broke away, and attacked the Me 109s together with another section of Hurricanes. After firing a few bursts, an Me 109 began to smoke and eventually burst into flames. I was then hit from the rear by a cannon shell and landed wounded.

BATTLE OF BRITAIN DAY

They chase the enemy as they retreat towards France. Pilot Officer Ludwick Paszkiewicz, who had been responsible for 303 (Polish) Squadron's first kill on 30 August, which led to their becoming operational, reports:

> Flying at 20,000 ft [6,096 metres] in the region of Folkestone, we caught up with two formations of Me 109s and Me 110s above us. The leading aircraft of my section attacked the formation and I followed. Four Me 109s then attacked from the rear. I engaged them and shot down one which fell in flames in the sea, and the other three fled to France.

Sergeant Miroslaw Wojciechowski recounts:

> I noticed a Me 109 returning towards France. I attacked him from the rear and fired at very close range, and [the] Me Burst into flames, losing height. There was no other machine in the vicinity. I followed him down to earth, where he crashed, but the pilot stepped out of the plane and was arrested. I again climbed and another machine joining me, we attacked a Dornier, and firing two bursts, enemy aircraft crashed to earth and burst into flames.

Flying Officer Zdzislaw Henneberg, who had earlier downed a Do 215 continues his report:

> Flying south I came across three Me 109s making their way towards the Channel. I gave chase, and firing from a distance of about 300 yards [274 metres], saw one enemy aircraft dive in smoke and spin down. I again fired a burst, enemy aircraft slackened speed, and approaching to a distance of about 150 yards [137 metres], I fired a third burst from the rear left side. Enemy aircraft hit the water at an angle of about thirty degrees and disappeared six miles, or ten kilometres from the coast.

Pilot Officer Miroslaw Feric recalls:

> After an hour's flight looking for enemy aircraft, I was attacked by two Me 109s over the coast at Dungeness. These were

ENEMY SIGHTED

> reinforced by three other Me's, and in the ensuing fight I shot one down, firing a long burst from a distance of 300 yards [274 metres]. Being myself engaged, I could not follow subsequent flight of damaged enemy aircraft, but Flight Lieutenant Kent who was in the vicinity states that he saw enemy aircraft burst into flames and fall to earth.

Sergeant Tadeusz Andruszkow:

> While returning to Northolt flying as Red Two with Sergeant Wojciechowski, we saw a Do 215 lower and to our right. We both attacked and watched him fall in flames to the ground.

Flight Lieutenant Reginald Rimmer has led his twelve 'Keta' Hurricanes from Northolt.[31] Keta is the call sign for 229 Squadron. As they turn east to engage the enemy, the Hurricanes of 303 (Polish) Squadron, who are below and to the east, turn in behind them. In the ensuing dogfight 229 Squadron split up and lose touch with each other. Some combats with the Me 109s are inconclusive, but others are decisive. Rimmer recounts:

> I was Keta Leader. After evading enemy fighters I found myself below cloud and sighted a Do 215, flying in and out of seven tenths cloud, heading for coast near Maidstone. I carried out five head-on and quarter deflection attacks, with bursts of two to three seconds. Fire from rear gunner ceased and enemy aircraft lost height and crash landed one mile [1.6 kilometres] west of dummy Aerodrome near Sevenoaks.[32]

A dummy aerodrome is a decoy airfield, set up to divert enemy bombing away from their actual target. It is known as a 'Q' site.

229 Squadron's Pilot Officer Victor 'Vicky' Ortmans, born in London of Belgian ancestry, chases an Me 109 to the coast and then heads northwest until he sees a Do 215 in the direction of Tunbridge Wells, with two Hurricanes close by. He attacks it in conjunction with the other two, and the enemy aircraft crashes in flames near Cranbrook. Ortmans had made the final attack. Pilot Officer Bob Smith, a Canadian, leads Green Section to attack a second formation of Messerschmitts to prevent them from diving on 303 (Polish) Squadron's Hurricanes below. They go into line astern, and he opens fire on one enemy aircraft, which pulls up with a spurt of

white smoke. Smith is then himself hit, receiving a bullet wound to the leg. He bales out of his stricken Hurricane over Sevenoaks. Pilot Officer Georges Doutrepont, a Belgian, is next to attack. He too is hit, and the Merlin gives out a deafening cry, as his Hurricane dives uncontrollably towards the ground, destroying the railway station at Staplehurst. Doutrepont's lifeless body is still inside the remains of the cockpit.

The Germans bombed London believing its population would be cowed into submission. The treatment meted out to Feldwebel Robert Zehbe by the angry and frenzied crowd near the Oval Cricket Ground, horrific as it was, shows that far from being cowed, the public were in fact incensed. The Germans wanted to force the Royal Air Force into the air and into a battle of attrition, in the belief that Fighter Command was down to its last few fighters. The appearance of so many Hurricanes and Spitfires, in the right place and at the right time, has heralded that rather than being on the brink of collapse, Fighter Command is in fact rejuvenated. These lessons, as clear as they are, cannot be digested and understood quickly enough to stop the Luftwaffe from carrying out a second round of raids, planned for the afternoon.

Chapter 16

Battle of Britain Day

'The Finale'

At 13.45 hours, around one hour after the first raid has ended, British Radar stations detect more aircraft gathering across the Channel. Many of Fighter Command's aircraft, involved in the morning engagements, are still being refuelled, rearmed or repaired, and so it is fifteen minutes before the Senior Controller at Uxbridge is able to scramble his first squadrons. The Spitfires of 222 and 603 (City of Edinburgh) Squadrons from Hornchurch are vectored to fly over Sheerness at 20,000 ft (6,096 metres). The Hurricanes of 17 and 257 Squadrons fly from their base at Debden to cover Chelmsford at 15,000 ft (4,572 metres). The Hurricanes of 249 Squadron at North Weald and 504 (County of Nottingham) Squadron at Hendon are vectored to fly over Hornchurch at 15,000 ft. The Hurricanes of 605 (County of Warwick) Squadron at Croydon and 501 (City of Bristol) Squadron at Kenley are ordered to fly over Kenley at 5,000 ft (1,524 metres).

Five minutes later, Biggin Hill's two Spitfire squadrons, 92 and 41, are scrambled to fly over Hornchurch at 20,000 ft, and the Hurricanes of 229 and 1 (Canadian) Squadrons take off from Northolt to patrol base. Twelve squadrons are in the air to meet the enemy. A further five minutes and more fighters are sent into the air by Uxbridge. Number 46 Squadron's Hurricanes from Stapleford Tawney to patrol over the London Docks. The Spitfires of 66 and 72 Squadrons to patrol over their base at Biggin Hill at 20,000 ft. The six Hurricanes of 73 Squadron's 'B' Flight from Castle Camps to patrol over Maidstone at 15,000 ft. Now there are sixteen squadrons in the sky over London and the south-east of England.

At 14.15 hours, yet more fighters are scrambled into the air. Number 253 Squadron's Hurricanes take off from Kenley to patrol over their base at 15,000 ft. The Hurricanes of 607 (County of Durham) and 213 Squadrons are vectored from Tangmere to fly a patrol line between Biggin Hill and Kenley at 15,000 ft. 10 Group scramble 238 Squadron's Hurricanes, vectoring them to fly a patrol line between the Hawker Hurricane works

BATTLE OF BRITAIN DAY

at Brooklands and Kenley. 12 Group again scrambles its Big Wing of five squadrons, to fly over Hornchurch at 25,000 ft (7,620 metres). Soon there will be a total of thirty-one squadrons airborne, three from 10 Group, twenty-three from 11 Group, and five from 12 Group.

Between 14.15 and 14.20 hours, three Luftwaffe formations cross the English coast between Dungeness and Dover. There are many more bombers and fighters than in the earlier raid, and they now outnumber the defending aircraft. The enemy move inland on a broad front spanning many miles across. The most northerly formation is flying from Dover towards Gravesend and consists of He 111 bombers escorted by a similar number of Messerschmitt fighters. The central one also has He 111s, as well as some Do 17 bombers, and again a similar number of fighters. It is moving inland from Folkestone towards Maidstone. The third formation to the south has Do 17 bombers, with a Messerschmitt fighter escort.

The enemy are first engaged by 603 (City of Edinburgh) and 222 Squadrons, who attack the northern formation over Sheerness and Canterbury. Squadron Leader George Denholm of 603 (City of Edinburgh) Squadron reports:

> I attacked He 111 with a two second burst, diving from astern, then I fired a short burst at an Me 109 but observed no results. Sometime later I saw an unescorted formation of Do 17s over the coast and made a diving frontal quarter attack [number] one on the port flank of the formation from out of the sun. I fired a short burst and dived through the formation and turned to make an astern attack. I saw the two Do 17s at which I had fired lagging behind the formation, emitting black smoke. I was then fired at, and flames started to come through my instrument panel, which was broken, so I baled out.[1]

Another 603 (City of Edinburgh) pilot, Flying Officer Brian McNamara, very nearly becomes a casualty through friendly fire:

> After becoming separated from the squadron, I hung about the estuary for stragglers. I soon saw AA fire over the Isle of Sheppey and saw a Dornier just emerging from cloud. I carried out a stern chase and saw my incendiaries hitting his starboard engine and very soon black smoke came from it and the aircraft, which was steering east, started turning slowly

left towards the Essex coast. I had to break away, as I had run out of ammunition and was troubled by heavy AA fire. I did not see what happened to the Dornier. Throughout this attack I was troubled by heavy AA fire, which did not cease, despite the fact that I had commenced an attack on the enemy, and shells were continually bursting very close to my aircraft.[2]

Pilot Officer Gerald Stapleton of 603 (City of Edinburgh) Squadron fared somewhat better:

When patrolling with my squadron, I sighted twenty-five He 111s and fifty Me 109s. While diving to attack, I found myself going too fast to pull out on the enemy, so I continued my dive. About ten minutes later, I sighted two Me 109s in light vic. I fired two deflection bursts at one and glycol streams came from his radiator. They dived into cloud. Later I saw one Do 17 over the Thames Estuary heading for the clouds. I did several beam attacks and he dived to 100 ft [30 metres]. He flew very low indeed and pancaked on the sea five miles [eight kilometres] north-west of Ramsgate. I experienced no return fire.[3]

When attacking the enemy bombers, the Spitfires are themselves attacked by Me 109s. Flying Officer Eric Thomas of 222 Squadron reports:

Having been broken up by enemy fighters, I dropped to 10,000 ft [3,048 metres] in the direction of Chatham. By this time I was alone and saw the Do 17 flying alone due east. I disregarded the AA fire and went in a beam attack out of the sun and got in a short burst at long range of about 400 yards [366 metres]. The enemy aircraft then disappeared in a cloud bank. I set my course due east and kept above the clouds and about four miles, or six kilometres further on, the Do 17 arrived flying due east again. I did an astern attack and closed from 300 to 50 yards [274 to 46 metres], firing all the time. I saw pieces of aircraft flying off and rear gun fire stopped. Just then a yellow nosed Me 109 got on my tail. I broke off the attack and took cover in the cloud. The Do 17 had disappeared when I came up again to look for it.[4]

BATTLE OF BRITAIN DAY

Flight Lieutenant John 'Pancho' Villa leading 72 Squadron, engages a Heinkel He 111 in the central formation over the Dartford area:

> I attacked the Heinkel from the starboard side. I opened fire at 200 yards [183 metres] dead astern and closed to 20 yards [18 metres], firing short bursts all the time. His starboard engine caught fire and his undercarriage dropped out. I broke away and attacked again and finished my ammunition on his port engine, which stopped. My windscreen was covered in oil from enemy aircraft.[5]

Pilot Officer John Lloyd, also from 72 Squadron writes:

> I was flying as Blue Three when the squadron attacked a squadron of He 111s at 10,000 to 12,000 ft [3,048 to 3,658 metres]. I picked one machine and attacked from astern and slightly below with a five-second burst during which my fire appeared to enter the attacked machine. There was, however, no other visible signs of damage. The pilot of the machine following me reports that on this attack there was no return fire from the rear gunner. I later attacked a 111 which was being subjected to numerous attacks from five other Spitfires, delivering a burst of about four seconds from astern and above.[6]

As the central formation continues towards London, it is engaged by the Hurricanes of 249 and 46 Squadrons. Pilot Officer Tom Neil reports:

> At approximately 14.50 hours, 249 Squadron intercepted a formation of about fifteen Do 215s. I was Yellow Two. Over south-east London at 15,000 ft, the squadron did a quarter attack. I eventually found myself behind a Dornier. I gave a one-second burst to the port engine. Large pieces of cowling and engine flew apart. The crew immediately baled out while the aircraft went vertically into the clouds. Later I saw another Dornier flying about 16,000 ft. I climbed, chasing him. I finally caught, a little north of the estuary and fired several two to three second bursts. Faint smoke was seen to come from the port engine. The bomber flew out to sea, gradually losing

height. It passed over a convoy sailing south about ten miles, or seventeen kilometres out to sea. I fired all my ammunition at close range. The enemy aircraft gradually lost height and crashed into sea about thirty miles [forty-eight kilometres] off English coast. No evasive action was made by bomber.[7]

The Hurricanes of 213 Squadron meet around eighty Do 17s in two formations of forty heading towards London. Some members of the squadron see Me 110s flying to the east, but with the little help they give the bombers, it appears they are part of another raid. The Hurricanes carry out head-on attacks against the Dorniers. Flight Lieutenant John Sing picks out one enemy aircraft and shoots away the whole of the nose, including the pilot's cockpit. The aircraft enters a steep dive and Sing claims a probable destroyed. Sub-Lieutenant Dennis Jeram, Green Two, and Flying Officer Duryasg, Red Three, go right through the enemy formation, turn back, and attack a Do 17 each from behind, following them down through the clouds until they crash and burn. Flight Sergeant Charles Grayson, Green One, carries out an astern attack on another bomber and after several bursts sees it go down out of control in an absolute vertical dive, claiming it as a probable destroyed. Sergeant Gordon Bushell attacks another, damaging it. Sergeant Reginald Llewyllyn destroys a Do 17, but is then himself attacked by Me 110s, he sustains a bullet wound to his right shoulder and is forced to bale out of his damaged Hurricane over Tenterden. Pilot Officer Hubert Cottam, Blue Two, dives vertically on another Do 17, damaging it but then loses it. He proceeds to Dungeness where he sees a Spitfire attacking a Me 110 and helps to bring it down into the Channel. Sergeant Ernest Snowden, Green Three, also searches for stragglers over Dungeness and fires at another Me 110, sending it into the water.[8]

Flight Lieutenant Denis Parnall, also of 249 Squadron, reports:

> I was flying fast over south London by myself as I had lost the rest of my squadron after I had attacked Do's, when [a] large raid of He 111 was sighted heading due west over Central London. I turned north and did a vertical climbing attack on the last He of the formation. I fired a steady burst while climbing and then over the vertical upside down. The bullets struck the port motor of the He and large pieces of metal flew off the port wing. The motor slowed down and was almost stationary when I had to break away vertically downwards. I was able

BATTLE OF BRITAIN DAY

to return to observe what happened to the He but he seemed to be rapidly dropping back from the main formation. I claim this aircraft probable. After breaking away from encounter, a number of yellow nose Me 109s came down to 12,000 ft [3,658 metres] heading north. I was also heading north at the same height but to their west so turned right to give the leader of the Me 109s a four-second burst from the beam to port quarter astern when a number of pieces fell off this aircraft just behind the pilot's seat. I had to break immediately as there were six Me 109s diving down on me following their leader, and so was unable to observe any further effect of this fire. I claim this yellow nosed Me 109 damaged.[9]

Again the raiders are met over London by 12 Group's Big Wing. Douglas Bader recalls:

At 16,000 ft [4,877 metres] sighted large number of enemy aircraft through AA bursts at approx. 20,000 ft [6,096 metres]. Endeavoured to climb and catch them but unfortunately was attacked by Me 109s from above and behind. I told Spitfires to come on and get bombers and told Hurricanes to break up and engage fighters. On being attacked from behind by Me 109, I ordered break up and pulled up and turned violently. Coming off my back I eventually blacked out, almost collided with Yellow Two (242), spun off his slipstream and straightened out 5,000 ft [1,524 metres] below without firing a shot. Climbed up again and saw enemy aircraft twin-engine flying westwards. Just got in range and fired a short burst (three seconds) in a completely stalled position and then spun off again and lost more height.[10]

Bader's 302 (Polish) Squadron join the melee and get in among the enemy.[11] Squadron Leader William Satchell, Blue One, turns to attack a small formation of enemy aircraft heading east. Just before getting in position, he notices in his mirror, an Me 109 flying above him. He waits until it dives to attack and then pulls his Hurricane sharply up, letting the enemy aircraft pass below him. He then gets on its tail and gives several long bursts, causing the Messerschmitt to roll over on its back and discharge smoke from its engine. As it spins into clouds, Blue Two, Pilot Officer Edward Pilch, dives to attack the bombers. He notices that Red One, Flight Lieutenant Tadeusz Chlopik, has already attacked them, causing the formation to break up and attempt to hide in the cavernous layers of cloud. Pilch decides to wait under them and attacks a Do 17 from above and head on as it emerges from cover. He flies over the bomber and notices the rear gunner is silent. It is now attacked by a Spitfire from behind. Pilch turns around and continues to fire at the Dornier, getting in five one-second bursts, closing to zero feet. The stricken aircraft belches black smoke from its port engine and begins to burn fiercely as it turns and dives towards the Thames Estuary. It is seen to crash into the sea near Margate.

Red One, Flight Lieutenant Tadeusz Chlopik's Hurricane is hit, and he bales out. His parachute fails to open and he falls to his death. Flying at 15,000 ft, Red Two, Pilot Officer Stanislaw Lapka, dives to attack a Dornier from the beam, getting in a long burst, but at this moment his starboard machine-gun panel blows up, causing a very big drag. His Hurricane is hit by return fire from the rear gunner of the Dornier he is attacking. Lapka's cockpit is immediately filled with smoke, and he dives away. After some difficulty he too bales out and, unlike Chlopik, his parachute opens and he lands safely with only a minor injury to his foot. Following Lapka, Flying Officer Julian Kowalski, Red Three reports:

> I attacked against seven Dorniers flying over London northwards. After firing three long bursts at one Dornier, I saw the tail plane disintegrate and pieces of the wings joining the fuselage flew off. The enemy aircraft dived at about forty-five degrees towards the ground. Immediately after this I attacked a second Dornier of this group of seven and after my second burst of three seconds, I saw white smoke and pieces of fuselage flying away. The enemy aircraft lost height very quickly indeed and dived away. I could not finish him off completely through lack of ammunition.[12]

Also to engage the enemy are Bader's 310 (Czechoslovak) Squadron,[13] who are attacked from the port side and drawn into a general dog fight. The Hurricane flown by Sergeant Josef Hubacek, Green One, is hit by a cannon shell and he is forced to bale out with an injury to his left leg. Squadron Leader Alexander Hess' Hurricane is also hit by a cannon shell and he too bales out, uninjured. Sergeant Josef Rechka, Blue Three, along with two other Hurricanes, chases and attacks a Heinkel He 111 bomber,

BATTLE OF BRITAIN DAY

seeing it crash on Foulness Island. Pilot Officer Stanislav Fejfar, Red Two, attacks and shoots down a Dornier Do 17, which crashes near the Isle of Grain. Sergeant Bohumil Furst, Red Three, follows a formation of Dornier Do 215 and Heinkel He 111 bombers and attacks one of the He 111s, which was some distance from the formation, driving it down out of control into the ground. Sergeant Jan Kaucky, Green Three, attacks a Do 215 along with two Spitfires, also sending it down in smoke, into the ground.

The fact that many of the Combat Reports are initially handwritten in Polish or Czech and then typed into English shines a light on some of the concerns around communication, which had delayed the Polish and Czech squadrons entering the battle. Much more importantly, their flying prowess and fighting ability on this day shows demonstrably that their contribution is not only helpful, it is essential.

Many of the raiders head to the west and then turn south towards the coast, but as they retreat, they continue to be harassed by more Fighter Command aircraft. Sergeant Miroslaw Wojciechowski of 303 (Polish) Squadron, reports:

> We attacked a formation of Do's shielded by Me 109s. Being near an Me, I fired a burst after which he turned and made off towards the sea. I chased him for quite a long time before I was able to shoot him down. The pilot jumped, and I saw him arrested.[14]

The afternoon raid holds one further surprise for the defenders. Around 15.30 hours, as the main formation beats a retreat after attacking London, twenty to thirty unescorted bombers swoop across the Channel from the Cherbourg Peninsula, towards the Royal Naval Station at Portland. The Spitfires of 152 Squadron from 10 Group intercept the raiders, but only after the enemy have dropped their bombs. They sight the Luftwaffe aircraft flying southeast, seven miles (eleven kilometres) off Portland, at 15,000 ft. Sergeant Kenneth Holland, Green Three, attacks a straggler, which is then also attacked by Pilot Officer Peter O'Brian, a Canadian, who makes an astern attack, concentrating his fire on the starboard engine, and then breaking away left and downwards. Pilot Officer Arthur Watson, Green Two, then picks up the onslaught, giving the same aircraft a five-second burst. He sees smoke coming from both engines and the undercarriage fall. O'Brian then fires again, causing considerable smoke to emanate from the starboard engine. Watson attacks another straggler at 6,000 ft (1,829 metres), and after giving it an eight-second burst, the machine blows to pieces in mid-air and falls into the sea, about fifteen miles (twenty-four kilometres) south-west of Swanage.

Pilot Officer Eric Marrs, Blue One, selects an aircraft on the extreme left of the rearmost enemy section, approaching from astern and then breaking away downwards. Sergeant John Christie, Blue Two, then attacks it from astern and slightly to the starboard. Marrs comes up from underneath and makes a number two attack on another straggler, following up with an astern attack before breaking off, as they are getting too far out to sea.[15]

Finally, the reconnoitres, watching the enemy's movements from their Observer Corps Posts and Radar stations, inform the Operations Room at Uxbridge that the only Germans to be seen are those beating a hasty retreat. No fresh raids have been detected. As the last plot is removed from the map, Churchill and his wife Clementine come down from the gallery to address the Operations Room staff, who have skilfully and composedly helped to repel the German raids. He looks around at the sea of expectant faces, removes the unlit cigar from his mouth, and says, 'Well done.' Vera Saies' daughter recalls her mother, 'describing a wonderful moment when the Prime Minister and his wife Clementine congratulated all the team in the Bunker. She said he was in an exceptionally good mood, smiling and waving at everyone.'[16]

As he is escorted from the Bunker, Churchill confides that he believes the German attacks were 'repelled satisfactorily'. The interception rates of 11 Group,[17] along with those of 10 and 12 Group, have been exemplary, although Park is disappointed, wishing that more raiders had been intercepted. All of the squadrons detailed to intercept raids have gone into action against the enemy. The Dowding System has worked sublimely.

The daylight raids are not over yet. Around 17.40 hours, Chain Home detects a formation of thirty-plus aircraft over the Cherbourg Peninsula, heading towards the Isle of Wight. They are Do 17 bombers, with their escorting Me 110 fighters, and are en route to deliver the Luftwaffe's last coordinated attack of the day. Within twenty minutes, the enemy are over Southampton and it is clear that their target is the Supermarine Spitfire Factory at Woolston. The Operations Rooms at 10 and 11 Group are caught off guard and the only element of the integrated air defence system able to retaliate are Southampton's anti-aircraft guns. The bombs dropped by the raiders cause significant damage in the surrounding area, but – miraculously – causing only superficial damage to the Spitfire factory, the nursery where Britain's foremost fighter is created. As the raiders flee

BATTLE OF BRITAIN DAY

for home, they are engaged over the Channel by the vengeful Hurricanes of 607 (County of Durham) Squadron and Spitfires of 609 (West Riding) Squadron. A ferocious dogfight erupts to the south-west of the Needles, and several of the bombers are sent to their watery grave. This then brings to a close the tumultuous engagements which have been fought throughout the day, a point in history which will come to be known as Battle of Britain Day.

Why has it come to be known as Battle of Britain Day? There were certainly other days during the battle when more sorties were flown by Fighter Command; more enemy aircraft were sent over Britain; and more enemy aircraft were claimed destroyed. The British believe that on this day they have downed 185 German aircraft. This figure is unintentionally inflated, as several pilots could have engaged the same machine, with each claiming it as a kill. Analysis after the war will show the true number of Luftwaffe aircraft destroyed as sixty. Fighter Command has lost twenty-five aircraft, giving it a better than two to one kill ratio against the Luftwaffe. Crucially for the Germans, not only have they lost more aircraft, but many of them were bombers, which means more of their men have been killed, are missing, or are now prisoners of war. Fighter Command has lost thirteen of its pilots killed, missing, or taken prisoner of war, but of the remaining twelve, the majority of those who managed to bale out will be able to rejoin their squadrons.

Churchill views this day as 'the crux of the Battle of Britain'.[18] It is also clear to those Luftwaffe aircrew who have survived and returned to their airfields across the Channel, that their adversary remains unvanquished and still very formidable. The assurance their leaders gave to them, that they would meet only a handful of British fighters on this day, has proven to be spurious, if not delusory. They do not have air superiority over Britain, nor are they any nearer to achieving it. Their losses in aircrew and aircraft are unsustainable, their morale has been weakened, and their chances of launching an invasion before the weather turns against them are growing ever slimmer. What of the German High Command? The first indication of what the day has meant to the Führer is revealed through an intercept by the codebreakers at Bletchley Park, a Victorian mansion secreted in the Buckinghamshire countryside. Known as Station 'X', Churchill calls the organisation his 'geese that laid the golden eggs, but never cackled'. Unbeknown to the Germans, staff at the intelligence factory have broken the codes the enemy is using to encrypt their confidential communications. They do not realise that the codebreakers are 'listening' and 'watching'.

Information obtained in this way is marked as 'Ultra', because Churchill refers to Bletchley Park as his 'ultra-secret'. An intercept on 17 September 1940, two days after the momentous clash over southern England, reports that equipment at German airfields in Belgium for loading planes with paratroopers and their equipment is about to be dismantled. This is seen as a clear sign that Operation *Seelöwe* has been indefinitely postponed, if not cancelled.[19]

However, the Battle of Britain is not yet over and continues to be fought bitterly, as the Luftwaffe continues its assault over Britain. Realising that the attrition of bombers is unsustainable, only individual, or small groups of Dornier Do 215s and 17s and Heinkel He 111s are now used during daylight attacks. The large bomber formations that had operated over Britain previously, are now replaced by large formations of Messerschmitt Me 109 fighter bombers.[20]

The bomb load they carry is patently insufficient to bring London to its knees, but the Germans hope their fighter bombers will lure 11 Group's Hurricanes and Spitfires into the air, so that they can be destroyed. Park, at Uxbridge, maintains a frugal approach to deploying his fighters, denying the Luftwaffe an opportunity to finish off Fighter Command in the south-east of England. This situation leads Dowding to conclude later that the end of the battle came the following month: 'Serious as were our difficulties, however, those of the enemy were worse, and by the end of October the Germans abandoned their attempts to wear down the Fighter Command, and the country was delivered from the threat of immediate invasion.'[21]

Chapter 17

The Continuing & Immeasurable Contribution

It is worth saying, more out of interest than because of its contribution, something about the Italian involvement during the final phase of the battle. The Italian dictator Benito Mussolini had sent an unsolicited contingent of Fiat BR20 twin-engine bombers, Fiat CR42 biplane and Fiat G50 monoplane fighters, to operate against Britain from bases in Belgium. They carried out a night-time raid on 24 October over Harwich and Felixstowe in 12 Group, and so the Operations Room at Uxbridge was not involved. Their first incursion over 11 Group took place on 29 October, when a formation of Italian bombers and fighters were seen near Dover in the last attack of the day.[1] The formation consisted of around twelve BR20 bombers, with a similar number of escorting CR42 fighters. Their target was Ramsgate but, due to low cloud, they returned to base without releasing their bombs.[2]

Ramsgate was again targeted, on 1 November.[3] On this occasion the weather did not prevent bombs being dropped on the town of Deal. The raid itself was much larger, with fifteen bombers, escorted by thirty-nine CR42 biplane fighters and thirty-four monoplane G50 fighters, plus a dozen German Me 109s. While claims of kills were made by both Fighter Command and Corpo Aereo Italiano pilots, there are no records of any aircraft having been brought down as a result of aerial combat, although five aircraft were damaged by anti-aircraft fire and a number of aircrew were wounded as a result.[4] The Italians did lose aircraft due to other reasons and one of them, a CR42 biplane fighter, was forced to land over England and is now displayed at the Royal Air Force Museum, Hendon.

The total number of Fighter Command aircrew to lose their lives over the course of the last four months of fighting over Britain was 544. The Luftwaffe suffered an even greater loss of around 2,500. 'By the 31st of October, the battle is over. It did not cease dramatically. It died gradually away; but the British victory was none the less certain and complete. Bitter

ENEMY SIGHTED

experience had at last taught the enemy the cost of daylight attacks. He took to the cover of night.'[5]

The bombers, mainly relegated to raiding by night, continued their Blitz on London, returning to bomb it on over fifty-seven consecutive nights. The nocturnal raids continued until May of the following year, targeting not only London, but also other major cities, towns and ports across the British Isles. During this period, 43,500 civilians lost their lives and vast amounts of destruction and disruption was inflicted across the country and on the British people.

Final victory in the Battle of Britain not only prevented an invasion of the British Isles. Britain's survival, as had been the case after the evacuation from France, meant it could continue the fight against fascism and Nazi domination. The south-east of England, which had been so bitterly defended, would in time be used as the springboard from which to launch the assault on Hitler's Fortress Europe. The Bunker, it's existence still unknown to the enemy, remained relevant. Bound by its Latin motto *tutela cordis* ('Defence of the Heart'), it maintained a constant vigil, despatching and directing fighters around the clock to meet the Luftwaffe's unrelenting attacks against the capital.

In 1941, as well as responding to Luftwaffe incursions over the south-east of England, the Bunker was heavily engaged in Fighter Command's own incursions over north-west France. The offensive took the form of 'Rhubarbs', 'Rodeos', 'Circuses' and 'Ramrods'. Rhubarbs were where pairs of fighter aircraft were sent over the Channel during poor weather to search for potential ground targets and harass the enemy; Rodeos were large-scale fighter sweeps, flown at high altitude, in good weather, to do precisely what the Luftwaffe had done in the latter part of the Battle of Britain: to entice the enemy's fighters into combat; Circuses were where several squadrons of fighters escorted a small formation of bombers, using them as bait, to lure the German fighters into the air. Again, doing what the Luftwaffe had done over Britain the previous year; and Ramrods were where Hurricane bombers were sent to attack the enemy's coastal airfields and harbours.

On 19 August 1942, the Allies carried out the first large-scale assault, codenamed 'Operation Jubilee', against German forces in Occupied Europe. The main objective was for around 5,500 Canadian, British and American troops to temporarily seize and secure the French port of Dieppe. They were supported by around 237 ships from the Royal Navy, and 1,000 Allied aircraft, mainly from the Royal Air Force. The air component was directed and controlled from the Bunker, which pursued four objectives: to provide air superiority over the ships, landing grounds and troops as they advanced; to attack ground targets, which were either pre-designated by Headquarters 11 Group, or requested by the Headquarters Command Ship; to drop smoke to mask the landing and withdrawal of troops, or to block the vision of the enemy positions; and to fly tactical reconnaissance deeper into France, over the coastal roads and routes from Amiens, Rouen and Le Havre, for signs of enemy reinforcements. The Bunker had oversight of the command and control system for both pre-planned and responsive elements. Employing the telephone network and radio telephony, it maintained a constant listening watch on the communications link between the Portsmouth Station and the Headquarters ships, so that Force Commanders afloat were able to ask for special air support from fighters or bombers. The lessons learnt from Operation Jubilee were essential to the success of a much larger assault two years later, in Normandy.

In June 1943, many squadrons were transferred from Fighter Command to the newly formed 2nd Tactical Air Force (2TAF), which had its Headquarters in Hillingdon House at RAF Uxbridge. The 2TAF's role was to provide air support for British and Canadian Armies in Europe, as part of Operation Overlord, the Allied invasion of Europe. The remaining squadrons left in Fighter Command were reformed into the Air Defence of Great Britain (ADGB), whose role it was to defend Britain against aerial attack. The United States Ninth Air Force arrived at Uxbridge in February of the following year, and both British and American fighter squadrons were controlled from the Bunker, now renamed the Combined Control Centre (CCC).

On 6 June 1944, the long-awaited Second Front was opened, when 132,000 troops were landed at five beaches on France's Normandy coastline. Known as D-Day, the Normandy Landings were the first step towards liberating Europe from Nazi domination. Throughout the preparatory and assault periods, the control of the fighter bombers and the light and medium bombers of the two tactical air forces was exercised through a Combined Operations Room located at Uxbridge. This Operations Room was staffed by representatives of the United States Ninth Air Force and the Royal Air Force 2TAF.

The CCC was responsible, under Operation Neptune, for coordinating all Allied aerial activity involved in Operation Overlord, which included the over 13,000 sorties flown by British and American squadrons on the first day of the Operation. The CCC had been set up and was operated by the Air Officer Commanding 11 Group, with the full collaboration of the Commanding General, United States Ninth Fighter Command, and with authoritative

ENEMY SIGHTED

representation of the United States Army Eighth Fighter Command. This Combined Control Centre was manned by both British and American staff and was, in effect, the Operations Room of No. 11 Group, Air Defence of Great Britain, with the complete static signals system of the old organisation, developed over a long period and augmented by additional communication facilities. This Centre had planned, coordinated and controlled all fighter operations in the initial phases of the operation, and it was also responsible for issuing executive instructions for the fighter bombers.[6]

To ensure total air superiority, the CCC at Uxbridge deployed an astonishing 103 RAF fighter squadrons over the beachhead itself. Lines of communication were set up between 'Fighter Direction Ships' (FDS), the squadrons and the CCC at Uxbridge. Uxbridge was responsible for giving the order for squadrons to scramble towards Normandy and the FDS role was to vector the squadron to where it was required, dependent on events on the ground. The underground complex at Uxbridge was of absolute importance to the success of Operation Overlord. As with Operation *Seelöwe*, failure to gain and retain air superiority over the landing grounds would have ultimately resulted in failure:

> The 11 Group Controller had also to maintain such 'states' and was to order such fighter patrols to be flown as were required to maintain an adequate defence of these commitments over the 11 Group land and sea areas both by day and night, prior to, during and after the assault has taken place.[7]

On 13 June 1944, seven days after the launch of Operation Overlord, Uxbridge was again called upon to defend Britain from aerial attack. The new threat came in the form of an unmanned guided missile: the V1. It was the first of Hitler's *Vergeltungswaffen*. These were flying bombs, intended to bring carnage and destruction to the capital. The Führer had become ever more desperate as the Allied Armies gained a foothold in Europe and his cities came under constant attack from Allied bombers. Germany's leader hoped to destroy London, terrorise its population, and stop the Allies in their tracks. The objectives were no different to those in the preceding two years, but now the devastation which could be inflicted was much greater, and it could be brought about without risking his bombers or his aircrew. The pilotless planes, named Doodlebugs by the British, because of the distinctive noise made by the pulsing jet engine, travelled at 400 mph (644 kph). They were too fast to be intercepted by anything other than the Allies' most up-to-date fighters. The response was Operation Diver, coordinated from the CCC, which had recourse to squadrons of the latest Supermarine Spitfire Mk XIVs, Hawker Tempests, North American P51 Mustangs, De Havilland night fighter Mosquitos. From July, the Bunker also controlled a new ground-breaking aircraft, the Gloster Meteor Mk I, powered by Frank Whittle's jet engine. Flown by 616 Squadron at RAF Manston, it was the RAF's first jet fighter.

On 4 August, two of 616 Squadron's Meteors claimed the first ever kills made by a Royal Air Force jet fighter. Flying Officer Dean reported:

> At 15.45 hours I was scrambled for Anti *Diver* Patrol between Ashford and Robertsbridge. Flying at 4,500 ft [1,372 metres], 340 mph [547 kph]. At 16.16 hours, I saw one *Diver*, four to five miles [six to eight kilometres] south-east of Tenterden, flying at 1,000 ft [305 metres], on a course of 330 degrees, estimated speed of 365 mph [587 kph]. From two-and-a-half miles [four kilometres] behind the *Diver*, I dived down at 470 mph [756 kph]. Closing in to attack, I found my four 20 mm guns would not fire owing to a technical trouble now being investigated. I then flew my Meteor alongside the *Diver* for approximately twenty to thirty seconds. Gradually I manoeuvred my wing tip a few inches under the wing of the *Diver*, then pulling my aircraft upwards and sharply, I turned the *Diver* over on its back and sent it diving to earth approximately four miles [six kilometres] south of Tonbridge. This is the first pilotless aircraft to be destroyed by a jet propelled aircraft.[8]

Moments later, Flying Officer John Rodger, reported:

> At 16.40 hours I sighted a *Diver* near Tenterden flying on a course of 318 degrees at 3,000 ft [914 metres], estimated speed 340 mph [547 kph]. I immediately attacked from dead astern and fired a two-second burst at range of 300 yards [274 metres]. I observed hits and saw petrol or oil streaming out of *Diver,* which continued to fly straight and level. I fired another two-second burst from my four cannons, still at 300 yards. Both Meteor and *Diver* were flying at 340 miles per hour. The *Diver* then went down, and I saw it explode on ground about five miles, [eight kilometres] north-west of Tenterden.[9]

ENEMY SIGHTED

Fighters combined destroyed 1,771 Doodlebugs, by either shooting them down or by knocking them off balance using their wing tip, a method knowing as 'tipping'. A similar number were downed by anti-aircraft guns, and a further 200 by the balloon barrage.[10]

The V1 threat continued to test 11 Group's resolve for a further seven months, until their launch sites were overrun by the advancing Allied Armies. However, a further, more ominous threat remained. Since September the previous year, the German's had launched an even more powerful *Vergeltungswaffen* (Vengeance Weapon): the V2. It was the world's first long-range guided ballistic missile, and its trajectory and speed meant it could not be intercepted by Allied fighters. The only way to tackle them was to prevent them being built, or destroy them before they could be launched. Fighter aircraft under the direction and control of Uxbridge were sent on Operation Noball and Operation Crossbow sorties across the Channel to target the factories making V1s and V2s, or the sites from where they were launched.

In October 1944, the term ADGB was rescinded and the title 'Fighter Command' was used again. The Bunker continued its role of protecting London and the south-east of England. It also coordinated the fighters escorting Allied bombing raids over Germany. The fire started by the Nazis to satisfy their thirst for world domination was being extinguished.

When victory in Europe finally came, on 8 May 1945:

> All ranks were conscious of the significance of the day and were profoundly thankful and relieved that the hour for which they had strived and waited so long had arrived at last. They were, however, aware of the responsibilities for the defence of the country and had in mind the warning given by the AOC that even at this late stage 'the Hun' might attempt some treachery against this country by isolated irresponsible units or even on a greater and more organised scale.

The day was marked by a further speech from the AOC to the Operations Room personnel, he said:

> I think it only right that I should address the Watch which is now on duty at this historic moment. After all these years that 11 Group Operations Room has been manned, through the Battle of Britain time when we realise now that the safety of

> this country hung on a thread, on through the period of night blitzes when the situation was nearly as serious, and so slowly upwards during the time when the weight was slowly turned from defence to offence and finally to this conclusion. I feel this will be a moment that you will remember all your lives. I take this opportunity of thanking you for your loyalty and sense of duty, and I know well that each in his own articulate job has never spared himself to ensure that nothing was left undone which might impair the efficiency of our aircraft in whatever tasks they were employed.[11]

Together, the Bunker and the integrated air defence system of which it was a crucial part had not only made a comprehensive contribution to the fortunes of the Royal Air Force, or even this country, but to the world. Without them, defeat in France would have been a fatal hammer blow in the global conflict between democracy and fascism. Without them, sufficient troops would not have been rescued from the enemy's clutches to continue the fight between ideologies. Without them, the raid on Dieppe, albeit disastrous, would not have happened, and crucial lessons, would not have been learnt. Without them, command of the skies over Normandy would not have been won, and the Allies would have been pushed back into the sea. Without them, Hitler's vengeance weapons, would not have been successfully repelled and subdued. And finally, without them, Hitler's dream of invading this country would not have been so conclusively crushed.

How then to describe what is, perhaps, their greatest cumulative contribution? Well, an image comes to mind, when standing in the Bunker, looking at the faded and veritable map on the plotting table. It is a symbolic description of that epoch-defining moment in time when history was made. Britain was like a castle surrounded by her moat, the English Channel. The integrated air defence system was the drawbridge protecting that castle from being assailed. The Bunker was the gatehouse that controlled the drawbridge. What this inimitable assimilation allowed her to do, in the summer of 1940, was to pull up the drawbridge, and so deny the Germans entry into Britain. It was the Bunker's, and Britain's, 'finest hour'.

Endnotes

Introduction

1. Adolph Hitler, War Directive No.16, *Preparations for a Landing Operation Against England*, LCO 67/71.

Chapter 1

1. Imperial War Museum Collections.
2. *Daily Telegraph* (London), 11 December 1908.
3. *Mail Online*, 26 July 2009.
4. *The Literary Digest*, Volume XXXIX, July 1909–December 1909.

Chapter 2

1. Air Ministry, Air Defence Pamphlet Number 5, *The Operational Control of Fighter Aircraft*, A.P.NO.3145/5, April 1942, Part III, p.12.
2. www.roc-heritage.co.uk
3. Patrick Bishop, *Air Force Blue: The RAF in WW II, Spearhead of Victory*, William Collins, 2017, p.29.
4. Lawrence Holmes, *The First Blitz: German Air Raids on Great Britain, 1914 to 1918*, ROCA.
5. Minute 3 of 18th meeting of the War Cabinet, 11 July 1917.
6. Anthony Cumming, *The Battle for Britain: Inter-service Rivalry between the Royal Air Force and Royal Navy, 1909–40*, Naval Institute Press, 2015, p.23.
7. Royal Air Force, *War Cabinet Committee on Air Organisation and Home Defence Against Air Raids (2nd Report)*, Air Power Review, Spring 2013, p.143.

ENDNOTES

8. Royal Air Force, *War Cabinet Committee on Air Organisation and Home Defence Against Air Raids (2nd Report)*, Air Power Review, Spring 2013, pp.147–8.
9. Lawrence Holmes, *The First Blitz: German Air Raids on Great Britain*, 1914 to 1918, ROCA.

Chapter 3

1. Winston Churchill, *House of Commons Debate*, 30 July 1934, Hansard, vol.292, cc. 2325–447.
2. T.C.G. James, *The Growth of Fighter Command 1936–1940*, Routledge Taylor & Francis, 2014, p.2.
3. T.C.G. James, *The Growth of Fighter Command 1936–1940*, Routledge Taylor & Francis, 2014, p.3.
4. T.C.G. James, *The Growth of Fighter Command 1936–1940*, Routledge Taylor & Francis, 2014, p.4,6.
5. Derek Wood & Derek Dempster, *The Narrow Margin,* Pen & Sword, 2003, p.78.
6. ACM Sir Hugh Dowding, *Battle of Britain Despatch*, AIR 8/863, 1941, para.179.
7. Williamson Murray & Richard Hart Sinnreich, *Successful Strategies: Triumphing in War and Peace from Antiquity to the Present,* Cambridge University Press, 2014, p.268.
8. T.C.G. James, *The Growth of Fighter Command 1936–1940*, Routledge Taylor & Francis, 2014, pp.11–3.
9. T.C.G. James, *The Growth of Fighter Command 1936–1940*, Routledge Taylor & Francis, 2014, p.26.
10. Derek Wood & Derek Dempster, *The Narrow Margin*, Pen & Sword, 2003, pp.55–6.
11. T.C.G. James, *The Growth of Fighter Command 1936–1940*, Routledge Taylor & Francis, 2014, p.13.

Chapter 4

1. Headquarters Fighter Command, *A Memorandum on the Raid Reporting and Control Aspects of the UK Air Defence Organisation*, AHB Reference 198, p.45.

2. B. Mortimer, C. Holland, J.F.C. Windmill and F. Vollrath, *Unpicking the signal thread of the sector web spider Zygiella x-notata*, https://doi.org/10.1098/rsif.2015.0633.

Chapter 5

1. T.C.G. James, *The Growth of Fighter Command 1936–1940*, Routledge Taylor & Francis, 2014, p.71.
2. T.C.G. James, *The Growth of Fighter Command 1936–1940*, Routledge Taylor & Francis, 2014, p.71.
3. ACM Sir Hugh Dowding, Letter written to Sir Arthur Street, Permanent Under Secretary, Air Ministry, AIR 16/255, 25th September 1939.
4. Derek Wood & Derek Dempster, *The Narrow Margin,* Pen & Sword, 2003, p.40.
5. Derek Wood & Derek Dempster, *The Narrow Margin,* Pen & Sword, 2003, p.284.
6. Douglas Bader, *Fight for the Sky: The Story of the Spitfire and Hurricane*, Pen & Sword, 2008, Chapter 1.
7. T.C.G. James, *The Growth of Fighter Command 1936–1940*, Routledge Taylor & Francis, 2014, pp.61, 79.
8. Eric Morgan and Edward Shacklady, *Spitfire: The History,* Guild Publishing, 1987, pp.38, 46, 490.
9. Mick Spick, *Luftwaffe Fighter Aces*, Frontline Books, 2011, pp.51–3.
10. John Dibbs and Tony Holmes, *Spitfire, The Legend Lives On,* Osprey Publishing, 2016, p.206.
11. Mitch Peeke, 1940 *The Battles to Stop Hitler*, Pen & Sword, 2015, p.35.
12. Richard Haitch, *Who Helped Win the Battle of Britain*, The New York Times, 3 December 1978.
13. V.A. Kalichevsky, *The Amazing Petroleum Industry*, Reinhold Publishing Corporation, 1943, p.7.
14. Mick Spick, *Luftwaffe Fighter Aces*, Frontline Books, 2011, pp.51–3.
15. The Spitfire Society, *Merlin Engine,* spitfiresociety.org.
16. Peter Townsend, *Duel of Eagles,* Corgi Books, 1974, p.170.
17. Mitch Peeke, 1940 *The Battles to Stop Hitler*, Pen & Sword, 2015, p.35–6.
18. Andy Saunders, *Battle of Britain July to October 1940,* Haynes Publishing, 2015, p.61.

ENDNOTES

19. Dr Alfred Price, *Spitfire Pilots' Stories*, The History Press, 2012, p.141.
20. Dr Alfred Price, *Spitfire Pilots' Stories*, The History Press, 2012, pp.75–6.
21. Air Historical Branch (1), *Photographic Reconnaissance by the Royal Air Force in the War of 1939–45*, Volume 1, pp.73–157.
22. Derek Wood & Derek Dempster, *The Narrow Margin,* Pen & Sword, 2003, p.32.
23. *The Times* (London), 22 January 2020.
24. Winston Churchill, *The Second World War, Volume II, Their Finest Hour*, Cassell & Co. Ltd, 1949, p.293.

Chapter 6

1. ACM Sir Hugh Dowding, *Battle of Britain Despatch*, AIR 8/863, 1941, para.75.
2. Derek Wood & Derek Dempster, *The Narrow Margin,* Pen & Sword, 2003, p.86.
3. Richard Hough & Denis Richards, *The Battle of Britain, The Jubilee History,* Guild Publishing, 1990, p.113.
4. ACM Sir Keith Park, audio interview, *BBC*, 1961.
5. 11 Fighter Group Battle Orders 1937, AIR 16/221, p.1.
6. 11 Fighter Group Battle Orders 1937, AIR 16/221, p.5.
7. 11 Fighter Group Battle Orders 1937, AIR 16/221, p.10.
8. Derek Wood & Derek Dempster, *The Narrow Margin,* Pen & Sword, 2003, p.173.
9. Derek Wood & Derek Dempster, *The Narrow Margin*, Pen & Sword, 2003, pp.82–3.
10. Derek Wood & Derek Dempster, *The Narrow Margin,* Pen & Sword, 2003, p.87.
11. Derek Wood & Derek Dempster, *The Narrow Margin,* Pen & Sword, 2003, p.79.

Chapter 7

1. Sir William Henry Bragg, *The World of Sound; Six Lectures Delivered Before a Juvenile Auditory at the Royal Institution, Christmas 1919, London*, G. Bell & Sons Ltd, 1920, p.193.
2. Derek Wood & Derek Dempster, *The Narrow Margin,* Pen & Sword, 2003, p.55.

3. Winston Churchill, *The Second World War, Volume II, Their Finest Hour*, Cassell & Co. Ltd, 1949, p.337.
4. Derek Wood & Derek Dempster, *The Narrow Margin,* Pen & Sword, 2003, p.56.
5. Stanley Baldwin, *House of Commons Debate,* Hansard, 10th November 1932, vol 270, cc633.
6. Derek Wood & Derek Dempster, *The Narrow Margin,* Pen & Sword, 2003, p.61.
7. Derek Wood & Derek Dempster, *The Narrow Margin*, Pen & Sword, 2003, pp.63–4.
8. RDF Report on 11 Group Home Defence Exercise, 8–9 July 1939, AVIA 7/401, p.1.
9. Report on Number 11 (Fighter) Group Exercise, 25 July 1939, AVIA 7/401, p.4.
10. Mike Dean, Squadron Leader, *Chain of Command, Battle of Britain A Tribute to the Few*, Key Publishing Ltd, 2010.
11. 11 Group Operations Record, AIR 25/193, 6 September 1939.
12. Richard Hough & Denis Richards, *The Battle of Britain, The Jubilee History*, Guild Publishing, 1990, p.66–7.
13. Derek Wood & Derek Dempster, *The Narrow Margin*, Pen & Sword, 2003, pp.62–3.
14. Derek Wood & Derek Dempster, *The Narrow Margin,* Pen & Sword, 2003, p.60.
15. Derek Wood & Derek Dempster, *The Narrow Margin*, Pen & Sword, 2003, pp.62–3.
16. B.T. Neale, *CH – The First Operational Radar*, The G.E.C. Journal of Research, Volume 3, Number 2, 1985.
17. Memorandum of Experiments Carried Out at Biggin Hill Operations Room, 09 July 1939, AVIA 7/401, p.2.
18. Derek Wood & Derek Dempster, *The Narrow Margin*, Pen & Sword, 2003, pp.84–6.
19. ACM Sir Hugh Dowding, *Battle of Britain Despatch*, AIR 8/863, 1941, para.54.
20. ACM Sir Hugh Dowding, *Battle of Britain Despatch*, AIR 8/863, 1941, para.55.
21. Mark Frankland, *Radio Man – The Remarkable Rise and Fall of CO Stanley,* IET History of Technology, Series 30, p.89.
22. E.G. Bowen, *Radar Days*, Institute of Physics Publishing, 1987, p.77.
23. War Cabinet Resume No 8, 28 October 1939, WP (39) 101, P3, para. 11.

ENDNOTES

24. Ronald Dekker, *The EF50, the Tube that helped Win the War,* https://www.dos4ever.com/EF50/EF50.html
25. ACM Sir Hugh Dowding, *Battle of Britain Despatch*, AIR 8/863, 1941, para.56.
26. Mike Dean, Squadron Leader, *Chain of Command, Battle of Britain A Tribute to the Few*, Key Publishing Ltd, 2010.
27. Andy Saunders, *Battle of Britain July to October 1940*, Haynes Publishing, 2015, pp.16–8.
28. Len Deighton, *Fighter, The True Story of the Battle of Britain*, Vintage Books, 2008, pp.88–9.
29. David Irving, *The Rise and Fall of the Luftwaffe, The Life of Field Marshal Erhard Milch*, Parforce UK, 2002, p.67.
30. Peter Jensen, *Wireless at War*, Rosenberg Publishing, 2013, *Development of Radar Chapter*.
31. Derek Wood & Derek Dempster, *The Narrow Margin*, Pen & Sword, 2003, p.42.
32. Derek Wood & Derek Dempster, *The Narrow Margin*, Pen & Sword, 2003, p.63.
33. Derek Wood & Derek Dempster, *The Narrow Margin*, Pen & Sword, 2003, p.16.
34. Adolf Galland, *The First and the Last*, Reading Essentials, 2018, p.17.
35. ACM Sir Hugh Dowding, *Battle of Britain Despatch*, AIR 8/863, 1941, para.57.
36. ACM Sir Hugh Dowding, *Battle of Britain Despatch*, AIR 8/863, 1941, para 235–6.
37. 11 Group Operations Record, AIR 25/193, 23 July 1940.
38. This was the instruction given by the Sector Controller to activate the aircraft's airborne interception Radar.
39. Glyn Ashfield, Flying Officer, F.I.U. Tangmere, Combat Report, AIR 50/470/1, 22/23 July 1940.
40. James Phinney Baxter III, *Scientists Against Time*, Little, Brown, and Co, 1946, p.142.

Chapter 8

1. ACM Sir Hugh Dowding, *Battle of Britain Despatch*, AIR 8/863, 1941, para.58.
2. Winston Churchill, *The Second World War, Volume 1, The Gathering Storm*, Houghton Mifflin Company, 1948, p.141.

3. An Official History, *Royal Observer Corps, The 'Eyes and Ears' of the RAF in WW2*, Frontline Books, p.viii.
4. Derek Wood & Derek Dempster, *The Narrow Margin,* Pen & Sword, 2003, p.74.
5. An Official History, *Royal Observer Corps, The 'Eyes and Ears' of the RAF in WW2*, Frontline Books, p.41.
6. An Official History, *Royal Observer Corps, The 'Eyes and Ears' of the RAF in WW2*, Frontline Books, p.x–xi.
7. An Official History, *Royal Observer Corps, The 'Eyes and Ears' of the RAF in WW2*, Frontline Books, p.23.
8. An Official History, *Royal Observer Corps, The 'Eyes and Ears' of the RAF in WW2*, Frontline Books, p.44.
9. An Official History, *Royal Observer Corps, The 'Eyes and Ears' of the RAF in WW2*, Frontline Books, p.31–2.
10. Derek Wood, *The Battle Rethought – A Symposium on the Battle of Britain*, Airlife Publishing, 1991, p.5.
11. ACM Sir Hugh Dowding, *Battle of Britain Despatch*, AIR 8/863, 1941, para 60–6.
12. An Official History, *Royal Observer Corps, The 'Eyes and Ears' of the RAF in WW2*, Frontline Books, p.xii.
13. An Official History, *Royal Observer Corps, The 'Eyes and Ears' of the RAF in WW2*, Frontline Books, p.55.
14. An Official History, *Royal Observer Corps, The 'Eyes and Ears' of the RAF in WW2*, Frontline Books, p.45–6.
15. Air Defence Pamphlet Number 4, A.P. No. 3145/4, April 1942, Appendix 'D' p.3, Appendix 'E', pp.4, 5.
16. No 11 Group Instructions to Controllers No 4, AIR 25/197, 19 August 1940.
17. An Official History, *Royal Observer Corps, The 'Eyes and Ears' of the RAF in WW2*, Frontline Books, p.47–8.
18. No 11 Group Instructions to Controllers No 10, AIR 25/197, 5 September 1940.
19. An Official History, *Royal Observer Corps, The 'Eyes and Ears' of the RAF in WW2*, Frontline Books, p.71–3.
20. An Official History, *Royal Observer Corps, The 'Eyes and Ears' of the RAF in WW2*, Frontline Books, p.116–7.
21. Alex Tooley, *WW2 People's War, In the Royal Observer Corps, BBC*, contributed October 2005.
22. Royal Observer Corps Association, *Heritage of the Corps, Post/Observer Instrument,* roc.heritage-co.uk.

ENDNOTES

23. Derek Wood & Derek Dempster, *The Narrow Margin,* Pen & Sword, 2003, p.76.
24. An Official History, *Royal Observer Corps, The 'Eyes and Ears' of the RAF in WW2*, Frontline Books, p.40–1.
25. Derek Wood & Derek Dempster, *The Narrow Margin,* Pen & Sword, 2003, p.206.
26. Derek Wood & Derek Dempster, *The Narrow Margin,* Pen & Sword, 2003, p.71.

Chapter 9

1. T.C.G. James, *The Growth of Fighter Command 1936–1940*, Routledge Taylor & Francis, 2014, p.120.
2. General Sir Fredrick Pile, *Anti-Aircraft Defence Despatch, The London Gazette*, 16 December 1947, Part 1, paragraph 26.
3. T.C.G. James, *The Growth of Fighter Command 1936–1940*, Routledge Taylor & Francis, 2014, Appendix 13, Note on WP (40) 159, 18 May 1940.
4. General Sir Fredrick Pile, *Anti-Aircraft Defence Despatch, The London Gazette*, 16 December 1947, Part 1, paragraph 4.
5. No 11 Group Instructions to Controllers No 7, AIR 25/197, 27 August 1940.
6. ACM Sir Hugh Dowding, *Battle of Britain Despatch*, AIR 8/863, 1941, Appendix 'C', p.118.
7. General Sir Fredrick Pile, *Anti-Aircraft Defence Despatch, The London Gazette*, 16 December 1947, part 1, para.8.
8. Major Josef Schmid, *'German Intelligence Appreciation of the RAF and Comparison With Current Luftwaffe Strength,* presented by 5th Abteilung to Luftwaffe High Command on 16 July 1940.
9. General Sir Fredrick Pile, *Anti-Aircraft Defence Despatch, The London Gazette*, 16 December 1947, part 1, para.8.
10. Andy Saunders, *Battle of Britain July to October 1940*, Haynes Publishing, 2015, pp.142–4.
11. Andy Saunders, *Battle of Britain July to October 1940*, Haynes Publishing, 2015, pp.142–9.
12. ACM Sir Hugh Dowding, *Battle of Britain Despatch*, AIR 8/863, 1941, para 237.
13. ACM Sir Hugh Dowding, *Battle of Britain Despatch*, AIR 8/863, 1941, para 56.

14. 11 Group Operations Record, AIR 25/193, 14 September 1940.
15. Basil Collier, *The Defence of the United Kingdom*, Appendix IX, Disposition of Anti-aircraft guns, 11th July 1940, HMSO, 1957.
16. ACM Sir Hugh Dowding, *Battle of Britain Despatch*, AIR 8/863, 1941, Appendix 'C', p.118.
17. ACM Sir Hugh Dowding, *Battle of Britain Despatch*, AIR 8/863, 1941, Appendix 'C.C', p.128.
18. Derek Wood & Derek Dempster, *The Narrow Margin*, Pen & Sword, 2003, p.235.
19. Richard Hough & Denis Richards, *The Battle of Britain, The Jubilee History,* Guild Publishing, 1990, p.263.

Chapter 10

1. Mark Felton, *Castle of the Eagles,* Thomas Dunne Books, 2017.
2. T.C.G. James, *The Growth of Fighter Command 1936–1940*, Routledge Taylor & Francis, 2014, p.37.
3. Andy Saunders, *Battle of Britain July to October 1940,* Haynes Publishing, 2015, p.154.
4. Basil Collier, *The Defence of the United Kingdom*, Equipment and Location of Balloon Squadrons 31 August 1940, HMSO, 1957, p.455.
5. Andy Saunders, *Battle of Britain July to October 1940*, Haynes Publishing, 2015, pp.151–3.
6. Andy Saunders, *Battle of Britain July to October 1940,* Haynes Publishing, 2015, p.152.
7. Derek Wood & Derek Dempster, *The Narrow Margin,* Pen & Sword, 2003, p.153, 157, 192, 200, 202.
8. Balloon Barrage Reunion Club, *'Barrage Balloon Cables Collisions with Aircraft through 1939 to 1945'*, www.bbrclub.org
9. ACM Sir Hugh Dowding, *Battle of Britain Despatch*, AIR 8/863, 1941, para.53.
10. Major Josef Schmid, *'German Intelligence Appreciation of the RAF and Comparison With Current Luftwaffe Strength,* presented by 5th Abteilung to Luftwaffe High Command on 16 July 1940.
11. Derek Wood & Derek Dempster, *The Narrow Margin,* Pen & Sword, 2003, p.142.
12. Andy Saunders, *Battle of Britain July to October 1940,* Haynes Publishing, 2015, p.153.

ENDNOTES

13. ACM Sir Hugh Dowding, *Battle of Britain Despatch*, AIR 8/863, 1941, para.53.
14. T.C.G. James, *The Growth of Fighter Command 1936–1940*, Routledge Taylor & Francis, 2014, p.127.

Chapter 11

1. Hazel Crozier, *RAF Uxbridge, 90th Anniversary*, RAF High Wycombe: Air Command Media Services, 2007, pp.8–9.
2. Battle of Britain Bunker, London Borough of Hillingdon.
3. Neville Chamberlain, *Arriving at Heston Aerodrome, 30 September 1938, Pathé News*, https://youtu.be/e0uOsPBSKPo
4. Battle of Britain Bunker, London Borough of Hillingdon.
5. Minutes of Meeting Held at Headquarters Fighter Command, AIR 16/601, 27 October 1938.
6. Battle of Britain Bunker, London Borough of Hillingdon.
7. Battle of Britain Bunker, London Borough of Hillingdon.
8. Battle of Britain Bunker, London Borough of Hillingdon.
9. Air Ministry, *The growth and progress of Operations Rooms in Fighting Area now (No 11 Fighter Group)*, AIR 16/195, pp.85–6.
10. Vincent Orange, *Park: The Biography of A.C.M Sir Keith Park*, Grubb Street, 2013, p.101.

Chapter 12

1. Daphne Wallis, Battle of Britain London Monument, https://bbm.org.uk
2. A memorandum produced by Headquarters Fighter Command on the raid reporting and control aspects of the United Kingdom Air Defence Organisation, AIR 10/4183, 1944, para. 211, 214, 216.
3. *'The History of 11 Group in the First Ten Years'*, AIR 16/1098, 1946, p.2.
4. Battle of Britain Bunker, London Borough of Hillingdon.
5. *Reflections & Observations of a Group Controller*, AIR 25/197, 1940.
6. A memorandum produced by Headquarters Fighter Command on the raid reporting and control aspects of the United Kingdom Air Defence Organisation, AIR 10/4183, 1944, para. 179
7. No. 11 Group Instructions to Controllers No. 28, Air Power Review, Centre for Air Power Studies, 2015, p.64.

8. Hastings Ismay, *The Memoirs of General Lord Ismay*, Viking Press, 1960, pp.181–2.
9. Vincent Orange, *Park: The Biography of A.C.M Sir Keith Park,* Grubb Street, 2013, p.119.
10. ACM Sir Hugh Dowding, *Battle of Britain Despatch*, AIR 8/863, 1941, para.128–9.
11. Vincent Orange, *Park: The Biography of A.C.M Sir Keith Park,* Grubb Street, 2013, p.96.
12. Group Controllers Instruction No.8, AIR 25/197, 2 September 1940.
13. Group Controllers Instruction No.10, AIR 25/197, 5 September 1940.
14. Air Ministry, *The growth and progress of Operations Rooms in Fighting Area now (No 11 Fighter Group)*, AIR 16/195, p.58.
15. Air Defence Pamphlet Number 4, Appendix A, AIR 10/3760, April 1942.
16. Vincent Orange, *Park: The Biography of A.C.M Sir Keith Park,* Grubb Street, 2013, p.77.
17. A memorandum produced by Headquarters Fighter Command on the raid reporting and control aspects of the United Kingdom Air Defence Organisation, AHB Reference 198, p.80.
18. *Those Girls & Their Finest Hour*, Custodians of Air Power Supplement, https://www.raffca.org.uk, 2015.
19. Air defence Pamphlet Number 4, Appendix D, AIR 10/3760, April 1942.
20. Air Ministry, *The growth and progress of Operations Rooms in Fighting Area now (No 11 Fighter Group)*, AIR 16/195, p.60.
21. No. 11 Group Instructions to Controllers No. 28, Air Power Review, Centre for Air Power Studies, 2015, p.64.
22. Group Controllers Instruction No.7, AIR 25/197, 27 August 1940.
23. ACM Sir Hugh Dowding, *Battle of Britain Despatch*, AIR 8/863, 1941, para.18–201.
24. Air Ministry, Air Defence Pamphlet Number 5, *The Operational Control of Fighter Aircraft*, A.P.NO.3145/5, Part III, p.12.
25. No. 11 Fighter Group Battle Orders 1937, AIR 16/221, p.17 & Air Defence Pamphlet Number 4, Appendix E, AIR 10/3760, April 1942, p.2.
26. ACM Sir Hugh Dowding, *Battle of Britain Despatch*, AIR 8/863, 1941, para. 62.
27. Air Ministry, *The growth and progress of Operations Rooms in Fighting Area now (No 11 Fighter Group)*, AIR 16/195, p.48.

ENDNOTES

28. Air defence Pamphlet Number 4, Appendix F, AIR 10/3760, April 1942.
29. Air Ministry, *The growth and progress of Operations Rooms in Fighting Area now (No 11 Fighter Group)*, AIR 16/195, p.56.
30. Winston Churchill, *The Second World War, Volume II, Their Finest Hour*, Cassell & Co. Ltd, 1949, pp.293–4.
31. Air Ministry, *The growth and progress of Operations Rooms in Fighting Area now (No 11 Fighter Group)*, AIR 16/195, p.53.
32. Air Ministry, Air Defence Pamphlet Number 5, *The Operational Control of Fighter Aircraft*, A.P.NO.3145/5, April 1942, p.6–8.
33. Air Defence Pamphlet Number 5, The Operational Control of Fighter Aircraft, A.P.NO.3145/5, Part III, p.12.
34. Air Defence Pamphlet Number 4, Appendix C, AIR 10/3760, April 1942.
35. No. 11 Fighter Group Battle Orders 1937, AIR 16/221, pp.6,25–6.
36. No. 11 Fighter Group Battle Orders 1937, AIR 16/221, p.7.
37. No. 11 Fighter Group Battle Orders 1937, AIR 16/221, p.8.
38. *Reporting of 'Tally Ho' by Formation Leaders*, Part II, AIR 25/197, 29 August 1940.
39. No. 11 Fighter Group Battle Orders 1937, AIR 16/221, p.7.
40. No. 11 Group Instructions to Controllers No. 4, AIR 16/216/71A, 19 August 1940.
41. No. 11 Fighter Group Battle Orders 1937, AIR 16/221, p.18.
42. Air Ministry, Air Defence Pamphlet Number 5, *The Operational Control of Fighter Aircraft*, A.P.NO.3145/5, Part II, pp.9–10.
43. No. 11 Fighter Group Battle Orders 1937, AIR 16/221, p.19.
44. Air Defence Pamphlet Number 5, *The Operational Control of Fighter Aircraft*, A.P.NO.3145/5, Part II, p.16.

Chapter 13

1. Spitfire Production List, http://www.airhistory.org.uk
2. www.polishairforce.pl
3. Call sign for 303 (Polish) Squadron.
4. Ludwik Paszkiewicz, Lieutenant, 303 (Polish) Squadron, Combat Report, AIR 50/117/45, 30 August 1940.
5. https://www.rafmuseum.org.uk/blog/poles-and-czechoslovaks-in-the-battle-of-britain/
6. ACM Sir Hugh Dowding, *Battle of Britain Despatch*, AIR 8/863, 1941, para. 164.

ENEMY SIGHTED

7. Issued by the Ministry of Information on Behalf of the Air Ministry, *The Battle of Britain,* H.M.S.O, 1941.
8. Hastings Ismay, *The Memoirs of General Lord Ismay*, Viking Press, 1960, pp.181–2.
9. Winston Churchill, *House of Commons Debate*, Hansard, 20 August 1940, vol 364, cc1167.
10. F.W. Stannard, Group Captain, *letter to the Under Secretary of State, Air Ministry*, FC/S.49788/org. A.O.A, AIR 16/1231, 14 February 1955.
11. Henry Wilson, Monumental Masons & Sculptors, *letter confirming completion*, AIR 16/1231, 8 April 1958.
12. RAF, Various Documents Relating to Memorial Unveiling on 22 April 1958 , AIR 16/1231, 1958.
13. Battle of Britain Bunker, London Borough of Hillingdon.
14. 11 Group Operations Record, AIR 25/193, 26 August 1940.
15. Dr Richard Mayne, *Among Canada's 'Few': The RCAF's No.1 Squadron in the Battle of Britain,* http://www.rcaf-arc.forces.gc.ca, 11 September 2017.
16. 11 Group Operations Record, AIR 25/193, 5 October 1940.
17. Hartland de Montarville Molson Obituary, *The Telegraph,* 01 October 2002.
18. Spitfires (Kenley Fighter Station), *British Pathé,* https://youtu.be/y6JxSHmVB5g 1940.
19. Francis Dawson-Paul, Sub Lieutenant, 64 Squadron, Combat Report, AIR 50/24/90, 25 July 1940.
20. 11 Group Operations Record, AIR 25/193, 25 July 1940.
21. https://colnect.com/en/stamps/stamp/486412-Supermarine_Spitfire_L1035-Battle_of_Britain_70th_Anniv-Falkland_Islands
22. Vincent Orange, *Park: The Biography of A.C.M Sir Keith Park*, Grubb Street, 2013, p.143. & Murray Rowlands, *Air Marshal Sir Keith Park: Victor of the Battle of Britain, Defender of Malta*, Pen & Sword, 2021, p.35.

Chapter 14

1. Neville Chamberlain, House of *Commons Debate*, Hansard, 31 March 1939, vol.345, cc. 2415.
2. Neville Chamberlain, House of *Commons Debate*, Hansard, 03 September 1939, vol.351, cc. 292.

ENDNOTES

3. Operations by 11 Group Over France, AIR 16/352, 8 July 1940, para.3.
4. Alfred Duff Cooper, *House of Commons Debate*, Hansard, 12 March 1936, vol 309, cc2349.
5. Martin Gilbert, *Winston. S. Churchill, Companion Volume V, Part 3, The Coming of War*, Heinemann, 1882, p.1594.
6. Operations by 11 Group Over France, AIR 16/352, 8 July 1940, para.14.
7. Denis Richards, *The Fight at Odds,* HMSO, 1953, p.138.
8. Operations by 11 Group Over France, AIR 16/352, 8 July 1940, Appendix D *'Return of Casualties'*.
9. Operations by 11 Group Over France, AIR 16/352, 8 July 1940, Appendix D *'Return of Casualties'*.
10. Larry Forrester, *Fly For Your Life,* Arrow Books, 1990, p.102.
11. Larry Forrester, *Fly For Your Life*, Arrow Books, 1990, p.106.
12. 11 Group Operations Record, AIR 25/193, 26 May 1940.
13. Winston Churchill, *House of Commons Debate*, Hansard, 4 June 1940, vol.361, cc. 790–796.
14. Winston Churchill, *House of Commons Debate*, Hansard, 18 June 1940, vol.362, cc. 53–61.
15. ACM Sir Hugh Dowding, *Battle of Britain Despatch*, AIR 8/863, 1941, para. 43.
16. ACM Sir Hugh Dowding, *Battle of Britain Despatch*, AIR 8/863, 1941, para. 40.
17. T.C.G. James, *The Growth of Fighter Command 1936–1940*, Routledge Taylor & Francis, 2014, p.98.
18. Winston Churchill, *Speech before Canadian Parliament*, *British Pathe*, https://youtu.be/y6JxSHmVB5g 1942.
19. Some Fighter Command aircrew reported sightings of Do 215s, which were variants of the Do 17.
20. ACM Sir Hugh Dowding, *Battle of Britain Despatch*, AIR 8/863, 1941, para. 43.
21. ACM Sir Hugh Dowding, *Battle of Britain Despatch*, AIR 8/863, 1941, para. 11–3.
22. 11 Group Operations Record, AIR 25/193, 10 July 1940.
23. Report by Joint Intelligence Sub-Committee to War Cabinet, *Imminence of a German Invasion of Great Britain, 4 July 1940*, Air Power Review, Centre for Air Power Studies, 2015.
24. Adolph Hitler, War Directive No.16, *Preparations for a Landing Operation Against England*, LCO 67/71.
25. Stephen Bungay, *The Most Dangerous Enemy*, Aurum Press, 2000, p.94.

ENEMY SIGHTED

26. Derek Wood & Derek Dempster, *The Narrow Margin,* Pen & Sword, 2003, *Monthly Output of Fighter Aircraft,* Appendix 6, p.306 & *Fighter Command Battle Casualties,* Appendix 13, p.312.
27. Derek Wood & Derek Dempster, *The Narrow Margin,* Pen & Sword, 2003, *Monthly Output of Fighter Aircraft,* Appendix 11, p.310.
28. Derek Wood & Derek Dempster, *The Narrow Margin,* Pen & Sword, 2003, *Fighter Command Casualties,* Appendix 10, p.309.
29. Steve Darrow, *Five of the Few,* Grub Street, 2007, p.109.
30. 11 Group Operations Record, AIR 25/193, 29 July 1940.
31. Bob Carruthers, *Hitler's Wartime Orders, The Complete Führer Directives 1939–1945, Hitler's War Directive No. 17 For the Conduct of Air and Sea Warfare against England*, Pen & Sword Military, 2018, pp.51–2.
32. T.C.G. James, *The Battle of Britain*, Frank Cass Publishers, 2000, p.70.
33. 11 Group Operations Record, AIR 25/193, 12 August 1940.
34. 11 Group Operations Record, AIR 25/193, 13 August 1940.
35. W.H. Tantum & E.J. Hoffschmidt, *The Rise and Fall of the German Air Force 1933 to 1945*, WE Inc Publishers, 1969, p.80.
36. Williamson Murray, *Strategy for Defeat. The Luftwaffe. 1933–1945,* Air University Press, 1983, p.47.
37. *Report by A.V.M. Keith Park, German Air Attacks on England, 8th August – 10th September*, 11G/S.493, AIR 25/197, 12 September 1940.
38. Issued by the Ministry of Information on Behalf of the Air Ministry, *The Battle of Britain,* H.M.S.O, 1941.
39. W.H. Tantum & E.J. Hoffschmidt, *The Rise and Fall of the German Air Force 1933 to 1945*, WE Inc Publishers, 1969, p.79.
40. ACM Sir Hugh Dowding, *Battle of Britain Despatch*, AIR 8/863, 1941, para. 57.
41. 11 Group Operations Branch, Operational Notes to Controllers, AIR 25/197, 15 August 1940, Para. 3.
42. 11 Group Operations Branch, Operational Notes to Controllers, AIR 25/197, 15 August 1940, Para. 1.
43. 11 Group Operations Record, AIR 25/193, 16 August 1940.
44. Funeral of Fiske, *British Pathe*, https://youtu.be/VGmOl4DpBy4 1940.
45. Tom Moulson, *The Millionaires' Squadron: The Remarkable Story of 601 Squadron and The Flying Sword*, Pen, and Sword Aviation, 2014, p.94.
46. *The London Gazette*, Number 34993, Friday, 15 November 1940, P. 6569, Column 1.
47. Nicolson, Eric James Brindley, *BBC*, Imperial War Museum, 20238, 1940.

ENDNOTES

48. Andy Saunders, *History of War*, 24 January 2019, Issue 64, pp.76–9.
49. ACM Sir Hugh Dowding, *Battle of Britain Despatch*, AIR 8/863, 1941, para. 127.
50. W.H. Tantum & E.J. Hoffschmidt, *The Rise and Fall of the German Air Force 1933 to 1945*, WE Inc Publishers, 1969, p.82.
51. W.H. Tantum & E.J. Hoffschmidt, *The Rise and Fall of the German Air Force 1933 to 1945*, WE Inc Publishers, 1969, pp.85–6.
52. W.H. Tantum & E.J. Hoffschmidt, *The Rise and Fall of the German Air Force 1933 to 1945*, WE Inc Publishers, 1969, p.82.
53. Winston Churchill, House of Commons Debate, Hansard, 20 August 1940, vol.364, cc. 1167.
54. Mike Rossiter, *Bomber Flight Berlin,* Transworld Publishers, 2011, p.106.
55. 11 Group Operations Record, AIR 25/193, 25 August 1940.
56. *'The History of 11 Group in the First Ten Years'*, AIR 16/1098, 1946, p.4.
57. Graham Wallace, *RAF Biggin Hill,* Universal Tandem Publishing, 1975, p.176.
58. Graham Wallace, *RAF Biggin Hill*, Universal Tandem Publishing, 1975, p.182.
59. W.H. Tantum & E.J. Hoffschmidt, *The Rise and Fall of the German Air Force 1933 to 1945*, WE Inc Publishers, 1969, p.85.
60. W.H. Tantum & E.J. Hoffschmidt, *The Rise and Fall of the German Air Force 1933 to 1945*, WE Inc Publishers, 1969, p.85.
61. 11 Group Operations Record, AIR 25/193, 6 September 1940.
62. 11 Group Operations Record, AIR 25/193, 7 September 1940.
63. No 11 Group Instructions to Controllers No 12, AIR 25/197, 7 September 1940.
64. ACM Sir Hugh Dowding, *Battle of Britain Despatch*, AIR 8/863, 1941, para. 206–8.
65. 11 Group Operations Record, AIR 25/193, 13 September 1940.
66. 11 Group Operations Record, AIR 25/193, 14 September 1940.
67. 11 Group Operations Record, AIR 25/193, 14 September 1940.

Chapter 15

1. Dr Alfred Price, *Address at AGM Royal Air Force Historical Society*, 12 June 2002.
2. Vincent Orange, *Park: The Biography of A.C.M. Sir Keith Park*, Grubb Street, 2013, p.101.

3. Victoria Panton Bacon, *Remarkable Women of the Second World War: A Collection of Untold Stories,* The History Press, 2022, Part One: The British Memories. Vera Saies: A Battle of Britain Plotter.
4. Vincent Orange, *Park: The Biography of A.C.M. Sir Keith Park*, Grubb Street, 2013, p.110.
5. Tony Bartley, *Smoke Trails in the Sky*, Crecy Publishing, 1997, pp.31–2.
6. John Villa, Flight Lieutenant, 72 Squadron, Combat Report, AIR 50/30/80, 15 September 1940.
7. Robert Holland, Pilot Officer, 92 Squadron, Combat Report, AIR 50/40/5, 15 September 1940.
8. George Denholm, Squadron Leader, 603 (City of Edinburgh) Squadron, Combat Report, AIR 50/167/15, 15 September 1940.
9. James MacPhail, Pilot Officer, 603 (City of Edinburgh) Squadron, Combat Report, AIR 50/167/39, 15 September 1940.
10. William Read, Pilot Officer, 603 (City of Edinburgh) Squadron, Combat Report, AIR 50/167/58, 15 September 1940.
11. Intelligence Patrol Report, 501 (City of Bristol) Squadron, AIR 50/162/72, 15 September 1940.
12. Melody Foreman, *The Wreck Hunter, Battle of Britain & The Blitz,* Frontline Books, 2019, p.128.
13. Intelligence Patrol Report, 253 Squadron, AIR 50/97/47, 15 September 1940.
14. Raymond Duke-Woolley, Flight Lieutenant, 253 Squadron, Combat Report, AIR 50/97/14, 15 September 1940.
15. Edward Darling, Sergeant, 41 Squadron, Combat Report, AIR 50/18/60, 15 September 1940.
16. Anthony Lovell, Flying Officer, 41 Squadron, Combat Report, AIR 50/18/87, 15 September 1940.
17. Crelin Bodie, Flight Lieutenant, 66 Squadron, Combat Report, AIR 50/26/125, 15 September 1940.
18. Winston Churchill, *The Second World War, Volume II, Their Finest Hour*, Cassell & Co. Ltd, 1949, pp.295–6.
19. John Sample, Squadron Leader, 504 (County of Nottingham) Squadron, Combat Report, AIR 50/163/26, 15 September 1940.
20. Ray Holmes, Sergeant, 504 (County of Nottingham) Squadron, Combat Report, AIR 50/163/12, 15 September 1940.
21. *Search for the Lost Fighter Plane – Battle of Britain, You Tube,* https://youtu.be/lACDhxSLbYQ
22. John Crossman, Pilot Officer, 46 Squadron, Combat Report, AIR 50/20/13, 15 September 1940.

ENDNOTES

23. Douglas Bader, Squadron Leader, 242 (Canadian) Squadron, Combat Report, AIR 50/92/89, 15 September 1940.
24. Stan Turner, Pilot Officer, 242 (Canadian) Squadron, Combat Report, AIR 50/92/104, 15 September 1940.
25. William Leather, Flight Lieutenant, 611 (West Lancashire) Squadron, Combat Report, AIR 50/173/53, 15 September 1940.
26. John Dundas, Flying Officer, 609 (West Riding) Squadron, Combat Report, AIR 50/171/24, 15 September 1940.
27. John Curchin, Pilot Officer, 609 (West Riding) Squadron, Combat Report, AIR 50/171/16, 15 September 1940.
28. Archie McKellan, Flight Lieutenant, 605 (County of Warwick) Squadron, Combat Report, AIR 50/169/92, 15 September 1940.
29. George Pinkerton, Flight Lieutenant, 602 (City of Glasgow) Squadron, Combat Report, AIR 50/166/86, 16 October 1939.
30. Intelligence Patrol Report, 303 (Polish) Squadron, AIR 50/117/92, 15 September 1940.
31. Intelligence Patrol Report, 229 Squadron, AIR 50/86/15, 15 September 1940.
32. Reginald Rimmer, Flight Lieutenant, 229 Squadron, Combat Report, AIR 50/86/33, 15 September 1940.

Chapter 16

1. George Denholm, Squadron Leader, 603 (City of Edinburgh) Squadron, Combat Report, AIR 50/167/15, 15 September 1940.
2. Brian McNamara, Flying Officer, 603 (City of Edinburgh) Squadron, Combat Report, AIR 50/167/38, 15 September 1940.
3. Gerald Stapleton, Pilot Officer, 603 (City of Edinburgh) Squadron, Combat Report, AIR 50/167/68, 15 September 1940.
4. Eric Thomas, Pilot Officer, 222 Squadron, Combat Report, AIR 50/85/141, 15 September 1940.
5. John Villa, Flight Lieutenant, 72 Squadron, Combat Report, AIR 50/30/80, 15 September 1940.
6. John Lloyd, Pilot Officer, 72 Squadron, Combat Report, AIR 50/30/72, 15 September 1940.
7. Tom Neil, Pilot Officer, 249 Squadron, Combat Report, AIR 50/96/101, 15 September 1940.
8. Intelligence Patrol Report, 213 Squadron, AIR 50/83/74, 15 September 1940.

9. Denis Parnall, Flight Lieutenant, 249 Squadron, Combat Report, AIR 50/96/14, 15 September 1940.
10. Douglas Bader, Squadron Leader, 242 (Canadian) Squadron, Combat Report, AIR 50/92/89, 15 September 1940.
11. Intelligence Patrol Report, 302 (Polish) Squadron, AIR 50/116/49, 15 September 1940.
12. Julian Kowalski, Flying Officer, 302 (Polish) Squadron, Combat Report, AIR 50/116/15, 15 September 1940.
13. Intelligence Patrol Report, 310 (Czechoslovak) Squadron, AIR 50/122/54, 15 September 1940.
14. Miroslaw Wojciechowski, Sergeant, 303 Squadron, Combat Report, AIR 50/117/62, 15 September 1940.
15. Intelligence Patrol Report, 152 Squadron, AIR 50/64/30, 15 September 1940.
16. Victoria Panton Bacon, *Remarkable Women of the Second World War: A Collection of Untold Stories,* The History Press, 2022, Part One: The British Memories. Vera Saies: A Battle of Britain Plotter.
17. 11 Group Operations Record, AIR 25/193, 15 September 1940.
18. Winston Churchill, *The Second World War, Volume II, Their Finest Hour*, Cassell & Co. Ltd, 1949, p.297.
19. Fredrick Winterbotham, *The Ultra Secret*, Weidenfeld and Nicholson, 1974, pp.56–8.
20. 11 Group Operations Record, AIR 25/193, 16 September to 31 October 1940.
21. ACM Sir Hugh Dowding, *Battle of Britain Despatch*, AIR 8/863, 1941, para. 210.

Chapter 17

1. 11 Group Operations Record, AIR 25/193, 29 October 1940.
2. Peter Haining, *The Chianti Raiders: The Extraordinary Story of The Italian Air Force in The Battle of Britain*, Robson Books, 2005, p.7.
3. 11 Group Operations Record, AIR 25/193, 1 November 1940.
4. Peter Haining, *The Chianti Raiders: The Extraordinary Story of The Italian Air Force in The Battle of Britain*, Robson Books, 2005, p.76–7.
5. Issued by the Ministry of Information on Behalf of the Air Ministry, *The Battle of Britain*, H.M.S.O, 1941, pp.32–3.

ENDNOTES

6. ACM Sir Trafford Leigh-Mallory, *Air Operations By The Allied Expeditionary Air Force In N.W. Europe Despatch*, AIR 8/863, 1944, para. 13.
7. Hazel Crozier, *RAF Uxbridge, 90th Anniversary,* RAF High Wycombe: Air Command Media Services, 2007, p.16.
8. T.D. 'Dixie' Dean, Flying Officer, 616 Squadron, Combat Report, AIR 50/176/19, 4 August 1944.
9. John Rodger, Flying Officer, 616 Squadron, Combat Report, AIR 50/176/53, 4 August 1944.
10. *Imperial War Museum, The Terrifying German 'Revenge Weapons' of the Second World War.*
11. Hazel Crozier, *RAF Uxbridge, 90th Anniversary,* RAF High Wycombe: Air Command Media Services, 2007, p.18.

Index

Adler Angriff, Attack of the Eagles, 143
Adler Tag, Eagle Day, 143–5
Air Council, 18
Air Defence of Great Britain (ADGB), 10–14, 29, 53, 80, 195, 198
Air Fighting Zone, 68, 70
Air Ministry, 7, 11–12, 20, 23–4, 29, 43, 45, 57, 60, 75, 83–4, 100–101, 112, 117
America, *also* American, 2, 41, 54–6, 86, 124–5, 131, 146–7, 194–7
   See Fiske, William 'Billy'
   See Petroleum Industry
   See United States Army Eighth Fighter Command
   See United States Army Ninth Air Force
   See United States Army Ninth Fighter Command
Anti-Aircraft, 8, 30, 51, 61, 73, 142, 193
   Command, ix, 14, 69, 70–3
   Gun Defended Area, 70
   Anti-aircraft gun, ix, x, 5–6, 8, 11–12, 15, 57, 68, 69, 70–4, 78–90, 113, 190, 198

Searchlight, ix, x, 11–12, 14–15, 30, 43, 63, 68–70, 72–3, 78–9, 90, 159
Ardennes Forest, 27, 128
Ashmore, 'Splash', 7–9, 13
Australia, 124

Bader, Douglas, 21, 85, 103, 165, 174, 187–8
Balloon, ix, x, 8, 12, 42, 68, 73, 75–9, 113, 198
   Command, x, 14–15, 30, 69, 75
   Group, 76
   Centre, 76
   Squadron, 76
   KH, 76
Barbados, 124
Barking Creek, battle of, 43–4
Battle of Britain, vii–viii, 2, 18, 21–6, 30, 32, 34, 42, 48, 50, 52, 58, 66, 71, 75–6, 81, 84, 91, 93, 107, 109–10, 114, 116–22, 124–5, 129, 136, 138–9, 144, 148, 191–2, 194, 198
Battle of Britain, Film, 40, 116, 146, 153, 160
Battle of Britain Bunker, *see* Operations Room
Bawdsey, *see* Radar

220

INDEX

Beaverbrook, Maxwell Aitken, 18, 23, 28, 135, 140
Belgium, 17–18, 33, 39, 124, 127–8, 137, 144, 146, 192–3
Bentley Priory, *see* Fighter Command
Big Wing, 103, 105, 174, 183, 187
Biggin Hill, RAF Station, *see* Fighter Command
Blenheim, Bristol, 18–20, 54, 72, 89, 107, 109, 115, 138, 159
Bleriot, Louis, 4
Blitz, 19, 73, 156, 194, 199
Blitzkrieg, 22
  Operation *Case Yellow*, 128
Bomber Command, 30, 63, 81, 89, 101, 145, 151–2
Box, RAF Station, *see* Fighter Command
Boyd, Owen, 75, 77
Brand, Christopher Joseph Quintin, 31
British Expeditionary Force (BEF), 17, 52, 127, 129
Bushell, Roger, 28, 45, 131

Calais, vii, 2, 4, 45, 130–1, 137, 161–2
Camm, Sydney, 12
Canada, *also* Canadian, 103, 107, 121–2, 124, 138, 146, 165–6, 174–7, 180, 182, 189, 194–5
Canewdon, *see* Radar
Cazenove, Peter, *see* Dunkirk
Chain Home (CH), *see* Radar
Chain Home Low (CHL), *see* Radar
Chamberlain, Neville, 17, 82, 126
Churchill, Winston, vii-viii, 10, 28, 40, 55, 57, 66, 69, 86, 107, 118–19, 132–5, 138, 151–2, 162–3, 171, 190–2
  Clementine, 86, 162, 190
Cierva C.30, *see* Radar
Clerk, Special Duties, 100–101
  Plotter, 8, 30, 32, 35, 59, 66, 91, 99–101, 105–106, 162, 171
  Teller, 30, 47, 59, 61, 66, 91, 99–101, 162
Colditz,
  Mussolini's, 75
  Oflag IV-C, 131
Combined Control Centre (CCC), *see* D-Day
Committee for the Scientific Survey of Air Defence (CSSAD), 12, 55–6
Controller, 5, 31
  Group, Senior, ix, 32, 43, 62, 65–6, 80, 83, 87, 89–97, 99, 102, 104–13, 129, 145–6, 149, 157, 160–3, 165–6, 182, 196
    Douglas-Jones, Eric, 93–4
    Lang, Thomas, 93–4
    Willoughby De Broke, John Verney, 93–4, 163, 166
  Sector, 32–6, 43–4, 59, 61, 63, 65, 93–6, 106, 108, 110–13, 146, 157, 160, 164, 166, 205
Cooper, Alfred Duff, 127
Corpo Aereo Italiano, 193
Creer, Robert Mason, 83
Croydon, RAF Station, *see* Fighter Command
Czechoslovakia, *also* Czech, 82, 103, 117, 124, 128, 165, 173–4, 178, 188–9

221

ENEMY SIGHTED

D-Day, 114, 195
   Combined Control Centre (CCC), 195–6
   Fighter Direction Ships (FDS), 196
   Fortress Europe, viii, 194
   Normandy, x, 1, 28, 79, 114, 195–6, 199
   Operation *Neptune*, 195
   Operation *Overlord*, viii, 195–6
   United States Army Eighth Fighter Command, 196
   United States Ninth Air Force, 195
   United States Ninth Fighter Command, 195
   2nd Tactical Air Force (2TAF), 195
Daimler Benz, 23, 28
Daventry, *see* Radar
Dawson-Paul, Francis, *see* Uxbridge
Debden, RAF Station, *see* Fighter Command
Defiant, Boulton Paul, 18–20, 23, 27, 107–108, 122, 129, 133, 138
De Gaulle, Charles, 86
Detling, RAF Station, *see* Fighter Command
Dieppe, x, 79, 194, 199
   Operation *Jubilee*, 194–5
Direction Finding Station, 35
Douglas-Jones, Eric, *see* Controller
Dover, vii, ix, 4, 59, 70, 76, 97, 110, 113, 123–4, 142–3, 165–6, 168, 170, 183, 193
   See also Radar
Dowding, Hugh Caswall Tremenheere, viii–ix, 11–13, 17–18, 24, 31–2, 40, 48, 53–4, 57, 59, 69, 72–3, 75, 77, 81–2, 84, 94–5, 104–105, 117, 119–20, 135, 137–9, 144, 150, 158, 190, 192
Dunkirk, x, 20, 32, 128–9
   Cazenove, Peter, 130–1
   Operation *Aerial*, 137
   Operation *Cycle*, 137
   Operation *Dynamo*, 129, 133
   Stephenson, Geoffrey, 131
   Supporting evacuation, 79, 94, 97, 104, 129–31, 135–6, 146
   See also Radar
Duxford, RAF Station, 43, 103, 165, 174

Eastchurch, RAF Station, 143
Eisenhower, Dwight, 86
English Channel, vii, 2, 4, 6, 10, 30–1, 41, 44, 49, 79, 97, 102, 105, 129, 138–9, 142, 199

Fiat, 193
   BR20, 193
   CR42, 193
   G50, 193
Fighter Command, vii, ix–x, 1, 5, 11, 13–15, 17–22, 24–5, 27–33, 40–4, 47, 53–4, 57, 59–60, 62–3, 65, 67–70, 75, 78, 81, 83, 85–6, 90, 93–4, 98, 101, 103–104, 106, 113–14, 117, 119–20, 122–4, 127, 129–30, 135, 137–45, 147–51, 154–6, 158, 160–2, 164, 181, 191–6
   Headquarters, Bentley Priory, 13, 29–30, 32, 35, 41, 47, 52, 58–9, 91–2, 106, 162

INDEX

Filter Room, x, 29, 30, 47, 52, 59, 101
Group, 47
  Box, 10 Group, 31–2, 95–7, 148, 157, 165, 175, 182–3, 189–90
  Kenton, 13 Group, 31–2
  Uxbridge, 11 Group, vii, ix–x, 1, 11, 14, 23, 26, 28, 30–4, 40–4, 53–4, 58–9, 61–4, 66, 68–70, 73, 75–6, 79–81, 83–98, 101–15, 117–22, 125, 127–31, 133, 137, 139, 141–55, 157–62, 164–6, 174–5, 177, 182–3, 190, 192–3, 195–6, 198
  Watnall, 12 Group, 31, 43, 69, 96–7, 103–104, 149, 157, 165, 174, 183, 187, 190, 193
Sector, 11 Group, 33–5, 41, 59, 66, 70, 108, 110, 112, 152, 157
  Biggin Hill, 34, 39, 66, 70, 96, 107, 110, 114, 141–2, 152–4, 164, 166–7, 182
  Debden, 34, 70, 96, 107, 110, 112–13, 164-5, 182
  Hornchurch, 34, 70, 73, 94, 96, 107, 110, 131, 142, 165–7, 182–3
  Kenley, 34, 70, 96, 102, 107, 110, 122–3, 164, 166, 168–9, 176, 182–3
  North Weald, 34, 43–4, 70, 72, 107, 109–10, 120, 159, 165–6, 182
  Northolt, 26, 34, 70, 102, 107–8, 110, 112, 114–16, 119–21, 164–6, 176–7, 180, 182
  Tangmere, 34, 54, 94, 96, 107, 110, 115, 146–7, 149, 182
Satellite, 11 Group, ix, 14, 29, 33–5
  Croydon, 34, 96, 130, 166, 177, 182
  Detling, 34, 143, 168
  Gravesend, 34, 113, 166, 170, 183
  Hawkinge, 34, 96, 123, 141–2, 145, 150
  Hendon, 34, 113, 125, 182, 193
  Heston, 26, 82
  Lympne, 34, 114, 142–3, 145, 152
  Manston, 34, 96, 142–3, 145, 150, 152, 197
  Martlesham Heath, 34, 165
  Redhill, 34
  Rochford, 34, 96, 145
  Stapleford Tawney, 34, 96, 182
  West Malling, 34
  Westhampnett, 28, 34, 115
Offensive, 194
  Circuses, Ramrods, Rhubarbs and Rodeos, 194
Fighter Direction Ships (FDS), *see* D-Day
Fiske, William 'Billy', 146–7
Fortress Europe, *see* D-Day
France, *also* French, vii, x, 1–2, 7, 10–11, 17–20, 22, 25–7, 30–1,

33–4, 45, 52, 71, 79, 82, 86, 91–2, 94, 97, 114–17, 123–4, 126–30, 132–40, 144–6, 162, 170, 175, 179, 194–5, 199

Galland, Adolf, 52
General Post Office (GPO), 34, 47, 87, 106
  Defence Telecommunications Control (DTC), 47
  Defence Teleprinter Network (DTN), 47
  Engineers, 34
Germany, *also* German, vii-ix, 1, 4, 7, 11, 14–15, 17–20, 24–8, 32–3, 35, 42–3, 45, 49, 51–2, 54, 57–8, 62, 68, 70, 72, 75, 77, 81–4, 86, 97–9, 102, 113, 115, 117, 122, 124–6, 128, 131–3, 135–41, 143–4, 147–8, 150–3, 155–6, 158, 160–4, 168, 172–3, 181, 190–4, 196, 198–9
  Nazi, vii, x, 1, 14–15, 28, 42, 45, 54, 75, 79, 81–3, 128, 134, 151, 194–5, 198
Gladiator, Gloster, 18, 20, 94
Goering, Hermann, 31, 138, 150, 154, 160
Gossage, Leslie, 75, 81, 84
Gravesend, RAF Station, *see* Fighter Command

Hanbury, Felicity, 153–4
Hawkinge, RAF Station, *see* Fighter Command
Henderson, Elspeth, 154
Hendon, RAF Station, *see* Fighter Command
Heston, RAF Station, see Fighter Command
Hillingdon House, 11, 80–1, 95, 195
Hitler, Adolf, Fuhrer, vii-viii, x, 10, 12, 17, 27–8, 52, 79, 82, 128, 134–5, 137, 139–40, 142, 152, 155, 191, 194, 196, 199
Hornchurch, RAF Station, see Fighter Command
Huff Duff, 30, 35, Hurricane, Hawker, viii-ix, 12, 18, 20–5, 27–8, 43–4, 62–3, 66, 68–9, 73, 82, 86, 93–6, 102–103, 107–108, 110, 114–16, 118, 120–22, 125, 128–30, 133, 135, 137–41, 143, 146–50, 154, 156–7, 159–60, 162, 164–6, 168–9, 171–8, 180–2, 185–8, 191–2, 194

Identification Friend or Foe (IFF), 44
Instructions to Controllers, 95
Integrated air defence system, ix, 3, 7, 14, 31, 53, 67
Invasion, of the British Isles, vii-viii, x, 2, 32, 62, 67–8, 79, 105, 125, 135, 138–40, 143, 151, 161, 191–2, 194
Operation *Sealion,* vii, 138

Jamaica, 124

Kanalkampf, Channel Fight, 139
Kenley, RAF Station, *see* Fighter Command
Kenton, RAF Station, *see* Fighter Command
King George VI, 64, 86, 96, 100, 131, 155

INDEX

Lang, Thomas, *see* Controller
Leigh-Mallory, Trafford, 31, 103
Luftwaffe, vii, x, 14, 18–20, 22–6, 28, 31–3, 40, 42–3, 45, 47–54, 58–9, 61–3, 67–9, 72–3, 76–7, 79, 81, 83–4, 91, 93, 103, 105, 113, 120–1, 125, 128–31, 138–45, 148–50, 152, 154–7, 159–63, 165, 181, 183, 189–94, 202, 205, 207–208, 214
    Signals, 15, 51, 143
Lympne, RAF Station, *see* Fighter Command

Maginot Line, 128
Manston, RAF Station, *see* Fighter Command
Martlesham Heath, RAF Station, *see* Fighter Command
McAlpine, Robert, 83
McGregor, Gordon, *see* Uxbridge
Messerschmitt, 160
    Willy, 19, 109, 19–26, 28, 40, 62, 115–16, 121, 123, 125, 127, 131, 138–40, 145, 148, 164–7, 169, 175, 180, 183, 187, 192, 110, 19, 21, 40, 116, 121–3, 125, 127, 130, 138, 140, 145, 148
Milch, Erhard, 51
Mitchell, Reginald, 12, 26
Molson, Hartland de Montarville, *see* Uxbridge
Montgomery, Bernard, 86
Mortimer, Joan, 154
Mosquito, De Havilland, 197
Mussolini, Benito, 75, 193
    Leader of fascist Italy, 82

New Zealand, *also* New Zealander, 31, 124–5
Nicolson, James Brindley, 147–9
Normandy, *see* D-Day
North Weald, RAF Station, *see* Fighter Command
Northolt, RAF Station, *see* Fighter Command

Observer Corps, ix-x, 2, 12, 14, 30, 32, 35, 44, 57–63, 66–7, 79, 91, 98, 156, 162, 190
    Air raid warning, 59–63
    Observer Centre, 59–63, 65–6
    Observer Post, 58–60, 63–5
    Observer Post Instrument, 64
    Operation *Totter*, 63
    Satellite Observer Post, 63
    Sea Teller, 59
Operation *Aerial*, *see* Dunkirk
Operation *Case Yellow*, *see* Blitzkrieg
Operation *Crossbow*, *see* Vengeance weapon
Operation *Cycle*, *see* Dunkirk
Operation *Diver*, *see* Vengeance weapon
Operation *Dynamo*, *see* Dunkirk
Operation Jubilee, *see* Dieppe
Operation *Neptune*, *see* D-Day
Operation *Noball*, *see* Vengeance weapon
Operation *Overlord*, *see* D-Day
Operation *Sealion*, *see* Invasion
Operation *Totter*, *see* Observer Corps
Operations Room, vii, ix–x, 1, 8, 11, 14–15, 23, 30, 32, 34–5, 41, 43, 53, 58–9, 61, 63, 66, 70, 73,

76, 79, 80–90, 93–5, 97–101,
105–106, 108, 110, 112, 118–20,
129, 133, 139, 142–3, 153, 159,
161, 175, 190, 193, 195–6, 198
Battle of Britain Bunker,
  vii–viii, x, 11, 58–9, 79, 81,
  84–7, 89–90, 93, 95–7, 99,
  107, 114, 117, 120, 122, 127,
  129, 151, 155, 161–2, 190,
  194–5, 197–9
Building 76, 82
Dais, 35, 80, 89–90, 162
Gallery, 90–2, 96–7, 102, 107,
  119, 162, 190
General Situation Map, 30, 32,
  35–6, 61–2, 89, 99, 102,
  105, 162
Plotting Room, 89
Porton Air Filtration Unit, 84,
  87, 162
Royal Box, 96
Sector Clock, 105–106
Totaliser, Squadron Indicator
  Panel, 32, 35, 89, 106–13

Park, Keith Rodney, 31–2, 62, 69,
  81, 88, 93–5, 100, 103–104,
  119, 124–5, 135, 144, 146,
  149–50, 152, 156–8, 162–3,
  166, 171–2, 190, 192
Petroleum Industry, 23
Pickering, Tony, 141
Pile, Fredrick, 69
Pip Squeak, 30, 35, 44, 60
Plotter, *see* Clerk, Special Duties
Poland, *also* Polish, 33–4, 102,
  107, 110, 112, 114–17, 124, 126,
  128, 144, 155–6, 164–5, 174,
  177–80, 187, 189

Poling, *see* Radar
Principle of Equal Angles, Tizzy
  Angle, 35–6, 42, 60
P51 Mustang, North American, 197

Queen Elizabeth, Consort, 64, 86,
  97, 155
Queen Elizabeth, II, 64

Radar, ix–x, 2, 6, 13, 19–20, 30,
  39–57, 59, 65–7, 73, 79, 91–2,
  142–3, 156, 161–2, 182, 190
  A.C. Cossor, 45
  Airborne Interception (AI), 19,
    48, 53–5
  AMES, 45–6, 48
  Chain Home (CH), ix, 30,
    45–50, 52–3, 79, 190
  Chain Home Low (CHL), ix, 30,
    48–50, 53, 79
  Cierva C.30, 43
  EF50 Valve, 49–50
  French military, 52
  GEC, 54
  Magnetron, 49, 53–6
  Metropolitan Vickers, 45
  Philips, 49
  PYE, 48-50
  Radar Station,
    Bawdsey, 41, 44, 48, 50, 65
    Canewdon, 43, 44
    Daventry, 12–13, 41
    Dover, 42
    Dunkirk, 143
    Pevensey, 42
    Poling, 54
    Ventnor, 42, 143
  Rota, Avro, 43
  Sound Mirror, 39–40

INDEX

Ramsay, Bertram, 129–30
Recognised air picture, ix, 29–31, 43, 47, 57, 87
Redhill, RAF Station, *see* Fighter Command
Rochford, RAF Station, *see* Fighter Command
Rolls-Royce, 3, 20
   Merlin, 20, 27
   Griffon, 28
Romer Committee, 10
Rota, Avro, *see* Radar
Royal Air Force (RAF), vii, 8, 13, 17, 24, 26, 28–9, 31, 33, 51, 63, 79, 80–2, 84, 86, 100–101, 106, 115, 118–20, 122–5, 130, 132–3, 137–9, 143–4, 146–7, 151–2, 154, 161, 163, 181, 193–7
Royal Auxiliary Air Force (RAAF), 17
Royal Flying Corps (RFC), 7–8, 32
Royal Naval Air Service (RNAS), 7–8
   Fleet Air Arm, 122–3
Royal Navy (RN), viii, 3, 18, 45, 70, 90, 129, 137, 139, 194

Saies, Vera, 163, 190
Salmond, John, 11
Satellite, *see* Fighter Command
Saul, Richard Ernest, 31, 83
Scramble, 8, 35, 40, 42–4, 53, 60, 63, 92, 98, 108–109, 121–2, 141, 143, 146, 155, 158, 163–6, 176, 182–3, 196–7
Searchlight, *see* Anti-aircraft
Sector, *see* Fighter Command
Sector Clock, *see* Operations Room
Shilling, Beatrice, 24

South Africa, 124
Squadrons,
   1 (Canadian) Squadron, 107, 121, 166, 176, 182
   17 Squadron, 107, 164, 182
   19 Squadron, 103, 131, 165, 174
   23 Squadron, 107
   25 Squadron, 72, 107, 109, 159
   32 Squadron, 141
   33 Squadron, 114
   41 Squadron, 107, 166, 170, 182
   46 Squadron, 107, 166, 173, 182, 185
   56 Squadron, 44
   64 Squadron, 122
   66 Squadron, 107, 166, 170–1, 182
   72 Squadron, 107, 164–6, 182, 185
   73 Squadron, 107, 164, 182
   74 Squadron, 44
   92 Squadron, 107, 130–1, 164–7, 182
   141 Squadron, 107
   145 Squadron, 115
   213 Squadron, 107, 182, 186
   222 Squadron, 107, 182–4
   229 Squadron, 102, 107, 164, 177, 180, 182
   249 Squadron, 107, 147–8, 166, 172, 182, 185–6
   253 Squadron, 107, 164, 166, 168–9, 182
   257 Squadron, 107, 165, 182
   264 Squadron, 107
   302 (Polish) Squadron, 103, 165, 174, 187
   303 (Polish) Squadron, 102, 107, 112, 114–17, 164, 177–80, 189

ENEMY SIGHTED

310 (Czechoslovak) Squadron, 103, 165, 173, 188
341 (Free French) Squadron, 114
501 (City of Bristol) Squadron, 107, 164, 166, 168–9, 182
504 (County of Nottingham) Squadron, 107, 165, 172, 182
600 (City of London) Squadron, 107
601 (County of London) Squadron, 146–7
602 (City of Glasgow) Squadron, 107
603 (City of Edinburgh) Squadron, 107, 165, 167–8, 182–4
605 (County of Warwick) Squadron, 94, 107, 125, 166, 176, 182
607 (County of Durham) Squadron, 107, 182, 191
616 (South Yorkshire) Squadron, 197
804 (Fleet Air Arm) Squadron, 123
808 (Fleet Air Arm) Squadron, 123
Fighter Interception Unit, 54
Stalag Luft III, 'Great Escape', 28, 45, 131
Stapleford Tawney, RAF Station, *see* Fighter Command
Steel-Bartholomew Committee, 10
Stephenson, Geoffrey, *see* Dunkirk

Tangmere, RAF Station, *see* Fighter Command
Teller, *see* Clerk, Special Duties
Tally Ho, 111, 166

Tempest, Hawker, 197
Tizard, Henry, 12–13, 36, 55–6
Tizzy Angle, 36, 42, 60
Totaliser board, *see* Operations Room
Turner, Helen, 153–4

United States Army Eighth Fighter Command, 196
United States Army Ninth Air Force, 195
United States Army Ninth Fighter Command, 195
Urbanowicz, Witold, *see* Uxbridge
Uxbridge, RAF Station
   Flags, 118, 124
   Hurricane, serial number P3901, 114, 116–17
     Urbanowicz, Witold, 114–17
     303 (Polish) Squadron, 114
   Hurricane, serial number, P3873, 120–1
     McGregor, Gordon, 121
     Molson, Hartland de Montarville, 121–2
     1 (Canadian) Squadron, 121
   Monument, 118–20
   Spitfire, serial number BS239, 114
     341 (Free French) Squadron, 114
     33 Squadron, 114
   Spitfire, serial number L1035, 120, 124
     Dawson-Paul, Francis, 122–4
     64 Squadron, 122

Visitor and Exhibition Centre, 82
Vector, 35, 42–3, 54–5, 164–6, 168, 182, 196

INDEX

Vengeance weapon, x, 198–9
   Operation Crossbow, 198
   Operation *Diver*, 197
   Operation *Noball*, 198
   V1, Doodle Bug, 64, 79, 196, 198
   V2, x, 79, 198

Watnall, RAF Station, *see* Fighter Command
Watson-Watt, Robert, 12–13, 49
Welsh, William, 81, 84
West Malling, RAF Station, *see* Fighter Command

Westhampnett, RAF Station, *see* Fighter Command
Willoughby De Broke, John Verney, *see* Controller
Women's Auxiliary Air Force (WAAF), 30, 47, 87, 90, 100–101, 153–4

Zimbabwe, formerly Southern Rhodesia, 124

2nd Tactical Air Force (2TAF), *see* D-Day